SOFT COMPUTING APPROACH FOR MATHEMATICAL MODELING OF ENGINEERING PROBLEMS

SOFT COMPUTING APPROACH FOR MATHEMATICAL MODELING OF ENGINEERING PROBLEMS

Edited by
Ali Ahmadian and Soheil Salahshour

CRC Press
Taylor & Francis Group
Boca Raton London New York

CRC Press is an imprint of the
Taylor & Francis Group, an **informa** business

First edition published 2022
by CRC Press
6000 Broken Sound Parkway NW, Suite 300, Boca Raton, FL 33487-2742

and by CRC Press
2 Park Square, Milton Park, Abingdon, Oxon, OX14 4RN

Library of Congress Cataloging-in-Publication Data
Names: Ahmadian, Ali, editor. I Salahshour, Soheil, editor.
Title: Soft computing approach for mathematical modeling of engineering problems / edited by Ali Ahmadian, Soheil Salahshour.
Description: First edition. I Abingdon, Oxon ; Boca Raton, FL : CRC Press, 2022. I Includes bibliographical references and index. I Summary: "This book describes the use of different mathematical modeling and soft computing techniques used to solve real world engineering problems. The book gives an overview of the current state of soft computing techniques and describes the advantages and disadvantages of soft computing compared to traditional hard computing techniques"– Provided by publisher.
Identifiers: LCCN 2021010426 (print) I LCCN 2021010427 (ebook) I ISBN 9780367685997 (hbk) I ISBN 9780367686345 (pbk) I ISBN 9781003138341 (ebk)
Subjects: LCSH: Engineering–Data processing. I Soft computing.
Classification: LCC TA345 .S589 2022 (print) I LCC TA345 (ebook) I DDC 620.00285/63–dc23
LC record available at https://lccn.loc.gov/2021010426
LC ebook record available at https://lccn.loc.gov/2021010427

ISBN: 978-0-367-68599-7 (hbk)
ISBN: 978-0-367-68634-5 (pbk)
ISBN: 978-1-003-13834-1 (ebk)

Typeset in Times
by MPS Limited, Dehradun

Dedication

To our lovely wives, Ferial and Adeleh

Contents

Preface

Soft computing is one of the hot research fields in advanced artificial intelligence, while mathematical modeling and analysis (MMA) plays a key role in soft computing. We aim to promote the research, development, and applications of MMA for soft computing by providing a high-level international forum for researchers and practitioners to exchange research results and share development experiences. The edited book **Soft Computing Approach for Mathematical Modeling of Engineering Problems** prescribes various mathematical modeling and soft computing techniques in engineering problems. This book will highlight that the models use some basic assumptions and mathematics to find parameters for different engineering problems and use those parameters to calculate the effects of different interferences, such as medical compartment models, weather, cryptoanalysis, image processing, industry revolution 4.0 and etc. This book will walk through the emerging trends in modeling engineering problems as a tool that has been used to study the mechanisms by which natural and physical phenomena defined, to predict the future vision and horizon and to recognize the potentials existing in different branches of engineering. It will help the researchers to appreciate the *Soft Computing Approach for Mathematical Modeling of Engineering Problems*.

The objective is to bring the mathematical modeling and soft computing in engineering problems into a single volume, which can add to the existing knowledge of undergraduate and postgraduate students, researchers, academicians, and industry people. This book aims to cover the main aspects of mathematical modeling and soft computing in different branches of engineering problems, and its goal is to persuade engineers and scientists that mathematical modeling can be of use to them. The primary users of this book include researchers, academicians, postgraduate students, and specialists. Many researchers have made significant contributions to the research, education, and the development of soft computing. This book is dedicated to those pioneers and scientific and technical workers in research in this area.

We thank our esteemed authors for having shown confidence in this book and considering it as a platform to showcase and share their original research work. We would also wish to thank the authors whose papers were not published in this book, probably because of the minor shortcomings.

Editor Biographies

Ali Ahmadian is a Senior Lecturer at the *Institute of IR 4.0, The National University of Malaysia, Adjunct Lecturer at the Kean University (Wenzhou Campus), China and Visiting Professor at the Mediterranea University of Reggio Calabria.* As a young researcher, he is dedicated to research in applied mathematics. He received his Ph.D. in early of 2014 as the best postgraduate student from Universiti Putra Malaysia (UPM). After his Ph.D. He took a postdoctoral fellowship at same university as part of the numerical analysis research group and at the same time joint to the University of Malaya as an Associate Researcher. He was promoted as a Fellow Researcher on December 2017 in UPM and supervised a number of PhD and MSC students as the main and member of supervisory committee. 8th Rank based on citations to his research works recognized by Google Scholar for the field of "Fuzzy *Sets and Systems.*" In general, his primary mathematical focus is the development of computational methods and models for problems arising in computer science, biology, physics, and engineering under fuzzy and fractional calculus (FC); in this context, he has worked on projects related to nano-communication networks, drug delivery systems, acid hydrolysis in palm oil frond, and carbon nanotubes dynamics, nanofluids, viscosity, AI and etc. He could successfully receive 16 national and international research grants (Worth: $ 800,000) and selected as the 1% top reviewer in the fields of mathematics and computer sciences recognized by Publons during 2017–2020. He is a member of editorial board in *Progress in Fractional Differentiation and Applications* (Natural Sciences Publishing) and lead guest editor and guest editor in *International Journal of Fuzzy Systems (Springer), International Journal of Uncertainty, Fuzziness and Knowledge-Based Systems, Mathematical Methods in Applied Sciences* (Wiley), *Advances in Mechanical Engineering* (SAGE), *Symmetry* (MDPI), and *International Journal of Hybrid Intelligence (*Inderscience Publishers) and etc.* He is an author of more than 120 research papers published in the reputed journals including high prestigious publishers such as Nature, IEEE, Elsevier, Springer, Wiley and etc. He also presented his research works in 38 international conferences held in Canada, Serbia, China, Turkey, Malaysia and UAE. He was a conference chairman, editor and member of programme committee in a number of International conferences in AI at Japan, China, South Korea, Turkey, Bahrain, India and Malaysia. He is also serving as a referee for more than 90 reputed international journals.

 **Soheil Salahshour** is the associate professor in Bahcesehir University. As a trained mathematician and computer scientist, Soheil has developed a passion for multi- and interdisciplinary research. He is not only deeply involved in fundamental research in fuzzy applied mathematics, especially fuzzy differential equations, but he was pioneered in the world to develop new mathematical models for real-world systems based on fuzzy fractional calculus. He is a prolific writer who published more than 145 peer-reviewed journal papers, five book chapters and 38 contributions to international conference proceedings, accumulating more than 2100 Google Scholar citations (h-index 25). He is one of the pioneers in the world in the field of fuzzy differential equations.

He is actively serving the research community, in particular as member in charge of the editorial board of several journals, including Advances in Mathematical Physics (WOS, IF: 0.841), Advances in Fuzzy Systems (Emerging Sources Citation Index), International Journal of Fuzzy System Applications (Scopus). He is an outstanding reviewer in the Fuzzy sets and systems (Elsevier), Journal of intelligent and fuzzy systems (IOS Press), and mathematical science (Springer). Besides, Dr. Soheil also serves as a referee in more than 80 international journals in the world including IEEE, Elsevier, Springer, Wiley, IOP Press, World Scientific and etc.

Contributors

John A
School of Computing Science and
Engineering, Galgotias University
Greater Noida, India

A. M. A. Abdalla
Al-Zaytoonah University of Jordan
Adenan Nurul Nur Hanisah Adenan,
Institute for Mathematical Research,
Universiti Putra Malaysia, 43400
UPM Serdang
Selangor, Malaysia

Ali Ahmadian
Institute of IR 4.0, The National
University of Malaysia, Bangi, 43600
UKM
Selangor, Malaysia

Fadzilah Md Ali
Institute for Mathematical Research
and Department of Mathematics,
Universiti Putra Malaysia, 43400
UPM Serdang
Selangor, Malaysia

M.A. Al-Jabbar
The National University of Malaysia
Allahviranloo Tofigh Allahviranloo,
Department of Mathematics, Faculty
of Engineering and Natural Sciences,
Bahcesehir University
Istanbul, Turkey

Muhammad Rezal Kamel Ariffin
Institute for Mathematical Research
and Department of Mathematics,
Universiti Putra Malaysia, 43400
UPM Serdang
Selangor, Malaysia

Haslina Arshad
Institute of IR 4.0, Universiti Kebangsaan
Malaysia, 43600 Bangi
Selangor, Malaysia

Majid Darehmiraki
Department of Mathematics, Behbahan
Khatam Alanbia University of
Technology
Behbahan, Khuzestan, Iran

Yashar Falamarzi
Climate Modelling and Prediction
Group, Climatological Research
Institute (CRI), Atmospheric Science
and Meteorological Research Center
(ASMERC)
Mashhad, Iran

Madineh Farnam
Department of Electrical Engineering,
Shohadaye Hoveizeh University of
Technology
Dasht-e Azadegan, Khuzestan

Amir Hamzah Abd Ghafar Ghafar
Institute for Mathematical Research and
Department of Mathematics, Universiti
Putra Malaysia, 43400 UPM Serdang
Selangor, Malaysia

Arijit Ghosh
Department of Mathematics, St. Xavier's
College (Autonomous)
Kolkata, India

M. Keshavarz
Department of Mathematics, Science
and Research Branch, Islamic Azad
University
Tehran, Iran

Azadeh Zahedi Khameneh
Institute for Mathematical Research,
Universiti Putra Malaysia, 43400 UPM
Selangor, Malaysia

Adem Kilicman
Institute for Mathematical Research and
Department of Mathematics, Universiti
Putra Malaysia, 43400 UPM Serdang
Selangor, Malaysia

Suchitra Kumari
Department of Commerce, J.D. Birla
Institute, Kolkata, India Kumari
Suchitra Kumari, Department of
Commerce, J.D. Birla Institute
Kolkata, India

Zainal Rasyid Mahayuddin
Faculty of Information Science and
Technology, Universiti Kebangsaan
Malaysia
Malaysia

Senthil kumar Mohan
School of Information Technology and
Engineering, VIT University
Vellore, India

Sankar Prasad Mondal
Department of Applied Science Maulana
Abul Kalam Azad University of
Technology
West Bengal, India

Morteza Pakdaman
Disasters and Climate Change Group,
Climatological Research Institute
(CRI), Atmospheric Science and
Meteorological Research Center
(ASMERC)
Mashhad, Iran

Wan Nur Aqlili Wan Mohd Ruzai
Institute for Mathematical Research,
Universiti Putra Malaysia, 43400
UPM Serdang
Selangor, Malaysia

A. F. M. Saifuddin Saif
Faculty of Science and Technology,
American International University –
Bangladesh
Dhaka, Bangladesh

Soheil Salahshour
Faculty of Engineering and Natural
Sciences, Bahcesehir University
Istanbul, Turkey

R. Sulaiman
The National University of Malaysia
Tamilarasan Ananth kumar Tamil-
arasan, Dept of Computer Science
and Engineering, IFET College of
Engineering
Tamil Nadu, India

Siok Yee Tan
Fakulti Teknologi dan Sains Maklumat,
Universiti Kebangsaan Malaysia, 43600
Bangi
Selangor, Malaysia

1 Soft Computing Techniques: An Overview

Morteza Pakdaman[1], Ali Ahmadian[2] and Soheil Salahshour[3]
[1]Disasters and Climate Change Group, Climatological Research Institute (CRI), Atmospheric Science and Meteorological Research Center (ASMERC), Mashhad, Iran
[2]Institute of IR 4.0, The National University of Malaysia, Bangi, 43600UKM, Selangor, Malaysia
[3]Faculty of Engineering and Natural Sciences, Bahcesehir University, Istanbul, Turkey

1.1 INTRODUCTION

In the purview of the rapidly increasing complexity, size of data and uncertainty in real-world problems in various fields such as economy, environment, engineering, science, medicine, we need suitable tools for modeling the phenomena in our daily life. On the other hand, the increase in growth of data production caused many problems in the face of data analysis, forecasting and knowledge extraction due to voluminous data.

Soft computing is a flexible tool for modeling real-world phenomena. This flexibility supports both the computational complexity and uncertainty aspects of real-world phenomena. The two main factors that led to the growth of soft computing were the development of computational methods and development of computer hardware. In the field of method development, in addition to deepening and generalization of existing methods, new approaches were created in the face of computational complexity and uncertainty of real-world problems. In the field of uncertainty and its modeling, we can refer to fuzzy logic (Zadeh 1965) and the theory of possibility (Zadeh 1978), and in the field of dealing with computational complexity, we can refer to the theory of deep learning (e.g., see Lecun et al. 2015). With the advent of computers and rapid advances in the production of super-computers and computing systems, the knowledge of soft computing grew rapidly. This growth has been achieved in both the creation of new algorithms and approaches as well as the deepening of existing methods.

As it can be observed in Figure 1.1, the main components of real-world problems are complexity, uncertainty, scale largeness and using optimization. Soft computing

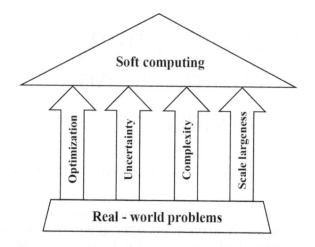

FIGURE 1.1   Soft computing is a flexible tool for modeling the real-world phenomena.

can adapt itself to the main components of real-world problems by several tools, which will be discussed in this chapter.

1.2   THE CONCEPT OF UNCERTAINTY: THE ROLE OF FUZZY LOGIC

Uncertainty is an integral part of real-world phenomena. It is clear that in order to model a real phenomenon, its uncertainty cannot be ignored. As a rule, a good realistic modeling method should be able to model degrees of uncertainty. There are various tools for uncertainty modeling, such as probability theory and interval calculation theory (for a simple application see Effati and Pakdaman 2012). Fuzzy logic is a powerful tool in modeling the uncertainty of real-world phenomena. In the field of soft computing, fuzzy logic has been able to grow significantly as a powerful tool for modeling uncertainty in the fields of economics, science, engineering, medicine and others. This theory was first proposed by Professor Zadeh in 1965 (Zadeh 1965), and since then, in addition to various generalizations, it has been able to have wide applications in various sectors.

Fuzzy logic, unlike classical logic, is a multivalued logic. Also, in fuzzy set theory, the membership degree of an element to a fuzzy set is a number between zero and one. In classical logic, however, a member may or may not belong to a set. The concept of the membership function is used in order to calculate and present the membership degree of an element to a fuzzy set. There are several types of membership functions. In Figure 1.2, two conventional fuzzy membership functions are depicted.

In the field of applications of fuzzy logic in mathematical models and concepts, we can refer to Effati and Pakdaman (2010) where the authors presented an artificial neural network approach for solving fuzzy differential equations. Effati et al. (2011) introduced a fuzzy neural network model for solving fuzzy linear programming problems. In this paper, they presented fuzzy shortest path problems as well as fuzzy maximum flow problems. Another important application of the fuzzy set

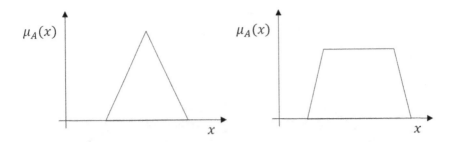

FIGURE 1.2 Triangular (left) and trapezoidal (right) fuzzy membership functions.

theory was for the approximation theory. Pakdaman and Effati (2016a) employed the fuzzy systems for approximating the solution of optimal control models.

From practical applications point of view, the applications of fuzzy logic cannot be limited to special cases. The use of fuzzy logic can be seen in a wide variety of practical applications such as economy, medicine, science, decision making, psychology and engineering. For example, we can refer to Hadi Sadoghi Yazi (2008) where the authors employed the concept of fuzzy uncertainty to model fuzzy current and fuzzy voltage for an electrical circuit. Dong et al. (2020) proposed a fuzzy best–worst method (BWM for short) based on triangular fuzzy numbers for multicriteria decision-making. Ren et al. (2020) proposed a multicriterion decision-making method based on the Dempster–Shafer (DS) theory and generalized Z-numbers. A Z-number is an ordered pair composed of two fuzzy numbers and DS theory is a tool for modeling uncertain information and provides weaker conditions than the traditional Bayes reasoning approach. They applied their approach to medicine selection for the patients with mild symptoms of the COVID-19. Some other applications of fuzzy logic in medicine can be found in Uzun Ozsahin et al. (2020). For the applications of fuzzy logic in the economy, we can refer to Padilla-Rivera et al. (2020) where the authors proposed an approach to identify key social indicators of circular economy (CE) through qualitative (Delphi) and quantitative (fuzzy logic) tools that objectively account for the uncertainty associated with data collection and judgment elicitation and a number of attributes (indicators) by considering the vagueness of the data. For another application of fuzzy logic in the economy, we can refer to Yu et al. (2020) where the authors studied the application of fractional-order chaotic system (based on the T–S fuzzy model) in the design of secure communication and its role in the construction of efficiency evaluation system for dispatching operation of energy-saving and power generation under a low carbon economy.

A general framework of a fuzzy system is depicted in Figure 1.3. Fuzzy logic is also used in several mathematical concepts. For example, we can refer to fuzzy calculus, fuzzy probability, fuzzy graph theory and fuzzy analysis. M. Pakdaman and Effati (2016b) and M. Pakdaman and Effati (2016c) defined the concept of fuzzy projection over the crisp set and also the meaning of fuzzy linear projection equation. The linear projection equation has several applications in the field of optimization and by defining the concept of fuzzy projection, the authors extended the applicability of fuzzy linear projection equation for fuzzy optimization problems. Lupulescu and O'Regan (2020) defined a new derivative concept for set-valued and fuzzy-valued

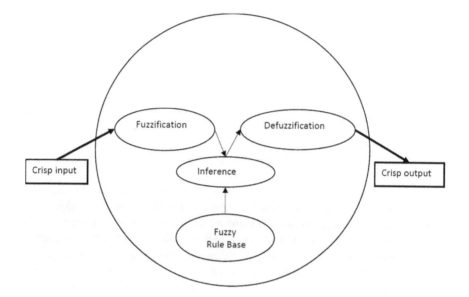

FIGURE 1.3   General structure of a fuzzy system.

functions. They employed this new derivative concept for differential and integral calculus in quasilinear metric spaces. Pakdaman et al. (2020) proposed an unsupervised kernel least mean squared algorithm for solving fuzzy differential equations. They applied the proposed solution procedure for solving the energy balance model. The proposed fuzzy energy balance model is a fuzzy initial value problem.

1.3   THE CONCEPT OF COMPLEXITY: THE ROLE OF ARTIFICIAL NEURAL NETWORKS

Artificial neural networks are simplified mathematical models of biological neural networks. Today, different types of neural networks are widely used in various scientific and technical fields. Artificial neural networks have different structures, topologies and models for different applications, including feedforward, recurrent, Hopfield, perceptron and convolutional neural networks (see, e.g., Haykin and Network 2004 and Hassoun 1995).

A general architecture of a multilayer ANN can be seen in Figure 1.4. The central processing unit of a neural network model can be considered as the artificial neuron. Neurons contain activation functions that can be of several types based on the under-study problem. Usually, for function approximation purposes, the sigmoid activation function is used as:

$$\sigma(y) = \frac{1}{1 + e^{-y}} \tag{1.1}$$

The use of ANN for function approximation is based on the universal approximation theorem (Cybenko 1989).

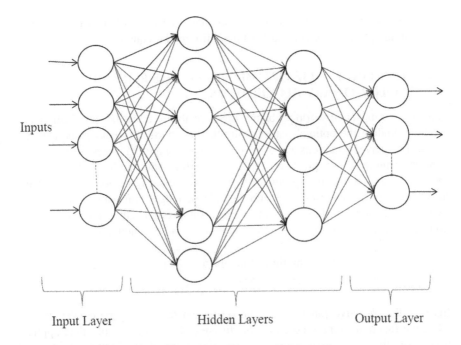

Input Layer   Hidden Layers   Output Layer

FIGURE 1.4   General architecture of a multilayer neural network.

Since there are several types of artificial neural networks (ANNs), they have a wide variety of applications in practice. For environmental sciences, the ANNs are applied for solving complicated problems arising in nature. Pakdaman Naghab et al. (2020) employed ANN and some other machine-learning techniques for lightning event prediction. Pakdaman et al. 2020) also employed the multilayer perceptron for the monthly forecast of precipitation by post-processing the North American multimodel ensemble data. Similar to fuzzy logic, ANNs have wide applications in medicine. You et al. (2020) proposed three predictive models of powder properties-tablet quality for simulated herbal medicine compound tablets. Their proposed models can be used to predict the tensile strength and disintegration time of tablets according to the powder properties. The models were based on combinations of four items: principal component analysis (PCA), radial basis function artificial neural network (RBF-ANN), backpropagation artificial neural network (BP-ANN) and multiple regression analysis (MRA). For a review on applications of ANN in medicine, one may study Lin et al. (2016). Finally, as an application of ANN in practice, we can refer to Pooya and Pakdaman (2017) where the authors proposed a neural network solution for production-inventory optimal control systems.

ANNs also applied for providing approximate-analytical solutions to mathematical problems. For example, Javad Sabouri et al. (2017) provided the solutions of fractional optimal control models by ANNs. They approximated the state and control functions of a fractional optimal control problem by multi-layer perceptron neural networks. Effati and Pakdaman (2013) used the ability of ANNs in function approximation to solve optimal control problems. Also, Pakdaman et al. (2017) proposed an approach for solving fractional differential equations.

1.4 THE CONCEPT OF OPTIMIZATION: THE ROLE OF EVOLUTIONARY ALGORITHMS

In the face of most real-world problems, there are always traces of optimization. For example, finding the optimal path, finding the best portfolio, making the best decisions in complex situations and even in many soft computing issues such as neural network training, we are practically solving an optimization problem. The methods for solving an optimization problem based on the linearity or nonlinearity of the model are very diverse. But in general, optimization algorithms can be divided into two main categories: classical mathematical optimization algorithms and evolutionary algorithms. A general optimization problem is presented in (1.2) as follows:

$$\begin{aligned} \text{minimize/maximize} \quad & f(x) \\ \text{s.t.} \quad & x \in \Omega \end{aligned} \tag{1.2}$$

In (1.2), the objective function and the set of constraints may be convex or not. Also, the function in the model may be differentiable or not. In practical applications, we may have nonsmooth and nonconvex problems. Although classical mathematical optimization algorithms are efficient in solving many problems and their convergence is guaranteed to be the optimal solution, but in real-world problems, there are many optimization problems that can be solved more easily and quickly with the help of evolutionary optimization algorithms. There are also similar conditions for solving multiobjective and multicriteria optimization problems. In addition to existing optimization methods to solve these problems, evolutionary algorithms have also been developed.

An Evolutionary algorithm uses mechanisms inspired by biological evolution, such as reproduction, mutation, recombination, crossover, generation and selection. Among the evolutionary optimization algorithms, the genetic algorithm (GA), in addition to being particularly popular, has many applications in practice. In what follows, we mention some successful applications of GA and other evolutionary algorithms in both practical and theoretical problems. As an application of GA in medicine, we can refer to Hilali-Jaghdam et al. (2020) where the authors proposed a multilevel segmentation method of medical images based on classical and quantum genetic algorithms. The difference between the classical and quantum GA is that the GA uses a binary coding approach while the quantum genetic algorithm (QGA) uses the qubit encoding of individuals. Yan et al. (2013) investigated the potential rules and knowledge of traditional Chinese medicine (TCM) and Western medicine (WM) treatment on chronic urticaria (CU) based on data-mining methods. They employed a genetic algorithm to discover the optimization model in the TCM and WM treatment on CU. As another application of GA, we can refer to Xiao et al. (2021), which proposed a highly scalable hybrid parallel genetic algorithm (HPGA) based on Sunway TaihuLight Supercomputer. Other industrial and engineering applications of GA and evolutionary algorithms can be found in Dasgupta and Michalewicz (1997) and Sanchez et al. (2012).

Evolutionary algorithms are not limited to genetic algorithms and are constantly evolving. For example, we can mention some other evolutionary algorithms such as particle swarm optimization (PSO) and ant colony optimization (OCA). In many cases, the evolutionary algorithms can be combined with other soft computing techniques. Combining evolutionary algorithms with the other soft computing algorithms and approaches, such as artificial neural networks as well as fuzzy systems, creates powerful modeling tools that have high performance to solve real-world problems. Especially, evolutionary algorithms can be used to train steps in several data mining techniques. This is due to the fact that the training process is indeed an optimization algorithm. For example, Hong et al. (2018) applied genetic algorithms to set the optimal combination of forest fire-related variables and modeled the forest fire susceptibility based on data mining models. They applied their approach to a real case in China. Chen et al. (2017) proposed a GIS-based new ensemble data mining technique that involves an adaptive neuro-fuzzy inference system (ANGIS) with a genetic algorithm, differential evolution and particle swarm optimization for landslide spatial modeling. They applied their algorithm for a real case in China.

1.5 CONCLUDING REMARKS

As briefly mentioned, in the face of complex real-world problems, we have to use newer tools with more capabilities instead of the classic modeling and solving tools. Soft computing is exactly the powerful tool that allows us to model and solve complex, large-scale real-world problems. Not only soft computing tools can be used individually, but also by combining them together, better tools can be obtained to model various aspects of real problems such as complexity and uncertainty simultaneously.

REFERENCES

Chen, W., Panahi, M., & Pourghasemi, H.R. (2017). Performance evaluation of GIS-based new ensemble data mining techniques of adaptive neuro-fuzzy inference system (ANFIS) with genetic algorithm (GA), differential evolution (DE), and particle swarm optimization (PSO) for landslide spatial modelling. *Catena, 157,* 310–324. https://doi.org/10.1016/j.catena.2017.05.034

Cybenko, G. (1989). Approximation by superpositions of a sigmoidal function. *Mathematics of Control, Signals, and Systems,* 2(4), 303–314. https://doi.org/10.1007/BF02551274

Dasgupta, D., & Michalewicz, Z. (1997). Evolutionary algorithms—an overview. In *Evolutionary Algorithms in Engineering Applications* (pp. 3–28). Springer, Berlin Heidelberg. https://doi.org/10.1007/978-3-662-03423-1_1

Dong, J., Wan, S., & Chen, S.-M. (2020). Fuzzy best-worst method based on triangular fuzzy numbers for multi-criteria decision-making. *Information Sciences.* https://doi.org/10.1016/j.ins.2020.09.014

Effati, S., Pakdaman, M., & Ranjbar, M. (2011). A new fuzzy neural network model for solving fuzzy linear programming problems and its applications. *Neural Computing and Applications,* 20(8). https://doi.org/10.1007/s00521-010-0491-4

Effati, Sohrab, & Pakdaman, M. (2010). Artificial neural network approach for solving fuzzy differential equations. *Information Sciences*, *180*(8), 1434–1457.

Effati, Sohrab, & Pakdaman, M. (2012). Solving the interval-valued linear fractional programming problem. *American Journal of Computational Mathematics*. https://doi.org/10.4236/ajcm.2012.21006

Effati, Sohrab, & Pakdaman, M. (2013). Optimal control problem via neural networks. *Neural Computing and Applications*, *23*(7–8), 2093–2100. https://doi.org/10.1007/s00521-012-1156-2

Hadi Sadoghi Yazdi, M.P. and S.E. (2008). Fuzzy circuit analysis. *International Journal of Applied Engineering Research*, *3*(8), 1061–1071.

Hassoun, M.H. (1995). *Fundamentals of artificial neural networks*. MIT press.

Haykin, S., & Network, N. (2004). A comprehensive foundation. *Neural Networks*, *2*, 41.

Hilali-Jaghdam, I., Ben Ishak, A., Abdel-Khalek, S., & Jamal, A. (2020). Quantum and classical genetic algorithms for multilevel segmentation of medical images: a comparative study. *Computer Communications*, *162*, 83–93. https://doi.org/10.1016/j.comcom.2020.08.010

Hong, H., Tsangaratos, P., Ilia, I., Liu, J., Zhu, A.X., & Xu, C. (2018). Applying genetic algorithms to set the optimal combination of forest fire related variables and model forest fire susceptibility based on data mining models. The case of Dayu County, China. *Science of the Total Environment*, *630*, 1044–1056. https://doi.org/10.1016/j.scitotenv.2018.02.278

Javad Sabouri, K, Effati, S., & Pakdaman, M. (2017). A neural network approach for solving a class of fractional optimal control problems. *Neural Processing Letters*, *45*(1). https://doi.org/10.1007/s11063-016-9510-5

Lecun, Y., Bengio, Y., & Hinton, G. (2015). Deep learning. In *Nature*. https://doi.org/10.1038/nature14539

Lin, D., Vasilakos, A.V., Tang, Y., & Yao, Y. (2016). Neural networks for computer-aided diagnosis in medicine: a review. *Neurocomputing*, *216*, 700–708. https://doi.org/10.1016/j.neucom.2016.08.039

Lupulescu, V., & O'Regan, D. (2020). A new derivative concept for set-valued and fuzzy-valued functions. Differential and integral calculus in quasilinear metric spaces. *Fuzzy Sets and Systems*. https://doi.org/10.1016/j.fss.2020.04.002

Padilla-Rivera, A., do Carmo, B.B.T., Arcese, G., & Merveille, N. (2020). Social circular economy indicators: selection through fuzzy Delphi method. *Sustainable Production and Consumption*. https://doi.org/10.1016/j.spc.2020.09.015

Pakdaman, M., Ahmadian, A., Effati, S., Salahshour, S., & Baleanu, D. (2017). Solving differential equations of fractional order using an optimization technique based on training artificial neural network. *Applied Mathematics and Computation*, *293*, 81–95. https://doi.org/10.1016/j.amc.2016.07.021

Pakdaman, M., & Effati, S. (2016a). Approximating the solution of optimal control problems by fuzzy systems. *Neural Processing Letters*, *43*(3). https://doi.org/10.1007/s11063-015-9440-7

Pakdaman, M., & Effati, S. (2016b). Fuzzy projection over a crisp set and applications. *International Journal of Fuzzy Systems*, *18*(2). https://doi.org/10.1007/s40815-015-0125-1

Pakdaman, M., & Effati, S. (2016c). On fuzzy linear projection equation and applications. *Fuzzy Optimization and Decision Making*, *15*(2). https://doi.org/10.1007/s10700-015-9222-8

Pakdaman, M., Falamarzi, Y., Sadoghi Yazdi, H., Ahmadian, A., Salahshour, S., & Ferrara, F. (2020). A kernel least mean square algorithm for fuzzy differential equations and its application in earth's energy balance model and climate. *Alexandria Engineering Journal*, *59*(4), 2803–2810. https://doi.org/10.1016/j.aej.2020.06.016

Pakdaman, M., Falamarzi, Y., Babaeian, I., & Javanshiri, Z. (2020). Post-processing of the North American multi-model ensemble for monthly forecast of precipitation based on neural network models. *Theoretical and Applied Climatology, 141*(1–2), 405–417. https://doi.org/10.1007/s00704-020-03211-6

Pakdaman, M., Naghab, S.S., Khazanedari, L., Malbousi, S., & Falamarzi, Y. (2020). Lightning prediction using an ensemble learning approach for northeast of Iran. *Journal of Atmospheric and Solar-Terrestrial Physics, 209*, 105417. https://doi.org/1 0.1016/j.jastp.2020.105417

Pooya, A., & Pakdaman, M. (2017). Analysing the solution of production-inventory optimal control systems by neural networks. *RAIRO - Operations Research, 51*(3). https:// doi.org/10.1051/ro/2016044

Ren, Z., Liao, H., & Liu, Y. (2020). Generalized Z-numbers with hesitant fuzzy linguistic information and its application to medicine selection for the patients with mild symptoms of the COVID-19. *Computers and Industrial Engineering, 145*, 106517. https://doi.org/10.1016/j.cie.2020.106517

Sanchez, E., Squillero, G., & Tonda, A. (2012). Industrial applications of evolutionary algorithms. *Intelligent Systems Reference Library, 34*, 1–130. https://doi.org/10.1007/ 978-3-642-27467-1

Uzun Ozsahin, D., Uzun, B., Ozsahin, I., Mustapha, M.T., & Musa, M.S. (2020). Fuzzy logic in medicine. In *Biomedical Signal Processing and Artificial Intelligence in Healthcare* (pp. 153–182). Elsevier. https://doi.org/10.1016/b978-0-12-818946-7.00006-8

Xiao, Z., Liu, X., Xu, J., Sun, Q., & Gan, L. (2021). Highly scalable parallel genetic algorithm on Sunway many-core processors. *Future Generation Computer Systems, 114*, 679–691. https://doi.org/10.1016/j.future.2020.08.028

Yan, M., Ye, F., Zhang, Y., Cai, X., Fu, Y., & Yang, X. (2013). Optimization model research on efficacy in treatment of chronic urticaria by Chinese and Western Medicine based on a genetic algorithm. *Journal of Traditional Chinese Medicine, 33*(1), 60–64. https:// doi.org/10.1016/s0254-6272(13)60101-6

You, G., Zhao, H., Gao, D., Wang, M., Ren, X., & Wang, Y. (2020). Predictive models of tensile strength and disintegration time for simulated Chinese herbal medicine extracts compound tablets based on artificial neural networks. *Journal of Drug Delivery Science and Technology, 60*, 102025. https://doi.org/10.1016/j.jddst.2020.102025

Yu, M., Ding, X., Sun, H., Yu, K., & Zhao, D. (2020). Role of fuzzy fractional differential equation in the construction of low carbon economy statistical evaluation system. *Alexandria Engineering Journal, 59*(4), 2765–2775. https://doi.org/10.1016/j.aej.202 0.05.031

Zadeh, L.A. (1978). Fuzzy sets as a basis for a theory of possibility. *Fuzzy Sets and Systems*. https://doi.org/10.1016/0165-0114(78)90029-5

Zadeh, Lotfi A. (1965). Fuzzy sets. *Information and Control, 8*(3), 338–353.

2 Solution of Linear Difference Equation in Interval Environment and Its Application

Mostafijur Rahaman[1], *Sankar Prasad Mondal*[2], *and Shariful Alam*[3]

[1]Department of Mathematics, Indian Institute of Engineering Science and Technology, Shibpur, Howrah 711103, India

[2]Department of Applied Science, Maulana Abul Kalam Azad University of Technology, West Bengal, Haringhata, Nadia 741249, West Bengal, India

[3]Department of Mathematics, Indian Institute of Engineering Science and Technology, Shibpur, Howrah 711103, India

2.1 INTRODUCTION

2.1.1 UNCERTAINTY VIA INTERVAL NUMBERS

Interval number theory is one of the dominant components of set-valued analysis. To define the sense of impreciseness, the theory of interval numbers is considered to be a very popular philosophy along with the fuzzy theory. When a set-valued function claims interval numbers in its range, it is called the interval-valued function. There are several worthy studies (Floudas 2000; Candau et al. 2006; Elishakoff and Miglis 2012; Popova 2012; Apt and Zoeteweij 2007; Hladík 2012; Jerrell 1994; Jiang et al. 2008; Žilinskas and Bogle 2007; Popova and Hladik 2013) which enrich the literature regarding the theory of interval numbers and interval-valued functions. On the application counterpart, the arithmetic of interval numbers and the calculus of interval-valued functions were accounted in the study of reliability optimization (Sahoo et al. 2014), design (Rao and Berke 1997), mechanical (Kulpa et al. 1998), and electrical (Oppenheimer and Michel 1988a, b, c; Kolev 1993) engineering problems and bio-mathematical models (Pal et al. 2013). The interval arithmetic oriented algorithms were improved to set the interval objectives in constrained optimization (Pal et al. 2015; Karmakar and Bhunia 2013), multi-objective optimization (Bhunia and Samanta 2014; Chanas and Kuchta 1996; Ishibuchi and Tanaka 1990), global optimization problems (Karmakar et al. 2008). The applications of interval numbers in the linear programming problems (LPP) were addressed by Shaocheng (1994) and Hladík (2011). Furthermore, Mahapatra and Mandal (2012) contributed a documentation of posynomial parametric geometric programming with coefficients as interval numbers. Also, a solution method of posynomial geometric programming with interval exponents and coefficients was credited by Liu (2008).

2.1.2 Difference Equation Versus Differential Equation

Applications of differential equation are very familiar to the researchers engaged in finding truth in the field of technology and management. The theory and applications of the integer-order differential equations (Mondal et al. 2013; Mondal and Roy 2013 a, b, c) and fractional order differential equation (Rahaman et al. 2020 a, b, c) enriched the research domain regarding the continuous process involved in a dynamical system. On the contrary, the literature on difference equation seems to be smaller in comparison to that of the differential equation. The discrete modeling between two given time-period can be traced and tackled by the difference equation. In the last three decades, the study of difference equations has gained enthusiasms among the academic to provide the mathematical structure for the dynamics involved in the field of science, technology, and management.

2.1.3 Relevance of Difference Equation Under Interval Uncertainty

The natural phenomena which describe the dynamical system in certain discrete period can be illustrated by the recurrence formula or the real or complex sequence. For analyzing these types of facts, the difference equation is coming into the picture. Now, most of the natural phenomena carry some ambiguities within its variables and parameters. Many discrete situations under uncertainty are frequently described by the fuzzy difference equation. But, when the impreciseness is measured in terms of interval uncertainty, then interval difference equation aptly provides the necessity. Furthermore, the interval version of the uncertain difference equation may be very easy and effective tool to tackle the mentioned situations. The difference equation having any one of the following three criteria is called an interval difference equation:

    i. Only initial condition of the difference equation is interval number,
    ii. Only the coefficients of the difference equation are interval number,
    iii. Both initial conditions and coefficients of the difference equation are both interval numbers.

The study of the imprecise difference equation faces a rapid development in the recent year. One of the major obstacles is that the solution of the imprecise difference equation does not follow strictly that of the crisp difference equation because of some exceptional characteristic of arithmetic in different uncertainty theory. We advocate for the interval difference equation over the fuzzy difference equation because of the simplicity to convert the interval difference to the system of crisp difference equations.

2.1.4 REVIEW ON IMPRECISE DIFFERENCE EQUATION

In this subsection, we are going through a brief review of the literature addressing the difference equation under uncertainty. The reviewed research works with their respective major contributions are presented in Table 2.1.

2.1.5 NOVELTIES

In spite of the few improvements of the theory of difference equation under uncertainty, we can claim the novelty of the work scripted in the present chapter under the following points of views:

i. The current chapter contributes to credit the study of difference equation interval environment in literature.
ii. The stability condition for interval difference equation is done here.
iii. The coefficients are taking positive and negative interval number both.
iv. The process is followed by numerical examples.
v. The proposed theory is validated by two worthy applications.

2.1.6 ARRANGEMENT OF THE CHAPTER

The rest of the paper is structured as follows: In section 2.2, we revisit the theory of interval analysis and difference equation. A flowchart describing the development of the philosophy regarding the interval difference equation is presented in section 2.3. The definition of interval difference equation along with its solutions and the stability conditions are discussed in section 2.4. In section 2.5, the numerical examples and the application are illustrated in favor of the proposed theory. The chapter ends with conclusions in section 2.6.

2.2 PRELIMINARIES

2.2.1 INTERVAL NUMBER

2.2.1.1 Representation of Interval Number

Definition 2.2.1: An interval number is a set of the real numbers and it is denoted by
$\hat{A} = [a_l, a_r] = \{a: a_l \leq a \leq a_r, a \in \mathbb{R}\}$, where a_l, a_r are two bounds on the upper and lower values of the interval number.

In this sense, the interval number is a generalization of the real number and in particular, any real number "a" can be viewed as the trivial interval $[a, a]$.

Definition 2.2.2: Let $\hat{A} = [a_l, a_r]$ be an interval number, and then the parametric representation of interval number can be defined by $A(k) = a_l^{(1-k)} a_r^k$ where $a_l > 0$, $a_r > 0$ and $k \in [0, 1]$.

TABLE 2.1

Lists of Work Associated with Imprecise Difference Equation

Author's Name	Imprecise Parameter	Major Contributions
Deeba et al. (1996)	Fuzzy	Introduction of Fuzzy difference equation and interpret that with an application
Deeba and De Korvin (1993)	Fuzzy	Modeling of the CO2 level in blood using the concept of fuzzy difference equation
Lakshmikatham and Vatsala (2002)	Fuzzy	Introduction of the fundamental theory of difference equations under fuzzy uncertainty
Papaschinopoulos and Papadopoulos (2002a)	Fuzzy	Discussion of two different types difference equation
Papaschinopoulos and Papadopoulos (2002b)	Fuzzy	Discussion of two different types difference equation
Papaschinopoulos and Schinas (2000)	Fuzzy	Analyzing the characteristic and possible solution of different types of fuzzy difference equations
Papaschinopoulos and Stefanidou (2003)	Fuzzy	Interpretation of boundedness and asymptotic characteristic of the solutions of a difference equation under fuzzy uncertainty
Umekkan et. al. (2014)	Fuzzy	Tracing an application of fuzzy difference equation on finance
Stefanidou et al. (2010)	Fuzzy	Brief discussion on an exponential type fuzzy difference equation
Din (2015)	Fuzzy	Interpreting the asymptotic behavior of a second order fuzzy difference equation
Zhang et al. (2012)	Fuzzy	Manifestation of the behavior of solutions to a fuzzy non-linear difference equation
Memarbashi and Ghasemabadi (2013)	Fuzzy	Introduction of the solution approach of fuzzy difference equation of volterra type
Stefanidou and Papaschinopoulos (2005)	Fuzzy	Introduction of the solution approach of a difference equation of rational form under fuzzy uncertainty
Chrysafis et al. (2008)	Fuzzy	Tracing an application of fuzzy difference equation on finance
Rahaman et al. (2021b)	Fuzzy	A detailed manifestation on Gaussian fuzzy difference equation is done considering the different combinations of Gaussian fuzzy initial value and coefficient inspired by extension principle scheme
Mondal et al. (2018a)	Fuzzy	Analyzing the existence and stability conditions of Fuzzy Difference Equation
Mondal et al. (2018b)	Fuzzy	Discussion of the application of non-linear interval-valued fuzzy numbers on difference equations

(*Continued*)

TABLE 2.1 (*Continued*)

Author's Name	Imprecise Parameter	Major Contributions
Alamin et al. (2020a)	Neutrosophic	Introduction of the solution of Neutrosophic Homogeneous Difference Equation
Alamin et al. (2020b)	Fuzzy	Establishment of the stability criteria of the fuzzy non-homogenous difference equation
Mondal et al. (2016)	Fuzzy	Finding the solution of the second order linear fuzzy difference equation by Lagrange's multiplier method
This Chapter	Interval number	Finding the solution of interval difference equation along with the interpretation of the stability conditions of the solutions

2.2.1.2 Arithmetic Operation in Interval Number

Definition 2.2.3: Let $\hat{A} = [a_l, a_r]$ and $\hat{B} = [b_l, b_r]$ be two interval numbers then their addition of the interval number is defined as

$$\hat{A} + \hat{B} = [a_l, b_r] + [a_l, b_r] = [a_l + b_l, a_r + b_r]$$

Definition 2.2.4: Let $\hat{A} = [a_l, a_r]$ and $\hat{B} = [b_l, b_r]$ be two interval numbers then their subtraction of the interval number is defined as

$$\hat{A} - \hat{B} = [a_l, b_r] - [a_l, b_r] = [a_l - b_r, a_r - b_l]$$

Definition 2.2.5: Let $\hat{A} = [a_l, a_r]$ and $\hat{B} = [b_l, b_r]$ be two interval numbers then their multiplication of jf the interval number is defined as

$$\hat{A} \times \hat{B} = [a_l, a_r] \times [b_l, b_r]$$
$$= [min\{a_l b_l, a_l b_r, a_r b_l, a_r b_r\}, max\{a_l b_l, a_l b_r, a_r b_l, a_r b_r\}]$$

Definition 2.2.6: Let $\hat{A} = [a_l, a_r]$ and $\hat{B} = [b_l, b_r]$ be two interval numbers such that $0 \notin [b_l, b_r]$ then their division of the interval number is defined as

$$\hat{A}/\hat{B} = [a_l, a_r]/[b_l, b_r] = \left[min\left(\frac{a_l}{b_r}, \frac{a_l}{b_l}, \frac{a_r}{b_r}, \frac{a_r}{b_l}\right), max\left(\frac{a_l}{b_r}, \frac{a_l}{b_l}, \frac{a_r}{b_r}, \frac{a_r}{b_l}\right) \right]$$

Definition 2.2.7: Let $\hat{A} = [a_l, a_r]$ be an interval number and μ be any crisp number, then the interval number is defined as follows

$$\mu\hat{A} = \mu[a_l, a_r] = \begin{cases} [\mu a_l, \mu a_r] & where \ \mu \geq 0 \\ [\mu a_r, \mu a_l] & where \ \mu < 0 \end{cases}$$

2.2.2 DIFFERENCE EQUATION

A linear difference equation of q-th order can be written as

$$x_n - (a_{n-1}x_{n-1} + a_{n-2}x_{n-2} + \ldots \ldots \ldots \ldots + a_{n-q}x_{n-q}) = r_n,$$

$$n = q, q + 1, \ldots \ldots \ldots \tag{2.1}$$

In equation (2.1), when $r_n = 0$ for each value of n, the equation (2.1) is said to be a homogeneous difference equation. For the nonzero values of r_n (called the forcing factor), the equation (2.1) is called the non-homogeneous difference equation. Furthermore, when a_i ($i = 1, 2, \ldots, n$) are independent of n, they are called constant coefficients.

2.2.3 STABILITY ANALYSIS OF LINEAR DIFFERENCE EQUATION (STEFANIDOU ET AL. 2010)

Suppose, a linear nonhomogeneous discrete difference equation with constant coefficients is given by

$$u_n = au_{n-1} + b(a \neq 0) \tag{2.2}$$

When, u^* is the equilibrium solution of (2.2), then $u_n = u_{n-1} = u^*$ and from (2.2)

$$au^* + b = u^* \ i. \ e. \ , u^* = \frac{b}{1-a}$$

The equilibrium point u^* is said to be stable if u_n tends to $\frac{b}{1-a}$ as n tends to infinity. The equilibrium point is unstable if all solutions (if exists) diverge from u^* to $\pm \infty$. The stability of the equilibrium solution depends on a. That is, u^* is stable when $|a| < 1$ and unstable when $|a| > 1$. For $a = \pm 1$, no remarks on the stability can be drawn.

2.2.3.1 Stability Analysis of System Linear Homogeneous Difference Equation

Suppose a system of linear homogeneous difference equations is given by

$$\begin{cases} u_{n+1} = au_n + bv_n \\ v_{n+1} = cu_n + dv_n \end{cases} \tag{2.3}$$

The matrix representation of the system (2.3) of difference equations is

$$\begin{pmatrix} u_{n+1} \\ v_{n+1} \end{pmatrix} = \begin{pmatrix} a & b \\ c & d \end{pmatrix} \begin{pmatrix} u_n \\ v_n \end{pmatrix}$$

Certainly, $(0, 0)$ is the equilibrium point of the system (2.3) of homogeneous difference equations.

Theorem 2.2.1: Let λ_1 and λ_2 be two real distinct eigenvalues of the coefficients matrix of the above system. Then the equilibrium point $(0, 0)$ is

    i. Stable if both $|\lambda_1| < 1$ and $|\lambda_2| < 1$
    ii. Unstable if both $|\lambda_1| > 1$ and $|\lambda_2| > 1$
    iii. Saddle if $|\lambda_1| < 1$ and $|\lambda_2| > 1$ or, $|\lambda_1| > 1$ and $|\lambda_2| < 1$.

Theorem 2.2.2: Let $\lambda_1 = \lambda_2 = \lambda^*$ be real and equal eigen value of the coefficients matrix then the equilibrium point $(0, 0)$ is

    i. Stable if $|\lambda^*| < 1$
    ii. Unstable if $|\lambda^*| > 1$.

Theorem 2.2.3: If $\alpha + i\beta$ and $\alpha - i\beta$ be the complex conjugate eigenvalues of the coefficients matrix the equilibrium point $(0, 0)$ is

    i. Stable if $|\alpha \pm i\beta| < 1$
    ii. Unstable if $|\alpha \pm i\beta| > 1$.

2.2.4 STABILITY ANALYSIS OF SYSTEM OF LINEAR NON-HOMOGENEOUS DIFFERENCE EQUATIONS

Suppose a system of linear homogeneous difference equations is given by

$$\begin{cases} u_{n+1} = au_n + bv_n + g \\ v_{n+1} = cu_n + dv_n + h \end{cases} \tag{2.4}$$

Now give such transformation so that it changes to

$$\begin{cases} x_{n+1} = ax_n + by_n \\ y_{n+1} = cx_n + dy_n \end{cases}$$

Then, the stability criterion of (2.4) can be easily checked following the approach describing the stability of the system (2.3).

2.3 FLOWCHART OF SOLUTION APPROACH

The understanding of the philosophy related to discrete modeling in an uncertain environment is a matter of great enthusiasm. The mathematical aspects to rich the

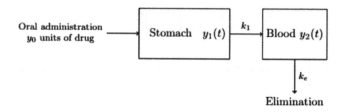

FIGURE 2.1 Flowchart.

interval difference equation through mathematical modeling is an emerging motive of the present study. The underlying reasoning of the notion established in the current chapter is visualized in Figure 2.1 as a flowchart.

2.4 DIFFERENCE EQUATION WITH INTERVAL ENVIRONMENT

An initial valued first-order non-homogeneous difference equation can be described by

$$\begin{cases} a_0 u_{n+1} = a_1 u_n + f(n) \\ \quad u_{n=0} = u_0 \end{cases} \tag{2.5}$$

The equation (2.5) will be called an interval difference equation if one of the following holds:

1. u_0 is an interval number
2. a_0, a_1 is an interval number
3. Both u_0, a_0 and a_1 are interval numbers.

2.4.1 SOLUTION WHEN U_0 IS AN INTERVAL NUMBER

The difference equation is

$$a_0 \hat{u}_{n+1} = a_1 \hat{u}_n + f(n)$$

with interval initial condition $\hat{u}_{n=0} = \hat{u}_0$

Here, four cases arise

  i. $a_0 > 0$, $a_1 > 0$
 ii. $a_0 > 0$, $a_1 < 0$
iii. $a_0 < 0$, $a_1 > 0$
 iv. $a_0 < 0$, $a_1 < 0$

2.4.1.1 When Coefficients Is Like $a_0 > 0$, $a_1 > 0$

2.4.1.1.1 Solution

The difference equation becomes

$$a_0 [u_{n+1,L}(n), u_{n+1,R}(n)] = a_1 [u_{n,L}(n), u_{n,R}(n)] + [f(n), f(n)]$$

Or,

$$a_0 u_{n+1,L}(n) = a_1 u_{n,L}(n) + f(n)$$

$$a_0 u_{n+1,R}(n) = a_1 u_{n,R}(n) + f(n)$$

with initial condition

$$u_{n=0,L}(n) = u_{0L}$$

$$u_{n=0,R}(n) = u_{0R}$$

The above are simply crisp systems of linear difference equation which can be easily solved for any numerical example.

2.4.1.1.2 Stability

Since this is a non homogeneous system we can give a transformation $u_{n,L}(n) = u'_{n,L}(n) + \epsilon_1$ and $u_{n,R}(n) = u'_{n,R}(n) + \epsilon_2$ so that the above system of difference equation transform to

$$a_0 u'_{n+1,L}(n) = a_1 u'_{n,L}(n)$$

$$a_0 u'_{n+1,R}(n) = a_1 u'_{n,R}(n)$$

So the equilibrium point (0, 0) is stable if $|\frac{a_1}{a_0}| < 1$ and saddle if $|\frac{a_1}{a_0}| > 1$

2.4.1.2   When Coefficients Is Like $a_0 > 0$, $a_1 < 0$

2.4.1.2.1 Solution

The difference equation becomes

$$a_0 [u_{n+1,L}(n), u_{n+1,R}(n)] = a_1 [u_{n,R}(n), u_{n,L}(n)] + [f(n), f(n)]$$

Or,

$$a_0 u_{n+1,L}(n) = a_1 u_{n,R}(n) + f(n)$$

$$a_0 u_{n+1,R}(n) = a_1 u_{n,L}(n) + f(n)$$

with initial condition

$$u_{n=0,L}(n) = u_{0L}$$

$$u_{n=0,R}(n) = u_{0R}$$

The above are simply crisp systems of linear difference equation which can be easily solved for any numerical example.

2.4.1.2.2 Stability

So the equilibrium point (0,0) is stable if $\left|\sqrt{\frac{a_1}{a_0}}\right| < 1$ and unstable if $\left|\sqrt{\frac{a_1}{a_0}}\right| > 1$

2.4.1.3   When Coefficients Is Like $a_0<0$, $a_1>0$

2.4.1.3.1 Solution

The difference equation becomes

$$a_0[u_{n+1,R}(n), u_{n+1,L}(n)] = a_1[u_{n,L}(n), u_{n,R}(n)] + [f(n), f(n)]$$

Or,

$$a_0 u_{n+1,R}(n) = a_1 u_{n,L}(n) + f(n)$$

$$a_0 u_{n+1,L}(n) = a_1 u_{n,R}(n) + f(n)$$

with initial condition

$$u_{n=0,L}(n) = u_{0L}$$

$$u_{n=0,R}(n) = u_{0R}$$

The above are simply crisp systems of linear difference equation which can be easily solved for any numerical example.

2.4.1.3.2 Stability

So the equilibrium point (0,0) is stable if $\left|\sqrt{\frac{a_1}{a_0}}\right| < 1$ and unstable if $\left|\sqrt{\frac{a_1}{a_0}}\right| > 1$

2.4.1.4   When Coefficients Is Like $a_0>0$, $a_1>0$

2.4.1.4.1 Solution

The difference equation becomes

$$a_0[u_{n+1,R}(n), u_{n+1,L}(n)] = a_1[u_{n,R}(n), u_{n,L}(n)] + [f(n), f(n)]$$

Or,

$$a_0 u_{n+1,R}(n) = a_1 u_{n,R}(n) + f(n)$$

$$a_0 u_{n+1,L}(n) = a_1 u_{n,L}(n) + f(n)$$

with initial condition

$$u_{n=0,L}(n) = u_{0L}$$

$$u_{n=0,R}(n) = u_{0R}$$

The above are simply crisp system of linear difference equation which can be easily solved for any numerical example.

2.4.1.4.2 Stability

The equilibrium point $(0,0)$ is stable if $|\frac{a_1}{a_0}| < 1$ and saddle if $|\frac{a_1}{a_0}| > 1$

2.5   NUMERICAL EXAMPLE AND APPLICATION

2.5.1   NUMERICAL EXAMPLE

Example 5.1: A difference equation is given by $a_0 u_{n+1} = a_1 u_n + 2n$ with $u_{n=0} = u_0$. Solve the problem when

   i. $a_0 = 4$ and $a_1 = 2$ with $u_0 = \hat{u}_0 = [10, 15]$

   Solution. Then given first order difference equation is

$$a_0 u_{n+1} = a_1 u_n + 2n$$

Taking in the interval form is

$$a_0 [u_{n+1,L}(n), u_{n+1,R}(n)] = a_1 [u_{n,L}(n), u_{n,R}(n)] + [2n, 2n]$$

$$4 [u_{n+1,L}(n), u_{n+1,R}(n)] = 2 [u_{n,L}(n), u_{n,R}(n)] + [2n, 2n]$$

i.e., $2 [u_{n+1,L}(n)] = [u_{n,L}(n)] + n$ and $2 [u_{n+1,R}(n)] = [u_{n,R}(n)] + n$
   The solution is

$$u_{n,L}(n) = c_1 \left(\frac{1}{2}\right)^n + n - 2$$

$$u_{n,R}(n) = c_1\left(\frac{1}{2}\right)^n + n - 2$$

Using the initial condition, we find the unknown

$$c_1 = 12, \ c_2 = 17$$

The general solution is

$$u_{n,L}(n) = 12\left(\frac{1}{2}\right)^n + n - 2$$

Similarly

$$u_{n,R}(n) = 17\left(\frac{1}{2}\right)^n + n - 2$$

The solution of interval difference equation is

$$[u_{n,L}(n), u_{n,R}(n)] = \left[12\left(\frac{1}{2}\right)^n + n - 2, \ 17\left(\frac{1}{2}\right)^n + n - 2\right]$$

ii $a_0 = 4$ and $a_1 = -2$ with $u_0 = \hat{u}_0 = [10, 15]$

Solution. The given difference equation is

$$a_0 u_{n+1} = a_1 u_n + 2n$$

Taking in interval number form is

$$a_0[u_{n+1,L}(n), u_{n+1,R}(n)] = a_1[u_{n,L}(n), u_{n,R}(n)] + [2n, 2n]$$

$$4[u_{n+1,L}(n), u_{n+1,R}(n)] = -2[u_{n,L}(n), u_{n,R}(n)] + [2n, 2n]$$

i.e.,

$$2\,u_{n+1,L}(n) = -u_{n,R}(n) + n \tag{2.6}$$

and

$$4u_{n+1,R}(n) = -2u_{n,L}(n) + 2n \tag{2.7}$$

This is the system of difference with interval number

On replacing $n = n + 1$ in equation (2.6) and substituting in equation (2.7)

$$4u_{n+2,L}(n) - u_{n,L}(n) = 2 + n$$

Solution is

$$u_{n,L}(n) = A\left(\frac{1}{2}\right)^n + B\left(-\frac{1}{2}\right)^n + \frac{3n - 2}{9}$$

Similarly

$$u_{n,R}(n) = -A\left(\frac{1}{2}\right)^n + B\left(-\frac{1}{2}\right)^n - \frac{2 - 3n}{9}$$

Using initial condition we find the unknown $A = \frac{-15}{6}$, $B = \frac{229}{18}$

The required solution of interval difference equation is

$$[u_{n,L}(n), u_{n,R}(n)] = \left[\left(\frac{-15}{6}\right)\left(\frac{1}{2}\right)^n + \frac{229}{18}\left(-\frac{1}{2}\right)^n + \frac{6n - 4}{9}, \left(\frac{15}{6}\right)\left(\frac{1}{2}\right)^n \right.$$
$$\left. + \frac{229}{18}\left(-\frac{1}{2}\right)^n + \frac{6n - 4}{9}\right]$$

iii $a_0 = -4$ and $a_1 = 2$ with $u_0 = \hat{u}_0 = [10, 15]$.

Solution. The difference equation is

$$a_0 u_{n+1} = a_1 u_n + f(n)$$

Taking in the interval form is

$$a_0[u_{n+1,L}(n), u_{n+1,R}(n)] = a_1[u_{n,L}(n), u_{n,R}(n)] + [f(n), f(n)]$$

$$- 4[u_{n+1,L}(n), u_{n+1,R}(n)] = 2[u_{n,L}(n), u_{n,R}(n)] + [2n, 2n]$$

i.e.,

$$- 2u_{n+1,R}(n) = u_{n,L}(n) + n \qquad (2.8)$$

and

$$- 2u_{n+1,L}(n) = u_{n,R}(n) + n \qquad (2.9)$$

Replacing $n = n + 1$ in equation (2.8)

$$- 2u_{n+2,R}(n) = u_{n+1,L}(n) + (n + 1) \tag{2.10}$$

From equation (2.9) and (2.10) we get

$$- 4u_{n+2,R}(n) + u_{n,R}(n) = n + 2$$

Solution is

$$u_{n,L}(n) = -k_1\left(\frac{1}{2}\right)^n + k_2\left(-\frac{1}{2}\right)^n - \frac{15n - 2}{9}$$

and

$$u_{n,R}(n) = k_1\left(\frac{1}{2}\right)^n + k_2\left(-\frac{1}{2}\right)^n + \frac{3n - 2}{9}$$

Using the initial condition we find the unknown k_1, k_2

$$k_1 = \frac{49}{18}, \; k_2 = \frac{25}{2}$$

The solution of the difference equation with interval number

$$[u_{n,L}(n), u_{n,R}(n)] = \left[\left(-\frac{49}{18}\right)\left(\frac{1}{2}\right)^n + \frac{25}{2}\left(-\frac{1}{2}\right)^n - \frac{15n - 2}{9}, \frac{49}{18}\left(\frac{1}{2}\right)^n \right.$$
$$\left. + \frac{25}{2}\left(-\frac{1}{2}\right)^n + \frac{3n - 2}{9}\right]$$

iv $a_0 = -4$ and $a_1 = -2$ with $u_0 = \hat{u}_0 = [10, 15]$.

Solution. The given difference equation is

$$a_0 u_{n+1} = a_1 u_n + 2n$$

Taking interval form of the interval number

$$a_0[u_{n+1,L}(n), u_{n+1,R}(n)] = a_1[u_{n,L}(n), u_{n,R}(n)] + [2n, 2n]$$

Or

$$- 4[u_{n+1,L}(n), u_{n+1,R}(n)] = -2[u_{n,L}(n), u_{n,R}(n)] + [2n, 2n]$$

Or

$$[-4u_{n+1,R}(n), -4u_{n+1,L}(n)] = [-2u_{n,R}(n), -2u_{n,L}(n)] + [2n, 2n]$$

i.e., $- 4u_{n+1,L}(n) = -2u_{n,L}(n) + 2n$ and $- 4u_{n+1,R}(n) = -2u_{n,R}(n) + 2n$

The general solution is

$$u_{n,L}(n) = a\left(\frac{1}{2}\right)^n + 2 - n$$

and

$$u_{n,R}(n) = b\left(\frac{1}{2}\right)^n + 2 - n$$

Using initial condition we find the unknown a, b

$$a = 8, b = 13$$

Hence

$$u_{n,L}(n) = 8\left(\frac{1}{2}\right)^n + 2 - n$$

$$u_{n,R}(n) = 13\left(\frac{1}{2}\right)^n + 2 - n$$

The required solution of difference equation with interval number

$$[u_{n,L}(n), u_{n,R}(n)] = \left[8\left(\frac{1}{2}\right)^n + 2 - n, 13\left(\frac{1}{2}\right)^n + 2 - n\right].$$

For different iteration step, the solutions of the above mentioned four examples are given by the Table 2.2.

2.5.2 APPLICATIONS

2.5.2.1 Bank Account Problem (Banerjee 2014)

Let us consider a situation of the opening of savings bank account. Suppose, the initial credit of the account is Rs. I_0 subjected to the $r\%$ yearly compound interest. Also, the account holder has to credit Rs. d at the end of each year and he/she can withdraw Rs. w at the end of each year. Now we want to find how much money is thereafter a certain time. Suppose a decision-maker tries to calculate before investing.

TABLE 2.2

Solution of the Difference Equations with Different Interval Number

n	Example 4.1 (i)		Example 4.1 (ii)		Example 4.1 (iii)		Example 4.1 (iv)	
	$u_{n,L}(n)$	$u_{n,R}(n)$	$u_{n,L}(n)$	$u_{n,R}(n)$	$u_{n,L}(n)$	$u_{n,R}(n)$	$u_{n,L}(n)$	$u_{n,R}(n)$
4	2.7500	3.0625	2.8611	3.1736	-5.8333	2.0625	-1.5000	-1.1875
6	4.1875	4.2656	3.7153	3.7934	-9.6250	2.0156	-3.8750	-3.7969
8	6.0469	6.0664	4.9288	4.9484	-13.0729	2.5039	-5.9688	-5.9492
10	8.0117	8.0166	6.2322	6.2371	-16.4349	3.1260	-7.9922	-7.9873
Stability	Stable		Stable		Stable		Stable	

He is not sure what amount he deposited. The only way now is to take the amount as an interval parameter.

Now sole the above problem when

    i. $r = 4\%$, $I_0 = [9800, 10200]$ and $d = 5000$
    ii. $r = 4\%$, $I_0 = [9800, 10200]$ and $w = 5000$

Find the solution after $t = 15$ and $t = 25$ for (i) and $t = 1$ and $t = 2$ for (ii).
    Solution.

    i. On the above application, we see that if the saving account makes a difference equation with interest money and ratio $r\%$ then the problem can be mathematically written as

$$I_{t+1} = \left(1 + \frac{r}{100}\right)^t + d$$

With initial condition $I_0 = [9800, 10200]$. Here $r = 4\%$, $d = 5000$
    The above solution of the problem is

$$I_{t,L}(t) = 134800\left(\frac{104}{100}\right)^t - 125000$$

$$I_{t,R}(t) = 135200\left(\frac{104}{100}\right)^t - 125000$$

The solution of the above problem with the interval

$$[I_{t,L}(t), I_{t,R}(t)] = \left[134800\left(\frac{104}{100}\right)^t - 125000, \; 135200\left(\frac{104}{100}\right)^t - 125000\right]$$

TABLE 2.3
Interval-valued Interest

t	Example 8.1.1	
	$I_{t,L}(t)$	$I_{t,R}(t)$
15	117767.1845	118487.5619
25	234354.7375	235421.0720
Stability	Stable	

The solution of the problem for different of discrete phases is given by the Table 2.3.

ii On the above application, we see that if the saving account makes a difference equation with interest money and ratio $r\%$ and withdrawn money then the problem can be mathematically written as

$$I_{t+1} = \left(1 + \frac{r}{100}\right)^t - w$$

With the initial condition is $I_0 = [9800, 10200]$. Here $r = 4\%$, $w = 5000$
The above solution of the problem

$$I_{t,L}(t) = -115200\left(\frac{104}{100}\right)^t + 125000$$

$$I_{t,R}(t) = -114800\left(\frac{104}{100}\right)^t + 125000$$

In interval number representation, the solution is

$$[I_{t,L}(t), I_{t,R}(t)] = \left[-115200\left(\frac{104}{100}\right)^t + 125000, -114800\left(\frac{104}{100}\right)^t + 125000\right].$$

The tabular visualization of the solutions for different discrete phases is provided by Table 2.4.

2.5.2.2 Drug Delivery Problem (Banerjee 2014)

Consider a phenomenon where a drug is induced to the body a patient to cure some infection. The primary measure of injected drug amount d_0 in the patient's bloodstream is noticed to be decreased at the rate of $R\%$ per hour. For sustainability

TABLE 2.4

Interval-valued Interest

t	Example 8.1.1	
	$I_{t,L}(t)$	$I_{t,R}(t)$
1	5192.0000	5608.0000
2	399.6800	832.3200
Stability		Stable

of drug level in a certain quanta, an injection to provide the drug of amount b unit is pushed in each hour. Now we want to the amount of drug in a patient's bloodstream after a certain time. Suppose the decision-maker tries to calculate it before giving the drug. It is obvious that the drug cannot be given inaccurately (no one can predict accurately how much drug is needed). So the amount of drug can be taken as an interval parameter.

Now solve the problem when

    i. $R = 50\%$, $d_0 = [3, 4]$ and $b = 0.2$.
    ii. $R = 60\%$, $d_0 = [5, 6]$ and $b = 0.4$. Find the solution after $t = 3$ and $t = 4$.

Solution.

$$d_{t+1} = \frac{R}{100} d_t + b$$

    i. On the above application, we see that if the drug delivery makes a difference equation, if d_n be the unit of the drug at the $R\%$, b unit be the bloodstream then we can write in the mathematically is

With the initial condition is $d_0 = [3, 4]$ and $b = 0.2$
    The solution of the above problem in the interval

$$[d_{t,L}(t), d_{t,R}(t)] = \left[\frac{13}{5}\left(\frac{1}{2}\right)^t + \frac{2}{5}, \frac{18}{5}\left(\frac{1}{2}\right)^t + \frac{2}{5} \right]$$

The tabular visualization of the solutions for different of discrete phases is provided in Table 2.5.

    ii. On the above application, we see that if the drug delivery makes a difference equation, if d_n be the unit of the drug at the $R\%$, b unit be the bloodstream then we can written in the mathematically is

TABLE 2.5
Interval-valued Interest

t	Example 8.1.1	
	$d_{t,L}(t)$	$d_{t,R}(t)$
4	0.5625	0.6250
6	0.4406	0.4563
Stability	Stable	

TABLE 2.6
Interval-valued Interest

t	Example 8.1.1	
	$d_{t,L}(t)$	$d_{t,R}(t)$
4	1.2283	1.3579
6	0.8688	0.9155
Stability	Stable	

$$d_{t+1} = \frac{R}{100}d_t + b$$

With the initial condition is $d_0 = [5, 6]$ and $b = 0.4$

The solution of the above problem in the interval form

$$[d_{t,L}(t), d_{t,R}(t)] = \left[\frac{13}{3}\left(\frac{3}{5}\right)^t + \frac{2}{3}, \frac{16}{3}\left(\frac{3}{5}\right)^t + \frac{2}{3} \right].$$

The solution of the problem for different of discrete phases is given by Table 2.6.

2.6   CONCLUSION

Interval-valued difference equation is one of the fruitful mathematical frame for the discrete modeling of dynamical systems with imprecise parameters. The chapter credits the solution approaches to a first-order linear difference equation with the initial condition as an interval number. We show that for a different sign of coefficient, the solution and behavior can change. The interval stability condition for interval difference equation for every case has been clarified. Two different numerical examples and two applications have been considered to see the validity of the work. The theory and results are interesting enough to carry out further research.

Finally, it is worthy to say that this present paper may be a potential documentation for an academic who deals with uncertainty modeling in discrete process. For limitation, we cannot give the solution of nonlinear difference equation. In future, we can take the system of a linear difference equation and nonlinear difference equation in a different imprecise environment and solve analytically and numerically.

REFERENCES

Alamin A., Mondal S.P., Alam S., Ahmadian A., Salahshour S., & Salimi M. (2020). Solution and interpretation of neutrosophic homogeneous difference equation. *Symmetry*, *12*(7), 1091. https://doi.org/10.3390/sym12071091.

Alamin, A., Mondal, S.P., Alam, S., & Goswamy, A. (2020). Solution and stability analysis of non-homogeneous difference equation followed by real life application in fuzzy environment. *Sādhanā*, *45*, 185. https://doi.org/10.1007/s12046-020-01422-1.

Apt, K.R., & Zoeteweij, P. (2007). An analysis of arithmetic constraints on integer intervals. *Constraints*, *12*(4), 429–468. https://doi.org/10.1007/s10601-007-9017-9.

Banerjee, S. (2014). *Mathematical modeling, models, analysis and applications.* CRC Press, Taylor and Francis Group.

Bhunia, A.K., & Samanta, S.S. (2014). A study of interval metric and its application in multiobjective optimization with interval objectives. *Computers and Industrial Engineering*, *74*, 169–178. https://doi.org/10.1016/j.cie.2014.05.014.

Candau, Y., Raissi, T., Ramdani, N., & Ibos, L. (2006). Complex interval arithmetic using polar form. *Reliable Computing*, *12*(1), 1–20. https://doi.org/10.1007/s11155-006-2966-7.

Chanas, S., & Kuchta, D. (1996). Multiobjective programming in optimization of interval objective functions a generalized approach. *European Journal of Operational Research*, *94*, 594–598. https://doi.org/10.1016/0377-2217(95)00055-0.

Chrysafis, K.A., Papadopoulos, B.K., & Papaschinopoulos, G. (2008). On the fuzzy difference equations of finance. *Fuzzy Sets and Systems*, *159*(24), 3259–3270. https://doi.org/10.1016/j.fss.2008.06.007.

Deeba, E.Y., De Korvin, A., & Koh, E.L. (1996). A fuzzy difference equation with an application. *Journal of Difference Equations and Applications*, *2*, 365–374. https://doi.org/10.1080/10236199608808071

Deeba, E.Y., & De Korvin, A. (1999). Analysis by fuzzy difference equations of a model of CO_2 level in the blood. *Applied Mathematical Letters*, *12*, 33–40. https://doi.org/10.1016/S0893-9659(98)00168-2

Din, Q. (2015). Asymptotic behavior of a second –order fuzzy rational difference equations. *Journal of Discrete Mathematics*, *2015*, 1–7. https://doi.org/10.1155/2015/524931

Elishakoff, I., & Miglis, Y. (2012). Overestimation-free computational version of interval analysis. International *Journal of Computational Methods in Engineering Science and Mechanics*, *13*(5), 319–328. https://doi.org/10.1080/15502287.2012.683134.

Floudas, A.C. (2000). *Deterministic global optimization, theory, methods and applications. Non-convex optimization and its applications.* Springer.

Hladík, M. (2011). Interval linear programming: a survey. In: Mann, Z.A. (ed.) *Linear Programming—New Frontiers in Theory and Applications*. Nova Science Publishers, New York.

Hladík, M. (2012). Complexity of necessary efficiency in interval linear programming and multiobjective linear programming. *Optimization Letters*, *6*(5), 893–899. https://doi.org/10.1007/s11590-011-0315-1.

Ishibuchi, H., & Tanaka, H. (1990). Multiobjective programming in optimization of the interval objective function. *European Journal of Operational Research*, 48, 219–225. https://doi.org/10.1016/0377-2217(90)90375-L.

Jerrell, M.E. (1994). Global optimization using interval arithmetic. *Computational Economics*, 7(1), 55–62. https://doi.org/10.1007/BF01299329.

Jiang, C., Han, X., Liu, G., & Liu, G. (2008). A nonlinear interval number programming method for uncertain optimization problems. *European Journal of Operational Research*, 188(1), 1–13. https://doi.org/10.1016/j.ejor.2007.03.031.

Karmakar, S., & Bhunia, A.K. (2013). Uncertain constrained optimization by interval- oriented algorithm. *Journal of the Operational Research Society*. 1–15. https://doi.org/1 0.1057/jors.2012.151.

Karmakar, S.,Mahato, S.K., & Bhunia, A.K. (2008). Interval oriented multi-section techniques for global optimization. *Journal of Computational and Applied Mathematics*, 224(2), 476–491. https://doi.org/10.1016/j.cam.2008.05.025.

Kolev, L.V. (1993). *Interval Methods for Circuit Analysis*. World Scientific, Singapore. https://doi.org/10.1142/2039.

Kulpa, K., Pownuk, A., & Skalna, I. (1998). Analysis of linear mechanical structures with uncertainties by means of interval methods. *Computer Assisted Mechanics and Engineering Sciences*, 5(4), 443–477.

Lakshmikatham, V., & Vatsala, A. S. (2002). Basic Theory of Fuzzy Difference Equations. *Journal of Difference Equations and Applications*, 8(11), 957–968. https://doi.org/10.1 080/1023619021000048850.

Liu, S.T. (2008). Posynomial geometric programming with interval exponents and coefficients. *European Journal of Operational Research*, 186(1), 17–27. https://doi.org/10.1 016/j.ejor.2007.01.031.

Mahapatra, G.S., & Mandal, T.K. (2012). Posynomial parametric geometric programming with interval valued coefficient. *Journal of Optimization Theory and Applications*, 154, 120–132. https://doi.org/10.1007/s10957-012-9996-6.

Memarbashi, R., & Ghasemabadi, A. (2013). Fuzzy difference equations of volterra type. *International Jouranal of Nonlinear Analysis and Applications*, 4(1), 74–78. https://dx.doi.org/10.22075/ijnaa.2013.56.

Mondal, S.P., Banerjee, S., & Roy, T.K. (2013). First order linear homogeneous ordinary differential equation in fuzzy environment. *International Journal of Pure and Applied Sciences and Technology*, 14(1), 16–26.

Mondal, S.P., Khan, N.A., Vishwakarma, D., & Saha, A.K. (2018). Existence and Stability of Difference Equation in Imprecise Environment. *Nonlinear Engineering*, 7(4), 263–271. https://doi.org/10.1515/nleng-2016-0085.

Mondal, S.P., Mandal, M., & Bhattacharya, D. (2018). Non-linear interval-valued fuzzy numbers and their application in difference equations. *Granular Computing*, 3(2), 177–189. https://doi.org/10.1007/s41066-017-0063-4.

Mondal, S.P., & Roy, T.K. (2013a). First order linear non homogeneous ordinary differential equation in fuzzy environment. *Mathematical Theory and Modeling*, 3(1), 85–95.

Mondal, S.P., & Roy, T.K. (2013b). First order linear homogeneous ordinary differential equation in fuzzy environment based on Laplace transform. *Journal of Fuzzy Set Valued Analysis*, 2013, 1–18.

Mondal, S.P., & Roy, T.K. (2013c). First order linear homogeneous fuzzy ordinary differential equation based on Lagrange multiplier method. *Journal of Soft Computing and Application*, 2013, 1–17. https://doi.org/10.5899/2013%2FJSCA-00032.

Mondal, S.P., Vishwakarma D.K., & Saha, A.K. (2016). Solution of second order linear fuzzy difference equation by Lagrange's multiplier method. *Journal of Soft Computing and Applications*. https://doi.org/10.5899/2016%2FJSCA-00063.

Oppenheimer, E.P., & Michel, A.N. (1988a). Application of interval analysis techniques to linear systems: Part-I—fundamental results. *IEEE Transactions on Circuits and Systems*, 35(9), 1243–1256. https://doi.org/10.1109/31.7573.

Oppenheimer, E.P., & Michel, A.N. (1988b). Application of interval analysis techniques to linear systems: part-II—the interval matrix exponential function. *IEEE Transactions on Circuits and Systems*, 35(10), 1230–1242. https://doi:10.1109/31.7598.

Oppenheimer, E.P., & Michel, A.N. (1988c). Application of interval analysis techniques to linear systems: part-III— interval value problems. *IEEE Transactions on Circuits and Systems*, 35(10), 1243–1256. https://doi.org/10.1109/31.7599.

Pal, D., & Mahapatra, G.S. (2015). Parametric functional representation of interval number with arithmetic operations. *International Journal of Applied and Computational Mathematics*, 3, 459–469. https://doi.org/10.1007/s40819-015-0113-z.

Pal, D., Mahapatra, G.S., & Samanta, G.P. (2013). Optimal harvesting of prey-predator system with interval biological parameters: a bioeconomic model. *Mathematical Biosciences*, 241(2), 181–187. https://doi.org/10.1016/j.mbs.2012.11.007.

Papaschinopoulos, G., & Papadopoulos, B. K. (2002). On the fuzzy difference equation $x_{n+1} = A + B/x_n$. *Soft Computing*, 6, 456–461.

Papaschinopoulos, G., & Papadopoulos, B.K. (2002). On the fuzzy difference equation $x_{n+1} = A + x_n/x_{n-m}$. *Fuzzy Sets and Systems*, 129, 73–81.

Papaschinopoulos, G., & Schinas, C. J. (2000). On the fuzzy difference equation $x_{n+1} \sum_{k=0}^{k=1} Ai/x_{n-i}^{pi} + 1/x_{n-k}^{pk}$. *Journal of Difference Equations and Applications*, 6(7), 85–89.

Papaschinopoulos, G., & Stefanidou, G. (2003). Boundedness and asymptotic behavior of the Solutions of a fuzzy difference equation. *Fuzzy Sets and Systems*, 140, 523–539. https://doi.org/10.1016/S0165-0114(03)00034-4.

Popova, E.D. (2012). Explicit description of AE solution sets for parametric linear systems. SIAM *Journal of Matrix Analysis and Applications*, 33(4), 1172–1189. https://doi.org/10.1137/120870359.

Popova, E.D., & Hladik, M. (2013). Outer enclosures to the parametric AE solution set. *Soft Computing*, 17(8), 1403–1414. https://doi.org/10.1007/s00500-013-1011-0.

Rahaman, M., Mondal, S.P., Shaikh, A.A., Ahmadian, A., Senu, N., & Salahshour, S. (2020). Arbitrary-order economic production quantity model with and without deterioration: generalized point of view. *Advances in Difference Equations*, 2020, 16. https://doi.org/10.1186/s13662-019-2465-x.

Rahaman, M., Mondal, S.P., Alam, S. Khan, N.A., & Biswas, A. (2020). Interpretation of exact solution for fuzzy fractional non-homogeneous differential equation under the Riemann–Liouville sense and its application on the inventory management control problem. *Granular Computing*. https://doi.org/10.1007/s41066-020-00241-3.

Rahaman, M., Mondal, S.P., Shaikh, A.A., Pramanik, P., Roy, S., Maity, M.K., Mondal, R., & De, D. (2020). Artificial bee colony optimization-inspired synergetic study of fractional-order economic production quantity model. *Soft Computing*, 24, 15341–15359. https://doi.org/10.1007/s00500-020-04867-y.

Rahaman, M., Mondal, S.P., Alam, S., & Goswami, A. (2021).Synergetic study of inventory management problem in uncertain environment based on memory and learning effects. *Sadhana*, 46(39), 1–20. https://doi.org/10.1007/s12046-021-01562-y.

Rahaman, M., Mondal, S.P., Algehyne, E.A. Biswas, A., & Alam, S. (2021). A method for solving linear difference equation in Gaussian fuzzy environments. *Granular Computing*. https://doi.org/10.1007/s41066-020-00251-1.

Rao, S.S., & Berke, L. (1997). Analysis of uncertain structural systems using interval analysis. *AIAA Jouranal*, 35(4), 727–735. https://doi.org/10.2514/2.164.

Sahoo, L., Bhunia, A.K., & Roy, D. (2014). Reliability optimization with and low level redundancies in interval environment via genetic algorithm. *International Journal of System Assurance Engineering and Management*, 5(4), 513–523. https://doi.org/10.1 007/s13198-013-0199-9.

Shaocheng, T. (1994). Interval number and fuzzy number linear programmings. *Fuzzy Sets and Systems*, 66(3), 301–306. https://doi.org/10.1016/0165-0114(94)90097-3.

Stefanidou, G., & Papaschinopoulos, G. (2005). A fuzzy difference equation of a rational form. *Journal of Nonlinear Mathematical Physics*, 12, 300–315. https://doi.org/10.2 991/jnmp.2005.12.s2.21.

Stefanidou, G., Papaschinopoulos, G., & Schinas, C.J. (2010). On an exponential –type fuzzy Difference equation. *Advanced in Difference Equations*, 2010, 1–19. https://doi.org/1 0.1155/2010/196920.

Umekkan, S.A., Can, E., & Bayrak, M.A. (2014). Fuzzy difference equation in finance. *International Journal of Scientific and Innovative Mathematical Research*, 2(8), 729–735.

Zhang, Q.H., Yang, L.H. and Liao, & D.X. (2012). Behaviour of solutions of to a fuzzy nonlinear difference equation. *Iranian Journal of Fuzzy Systems*, 9(2), 1–12. https://dx.doi.org/10.22111/ijfs.2012.186.

Žilinskas, J., & Bogle, I.D.L. (2007). A survey of methods for the estimation ranges of functions using interval arithmetic. *Models and Algorithms for Global Optimization. Appl*, 4, 97–108.

3 Industrial Internet of Things and Industry 4.0

Suchitra Kumari[1], Arijit Ghosh[2],
Sankar Prasad Mondal[3], Ali Ahmadian[4] and
Soheil Salahshour[5]

[1]Department of Commerce, J.D. Birla Institute, Kolkata, India
[2]Department of Mathematics, St. Xavier's College
(Autonomous), Kolkata, India
[3]Department of Applied Science MaulanaAbulKalam Azad
University of Technology, West Bengal, India
[4]Institute of IR 4.0, The National University of Malaysia,
Bangi, 43600 UKM, Selangor, Malaysia
[5]Faculty of Engineering and Natural Sciences, Bahcesehir
University, Istanbul, Turkey

3.1 INTRODUCTION

Industrial revolutions have always been the turning point of any economy. The first Industrial Revolution of 1784 gave us water and steam-powered engines, the second of 1870 pushed forward mass production using electrical energy, the third which occurred in 1970 used PLC and IT systems for automation while the fourth Industrial revolution which is happening at present has given Internet of Things (IoT) and Cyber Physical Systems(CPS) (Vaidya et al. 2018). These revolutions have made the manufacturing process simpler and the workers can operate the machines more steadily (Qin et al. 2016). The fourth Industrial revolution or Industry 4.0 as it is commonly known stands for a new level of control and organization over the value chain of the life cycle of the products and it is centered toward customizing the requirements (Rüßmann et al. 2015). The main aim of Industry 4.0 is satisfying the customer and a few of the impact able areas are research and development, from delivery up to the utilization, management of the orders and recycling of the products (Neugebauer et al. 2016). Industry 4.0 archetype endorses the union of the internet to the material systems like enterprise assets, devices and sensors and amongst the material assets themselves (Sipsas et al. 2016). Successful multidisciplinary integration can occur when there is drafting and designing of methods done in order to have a common hassle-free approach to product development (Rennung et al. 2016) which leads to improved litheness thereby reducing the difficulty of synchronization (Brettel et al. 2014). Industry 4.0 led to a new era of machines that had the capacity of self-learning and changing the output and the performance based on their dealings with their ambiance (Lee et al. 2014). The advantages of this were that there was the tracking of the status of the product on a real-time basis and any change in delivery instructions or specifications could be made on the go (Almada-Lobo 2015).

3.2 REVIEW OF LITERATURE

Atzori et al. (2017) affirm that Industry 4.0 is the sum of all the spheres of the economy which consist of fully automatic production processes which work using artificial intelligence and internet connectivity without human interventions. Pan et al. (2015) proposed that Industry 4.0 was the ability of the components to communicate with each other. Kovács and Kot (2016) stated that the quintessence of Industry 4.0 was the formation of network-linked smart systems in which products, equipment and machines communicated with one another. Almada-Lobo (2015) affirmed that Industry 4.0 was an umbrella expression for a set of interconnected technological advances which increases the digitization of the business. Sanders et al. (2016) stated that Industry 4.0 radically changes the execution of operations from a forecast-based production planning to dynamic self-optimization and real-time production planning. Prause and Atari (2017) in accord with Kagermann et al. (2013) confirmed that Industry 4.0 was synonymous with the fourth industrial revolution which facilitated smart logistics and manufacturing processes by using Internet of Services, Internet of Things and Big Data. The second set of definitions state how innovations have been introduced by Industry 4.0 to influence the business processes and dynamics and not just the firm's business model. Kinzel 2017 avowed that in the manufacturing sector Industry 4.0 was the new catchphrase consisting of the complete value chain process in manufacturing goods and providing services. Prause and Atari 2017 adopted Koether 2006 affirming that Industry 4.0 would be more robust and flexible than its predecessors since the former's value chains are established on adaptable and flexible business structures which have the ability to radically change the internal environment of the business so as to fit into the ever-changing business world. The third set of definitions co-joins industry 4.0 with "smart factory" concept. Radziwon et al. 2014 spoke about smart factory having flexible and adaptive production processes which help in solving problems at a dynamic pace in spite of the latter's complexity. Preuveneers and Ilie-Zudor 2017 state that smart factories will increase the productivity and efficiency of the manufacturing processes by using better technology. Weyer et al. 2015 say that Industry 4.0 and smart factory is not only a codeword for revolutionized changes in the factory structure which went from being a traditional factory using raw materials and human intervention to a smart factory without human involvement which also addresses the test of global competition, customized products and shorter product lifecycles. Further fourth set of definitions talk about competitiveness by joining it with innovations and Industry 4.0. Navickas et al. 2017 considered Industry 4.0 as the necessary instrument for maintaining competitiveness within the industry. Gerlitz 2016 defined Industry 4.0 as the reason for the critical success and the development of the firms in an industry. Müller et al. 2018 overtly added the secular fact that Industry 4.0 helped in protecting the competition amongst the firms in the long run. The fifth category is somewhat similar to the fourth one. It not only considers the long-term impact but also takes the strategy formulation into account, even if it is at the governmental level thereby on a whole labeling Industry 4.0 as a managerial strategy. Johansson et al. (2017) pointed out that the technological development represented in Industry 4.0 was a strategy used by the German government in 2013. Strange and Zucchella (2017) further backed the previous statement by adding that Industry 4.0 was indeed an expression used by the German government while describing a high-technology strategy earlier but now it is used in respect of cyber-physical systems and active data processes that utilize tons of data in order to oblige smart machines. The sixth category of definitions lays special stress on "Internet of Things" and uses it identically with Industry 4.0. Kiel et al. 2016 along with the definitions of (Kagermann et al. 2013) and (Hartmann and Halecker 2015) affirm that internationally Industry 4.0 is synonymous with Industrial Internet of Things since it refers to the harmonious relation of the Industrial value creation with the Internet of Things technologies thereby creating the value chains as digital, decentralized and smart. Atzori et al. 2017 pronounce that IoT is a theoretical outline that relies on the ability of diverse devices, amplified physical objects and interrelated solutions to have a universal worldwide range for representing the implicit level of both objects and people. Atzori et al. 2010 say that the Internet of Things is a fresh archetype because wireless communications are present in all aspects of our life. Due to its frequency, a bunch of objects like mobile phones, sensors, actuators, Radio Frequency Identification (RFID) tags is able to interact, communicate and co-operate with each other in order to fulfill the common target. Kim and Mauborgne 1999 proposed that Industry 4.0 would lead to the creation of new market space which would replace the concept of out-performing competitors with out-competent competitors as also propounded by Pitt and Clarke 1999. Ringberg et al. 2019 observed that with the onset of the fourth industrial revolution cost control and efficiency would take a backseat and would be overshadowed by disruption, flexibility and creativity. There are nine pillars of Industry 4.0 which will change the way manufacturing works by making the process more optimized, automated and integrated thereby leading to greater efficiency among machine, humans, producers as well as suppliers (Rüßmann et al. 2015).

3.2.1 AUGMENTED REALITY

Augmented reality-based systems carry on varied services like relaying repair instructions over mobile devices as well as choosing parts in a warehouse. The industries can make use of augmented reality in order to endow the workers with real-time information so that they can improve decision-making. The systems needing repair can be repaired using augmented reality (Rüßmann et al. 2015).

For example, if there is a chopper that is stuck in a ravine and they can only be saved if timely action is taken. Using the augmented reality glass on the pilot's head which is connected to the main computer, the repair actions can be taken in a timely manner.

3.2.2 Additive Manufacturing

Additive manufacturing methods produce customized products that are lightweight in terms of designing and give high-performance outputs, ultimately reducing the stock in hand and the transport distance (Rüßmann et al. 2015; Bueno et al. 2020). Additive Methods like selective laser sintering, fused deposition method and selective laser melting make the production process cheaper and faster (Landherr et al. 2016). With increased technological penetration, digitization in every sphere and higher demands for customization, customers can only be retained by reducing the time taken to get the product to market and eventually to the customers, reducing service time (Rennung et al. 2016). In these current times, complexity has increased due to the mounting demand for customized products which leads to makeover in the organization structure (Brettel et al. 2014).

For example, MacBook by Apple has many variations in the color, size, storage, specifications and even a configure to order option so that customers can make an informed decision about which they like best.

3.2.3 The Cloud

Cloud-based IT platform is the technological spine connecting the various fundamentals of the Application Centre Industry 4.0 (Landherr et al. 2016). In order to increase data sharing Industry 4.0 has forced data transfer to milliseconds thereby making it in real-time (Rüßmann et al. 2015; Xu et al. 2014). The theory of Digital production explains that different devices can connect to the same cloud for sharing information with one another and this is not limited to only nearby machines but also to the entire plant (Marilungo et al. 2017; Zhang et al. 2020).

3.2.4 The Industrial Internet of Things

The term Internet of Things stands for a global set-up of interconnected objects which communicate using standard protocols (Hozdić 2015). Internet of Things is synonymous with Internet of Everything which consists of Internet of People, Internet of Service, Integration of Information and Communication technology and Internet of Manufacturing Services (Neugebauer et al. 2016). The three main features of Internet of Things are Omnipresence, Context and Optimization. Omnipresence gives the details about the position and the atmospheric and physical conditions of the object, context provides the prospect of superior object dealings with an on-hand environment and instantaneous response when the slightest change is made and optimization refers to the fact that today's objects are more than mere connections at the human-machine interface (Witkowski, K. (2017). Agility and intelligence are key factors of the value chain and must be connected with human factors, smart sensors, production lines, physical objects, intelligent machines and production process (Schumacher et al. 2016). Data and software are the driving forces behind the smartsetting up and the control of machines and ultimately the future fate of the factories (Valdeza et al. 2015).

For example, Smart shelving in warehouses will help in modern inventory management and the goods can be tracked making information receivable more quick, safe and exact (Dutra and Silva 2016).

3.2.5 System Integration—Horizontal, Vertical and End to End

Industries majorly use self-optimization and integration (Schuh et al. 2014).Industry 4.0 displays three types of integration (a) horizontal integration across the entire value creation network (b) vertical integration and networked manufacturing systems (c) end-to-end integration over the entire product life cycle (Stock and Seliger 2016).

3.2.6 Simulation

Simulations are used to increase quality and decrease machine setup times by using virtual models of humans, products and machines in plant operations to leverage real-time data to match the virtual model with the physical model (Rüßmann et al. 2015). Using simulations of production processes not only lowers the downtime but also lessens the production failures made during start-up phase (Simons et al. 2017) thereby eventually leading to improved quality of decision making (Schuh et al. 2014).

3.2.7 Autonomous Robots

Robots are day-by-day becoming more flexible and human-like and the time is not far when a robot will co-exist with humans (Rüßmann et al. 2015). An autonomous robot is capable of executing autonomous production method and tasks intelligently and more accurately and even are able to work in places which are designated unsafe for humans thereby showing more versatility, safety, flexibility and collaboratively (Bahrin et al. 2016).

For example, Roberta used by Gomtec is a 6-axis industrial robot that is used for efficient and flexible automation. Kuka LBR iiwa by Kuka is a lightweight robot used for doing sensitive industrial tasks (Sipsas et al. 2016).

3.2.8 Big Data and Analytics

Forrester states that Big data has four proportions: Value of Data, Volume of Data, Velocity of generation of new data and analysis and variety of Data (Witkowski, K. 2017). Analysis of previous data points out the inefficiencies which have been occurring in the production process previously and give a solution to fix the problem as well as to forecast when the new issues will be occurring again (Bagheri et al. 2015).

3.2.9 Cyber Physical Systems and Cybersecurity

Cyber Physical Systems(CPS) stands for the system in which innate and synthetic systems ie. physical space are snugly incorporated with control systems (cyber-space), computation and communication (Bagheri et al. 2015). The two main features of CPS are autonomous behavior of the production process and decentralization. The advancement of CPS depends on the implementation and reconfiguration of the product structures supply networks which are used in different cyber-physical systems as well as in manufacturing (Ivanov et al. 2016). The continuous intermingling of data is done in real-time by joining the cloud system with the CPS (Stock and Seliger 2016). Using effective sensors in CPS will help to locate the breakdown of the machine and without human intervention relay the message of repairing the fault using CPS. It also finds out the finest utilization of each workstation using the cycle time required for the procedure carried out on that station (Kolberg and Zühlke 2015). Increased connectivity and set communication protocols which come from Industry 4.0 require proper safe keep of the manufacturing lines as well as the critical industrial systems from cyber threats. This raises the requirement for reliable and secure management of machines and users (Lu et al. 2019; Rüßmann et al. 2015). The well-built link between the service, physical and digital structure increases the information eminence which is required for the operation, optimization and planning of the manufacturing systems (Landherr et al. 2016; Lins and Oliveira 2020).

3.3   CHALLENGES AND FUNDAMENTAL ISSUES OF INDUSTRY 4.0

Newer technologies have developed the industry from mechanical systems to automated ones in order to suit the current market with more robustness, embedment and flexibility to unforeseen situations (Wang et al. 2016; Sisinni et al. 2018). Few challenges and fundamental issues which have arisen while implementing it in the current manufacturing industries are:

- Cyber security—With the increased usage of automated systems in manufacturing lines the security features need to be beefed up to ensure a smooth uninterrupted flow of information.
- Huge Investment required—A large amount of start-up investment is required to be done to make an enterprise compliant with the new technologies.
- Intelligent decision-making—More autonomy needs to be provided to the smart manufacturing system so that they can proceed without hiccups in their flows.
- Manufacturing Big Data and Analytics—The huge amount of data available from the manufacturing systems is highly diverse and needs specialized depositories for its analysis so that the integrity of data is maintained.
- High-speed IWN Protocols—The IWN networks used today cannot sustain the heavy data load and require more bandwidth for smooth transfer of data and communication.

3.4   FUTURE DIRECTION AND SCOPE

Internet connectivity has remodeled the way industries have been operating since time immemorial. With a single click, an array of interconnected machines jumpstart their designated work without any further ado or human intervention and ultimately produce the product. However, most of the research has been done on the production phase of the product life cycle and the other in-between stages have been done away with. This can be done in future researches. There is also scope for more research in preparing efficient logistic support for the end products to reach their destination which will further enhance the customer's experience. Further research can be done on transparent industrial management.

3.5 CONCLUSION

Industrial Internet of Things and Industry 4.0 have been focused on in this paper. Usage of augmented reality will make tough situations seem easier and more approachable. Additive manufacturing will make the "Customer is the queen" concept more prominent and real since the products will be more custom-made than mass-made. The Cloud will come to mean more than the sky and be used by people of all ages to store their data and information for a seamless experience. The Industrial Internet of Things will facilitate efficient, customized and effective production at cost-effective rates. The system integration channels will clearly direct the flow and aid the simulation process. The concept of Autonomous robots which are distinctive of Industry 5.0 is also making its impact felt and this could be studied in great detail to see how the age of robots will influence humans on the basic as well as the industrial levels. Big Data will be used to take into account the huge volume of data and analysis will be smooth due to the greater velocity of data. The cyber-physical systems will lead to a harmonious relationship between the components and help in keeping cybersecurity intact. When these systems will finally be put into action with the help of better sensors, smarter machines and less pricey data storage then the transmission of data will be like never before.

REFERENCES

Almada-Lobo, F. (2015). The Industry 4.0 revolution and the future of manufacturing execution systems (MES). *Journal of innovation management*, *3*(4), 16–21.

Atzori, L., Iera, A., & Morabito, G. (2010). The internet of things: a survey. *Computer networks*, *54*(15), 2787–2805.

Atzori, L., Iera, A., & Morabito, G. (2017). Understanding the Internet of Things: definition, potentials, and societal role of a fast evolving paradigm. *Ad Hoc Networks*, *56*, 122–140.

Bagheri, B., Yang, S., Kao, H.A., & Lee, J. (2015). Cyber-physical systems architecture for self-aware machines in industry 4.0 environment. *IFAC-PapersOnLine*, *48*(3), 1622–1627.

Bahrin, M.A.K., Othman, M.F., Azli, N.H.N., & Talib, M.F. (2016). Industry 4.0: a review on industrial automation and robotic. *JurnalTeknologi*, *78*, 6–13.

Brettel, M., Friederichsen, N., Keller, M., & Rosenberg, M. (2014). How virtualization, decentralization and network building change the manufacturing landscape: An Industry 4.0 Perspective. *International Journal of Mechanical, Industrial Science and Engineering*, *8*(1), 37–44.

Bueno, A.F., Godinho Filho, M., & Frank, A.G. (2020). Smart production planning and control in the industry 4.0 context: a systematic literature review. *Computers & Industrial Engineering*, *149*, 106774.

Dutra, D.D.S., & Silva, J.R. (2016). Product-service architecture (psa): toward a service engineering perspective in industry 4.0. *IFAC-PapersOnLine, 49*(31), 91–96.

Gerlitz, L. (2016). Design management as a domain of smart and sustainable enterprise: business modelling for innovation and smart growth in Industry 4.0. *Entrepreneurship and Sustainability Issues, 3*(3), 244–268.

Hartmann, M., & Halecker, B. (2015). Management of innovation in the industrial internet of things. In *ISPIM Conference Proceedings* (p. 1). The International Society for Professional Innovation Management (ISPIM).

Hozdić, E. (2015). Smart factory for industry 4.0: a review. *International Journal of Modern Manufacturing Technologies, 7*(1), 28–35.

Ivanov, D., Sokolov, B., & Ivanova, M. (2016). Schedule coordination in cyber-physical supply networks Industry 4.0. *IFAC-PapersOnLine, 49*(12), 839–844.

Johansson, J., Abrahamsson, L., Kåreborn, B.B., Fältholm, Y., Grane, C., & Wykowska, A. (2017). Work and organization in a digital industrial context. *Mrev Management Revue, 28*(3), 281–297.

Kagermann, H., Wahlster, W., & Helbig, J. (2013). Acatech–National Academy of Science and Engineering. *Recommendations for implementing the strategic initiative Industrie, 4*, 1–79.

Kiel, D., Arnold, C., Collisi, M.A., & Voigt, K.I. (2016, May). The impact of the industrial internet of things on established business models. In *Proceedings of the 25th international association for management of technology (IAMOT) conference* (pp. 673–695).

Kim, W.C., & Mauborgne, R. (1999). Creating new market space. *Harvard Business Review, 77*(1), 83–93.

Kinzel, H. (2017). Industry 4.0–where does this leave the human factor?. *Journal of Urban Culture Research, 15*, 70–83.

Koether, R. (2006). Koether, R.: Taschenbuch der Logistik.

Kolberg, D., & Zühlke, D. (2015). Lean automation enabled by industry 4.0 technologies. *IFAC-PapersOnLine, 48*(3), 1870–1875.

Kovács, G., & Kot, S. (2016). New logistics and production trends as the effect of global economy changes. *Polish Journal of Management Studies, 14*, 115–126.

Landherr, M., Schneider, U., & Bauernhansl, T. (2016). The Application Center Industrie 4.0-Industry-driven manufacturing, research and development. *Procedia CIRP, 57*, 26–31.

Lee, J., Kao, H.A., & Yang, S. (2014). Service innovation and smart analytics for industry 4.0 and big data environment. *Procedia Cirp, 16*(1), 3–8.

Lins, T., & Oliveira, R.A.R. (2020). Cyber-physical production systems retrofitting in context of industry 4.0. *Computers & Industrial Engineering, 139*, 106193.

Lu, Y., Huang, X., Dai, Y., Maharjan, S., & Zhang, Y. (2019). Blockchain and federated learning for privacy-preserved data sharing in industrial IoT. *IEEE Transactions on Industrial Informatics, 16*(6), 4177–4186.

Majeed, A.A., & Rupasinghe, T.D. (2017). Internet of things (IoT) embedded future supply chains for industry 4.0: An assessment from an ERP-based fashion apparel and footwear industry. *International Journal of Supply Chain Management, 6*(1), 25–40.

Marilungo, E., Papetti, A., Germani, M., & Peruzzini, M. (2017). From PSS to CPS design: a real industrial use case toward Industry 4.0. *Procedia Cirp, 64*, 357–362.

Müller, J.M., Buliga, O., & Voigt, K.I. (2018). Fortune favors the prepared: how SMEs approach business model innovations in Industry 4.0. *Technological Forecasting and Social Change, 132*, 2–17.

Navickas, V., Kuznetsova, S.A., & Gruzauskas, V. (2017). Cyber–physical systems expression in industry 4.0 context. *Фінансово-кредитнадіяльність: проблемитеоріїтапрактики, 2*(23), 188–197.

Neugebauer, R., Hippmann, S., Leis, M., & Landherr, M. (2016). Industrie 4.0-From the perspective of applied research.

Pan, M., Sikorski, J., Kastner, C.A., Akroyd, J., Mosbach, S., Lau, R., & Kraft, M. (2015). Applying industry 4.0 to the Jurong Island eco-industrial park. *Energy Procedia, 75,* 1536–1541.

Pitt, M., & Clarke, K. (1999). Competing on competence: a knowledge perspective on the management of strategic innovation. *Technology Analysis & Strategic Management, 11*(3), 301–316.

Prause, G., & Atari, S. (2017). On sustainable production networks for Industry 4.0.

Preuveneers, D., &Ilie-Zudor, E. (2017). The intelligent industry of the future: a survey on emerging trends, research challenges and opportunities in Industry 4.0. *Journal of Ambient Intelligence and Smart Environments, 9*(3), 287–298.

Qin, J., Liu, Y., & Grosvenor, R. (2016). A categorical framework of manufacturing for industry 4.0 and beyond. *Procedia cirp, 52,* 173–178.

Radziwon, A., Bilberg, A., Bogers, M., & Madsen, E.S. (2014). The smart factory: exploring adaptive and flexible manufacturing solutions. *Procedia engineering, 69,* 1184–1190.

Rennung, F., Luminosu, C.T., & Draghici, A. (2016). Service provision in the framework of Industry 4.0. *Procedia-Social and Behavioral Sciences, 221*(1), 372–377.

Ringberg, T., Reihlen, M., & Rydén, P. (2019). The technology-mindset interactions: leading to incremental, radical or revolutionary innovations. *Industrial Marketing Management, 79,* 102–113.

Rüßmann, M., Lorenz, M., Gerbert, P., Waldner, M., Justus, J., Engel, P., & Harnisch, M. (2015). Industry 4.0: the future of productivity and growth in manufacturing industries. *Boston Consulting Group, 9*(1), 54–89.

Sanders, A., Elangeswaran, C., & Wulfsberg, J.P. (2016). Industry 4.0 implies lean manufacturing: research activities in industry 4.0 function as enablers for lean manufacturing. *Journal of Industrial Engineering and Management (JIEM), 9*(3), 811–833.

Schuh, G., Potente, T., Wesch-Potente, C., Weber, A.R., & Prote, J.P. (2014). Collaboration Mechanisms to increase Productivity in the Context of Industrie 4.0. *Procedia Cirp, 19,* 51–56.

Schumacher, A., Erol, S., & Sihn, W. (2016). A maturity model for assessing Industry 4.0 readiness and maturity of manufacturing enterprises. *Procedia Cirp, 52*(1), 161–166.

Simons, S., Abé, P., & Neser, S. (2017). Learning in the AutFab–the fully automated Industrie 4.0 learning factory of the University of Applied Sciences Darmstadt. *Procedia Manufacturing, 9,* 81–88.

Sipsas, K., Alexopoulos, K., Xanthakis, V., Chryssolouris, G. (2016). Collaborative maintenance in flow-line manufacturing environments: An Industry 4.0 approach. *5th CIRP Global Web Conference Research and Innovation for Future Production, Procedia CIRP,* 55, 236–241.

Sipsas, K., Alexopoulos, K., Xanthakis, V., & Chryssolouris, G. (2016). Collaborative maintenance in flow-line manufacturing environments: An Industry 4.0 approach. *Procedia Cirp,* 55, 236–241.

Sisinni, E., Saifullah, A., Han, S., Jennehag, U., & Gidlund, M. (2018). Industrial internet of things: Challenges, opportunities, and directions. *IEEE Transactions on Industrial Informatics, 14*(11), 4724–4734.

Stock, T., &Seliger, G. (2016). Opportunities of sustainable manufacturing in industry 4.0. *Procedia Cirp, 40,* 536–541.

Strange, R., & Zucchella, A. (2017). Industry 4.0, global value chains and international business. *Multinational Business Review, 25*(3), 174–184.

Vaidya, S., Ambad, P., & Bhosle, S. (2018). Industry 4.0–a glimpse. *Procedia Manufacturing, 20,* 233–238.

Valdeza, A.C., Braunera, P., Schaara, A. K., Holzingerb, A., & Zieflea, M. (2015, August). Reducing complexity with simplicity-usability methods for industry 4.0. In *Proceedings 19th triennial congress of the IEA* (Vol. 9, p. 14).

Wang, S., Wan, J., Li, D., & Zhang, C. (2016). Implementing smart factory of industrie 4.0: an outlook. *International Journal of Distributed Sensor Networks, 12*(1), 3159805.

Weyer, S., Schmitt, M., Ohmer, M., & Gorecky, D. (2015). Towards Industry 4.0-Standardization as the crucial challenge for highly modular, multi-vendor production systems. *Ifac-Papersonline, 48*(3), 579–584.

Witkowski, K. (2017). Internet of things, big data, industry 4.0–innovative solutions in logistics and supply chains management. *Procedia Engineering, 182*, 763–769.

Xu, B., Da Xu, L., Cai, H., Xie, C., Hu, J., & Bu, F. (2014). Ubiquitous data accessing method in IoT-based information system for emergency medical services. *IEEE Transactions on Industrial informatics, 10*(2), 1578–1586.

Zhang, Z., Zhang, Y., Lu, J., Gao, F., & Xiao, G. (2020). A novel complex manufacturing business process decomposition approach in cloud manufacturing. *Computers & Industrial Engineering, 144*, 106442.

4 Industry 4.0 and Its Practice in Terms of Fuzzy Uncertain Environment

Arijit Ghosh[1], Suchitra Kumari[2],
Sankar Prasad Mondal[3] and Ali Ahmadian[4]
[1]Department of Mathematics, St. Xavier's College
(Autonomous), Kolkata, India
[2]Department of Commerce, J.D. Birla Institute, Kolkata, India
[3]Department of Applied Science Maulana Abul Kalam Azad
University of Technology, West Bengal, India
[4]Institute of IR 4.0, The National University of Malaysia,
Bangi, 43600 UKM, Selangor, Malaysia

4.1 INTRODUCTION

The first industrial revolution set the wheels turning for the conversion of the agrarian lifestyle to an industry-enabled one. Going forward all the human developments has been done keeping in mind the automation aspect. Industry 1.0 dealt with steam and water power (Kagermann et al. 2013; Qin et al. 2016; Schläpfer et al. 2015). Industry 2.0 which happened in 1870 used assembly lines. It was popularized by Ford in the 20th century by applying it to its own factories (Womak et al. 1990). Industry 3.0 consisted of programmable logic control system (Segovia and Theorin 2012). Due to this there was digitization in the industries which led the computer to be widely used thereby paving the path for Industry 4.0 (Lasi et al. 2014). Industry 4.0 is an industrial revolution which redesigns the way things are made. The things are automated, integrated and optimized to perk up the efficiency and modify the relationships between customers, suppliers and producers as well as build on the relationship between machines and humans (Rüßmann et al. 2015). Industry 4.0 plans to increase operational efficacy and change the way products, business models and services are viewed (Rüßmann et al. 2015; Hermann et al. 2016). It helps in setting up Internet technology-enabled factories i.e. smart factories which improve adaptability, ergonomics and resource efficiency thereby moulding the business partners and customers with the logistics and value chain (Lee et al. 2017; Stork 2015). Internet of Things is a ground for Industry 4.0 which refers to a networked interconnection of devices whose objective is to let free flow of communication between the devices and lets them communicate with each other on the basis of their condition and status (ElMaraghy and ElMaraghy 2016). The technologically advanced communication technology and information system like cyber physical systems and wireless sensor network transforms a traditional product into a smart connected product (Zheng et al. 2019; Porter and Heppelmann 2014). Smart connected products stand for the third sign of IT driven competition where the IT is embedded in the products and can easily collect, process and produce information (Zheng et al. 2020). IoT technology is embedded in various smart manufacturing resources like bar-coding and RFID which can communicate and interact with each other. The smart devices of industry 4.0 also have the capability of transferring their work status in real time to a manager who is central cloud-based (Zheng et al. 2018). Modern wireless communication has disrupted the natural flow of information since it has large amount and all kinds of data that are transmissible (Atzori et al. 2010). Information sharing is done so as to make the services more informative as well as to increase productivity and efficiency (Bandyopadhyay and Sen 2011). The real-time data obtained by the devices connected with Internet of Things can be used in smart logistics (Lee et al. 2018), logistic decisions (Zhong et al. 2017), smart cities (Keung et al. 2018) and in smart production (Lee et al. 2017). Sophisticated technologies are better in implementing automated guided vehicles (Lee et al. 2018; Lu et al. 2018) which sustain smart warehouse. Moreover, big data analysis helps in increasing the accuracy and speed for maintaining decision-making (Lee et al. 2017). Industry 4.0 will bring immense changes in the assembly process. Better collaboration between varied parts is expected since there will be real-time exchange of information which will eventually lead to better evaluation (ElMaraghy and ElMaraghy 2016).

4.1.1 FUZZY THEORY AND DEGREE OF UNCERTAINTY

In traditional set theory, a component can either belong to a set or not belong to it, in conventional Boolean logic, a testimonial can be either true or false and in optimization a solution can be feasible or not, but nothing in between (Zimmermann 1991). On the other hand, real-world models do not generally have well-defined values which leads to difficulty in decoding them. More the complexity of the system, the lower is its noteworthiness and clearness (Zadeh 1965). To deal with the turbulent behavior fuzzy sets were developed which handled the impreciseness of the statements (Zadeh 1965). There are various kinds of fuzzy sets proposed with few of them being hesitant fuzzy sets, type-2 fuzzy sets and intuitionistic fuzzy sets (Fournier-Viger et al. 2012; Oztaysi et al. 2017). The greatest advantage of intuitionistic fuzzy sets is its knack of representing supposed commitment in terms of mathematical expressions. This lack of information and vagueness about the system process can be dealt with using hesitant, non-membership and membership functions (Cuong and Kreinovich 2014; Tooranloo and Sadat Ayatollah 2016).

Uncertainty arises in Industry 4.0 due to the intricacies of the data being handled as well as the lack of a well-defined movement structure (Pan et al. 2015; Schumacher et al. 2016; Mosterman and Zander 2016; Oesterreich and Teuteberg 2016). It leads to a new relationship between all the components of an ecosystem wherein the loosening of any one component will disrupt the flow of data and cause a system failure. Uncertainty in behavioral terms is due to internal ie. Industry 4.0 as well as external factors ie. situational factors such as suppliers, customers, etc which makes it difficult to interpret the behavior of different stakeholders. Relational uncertainty occurs between organizations and the environment due to the indecisiveness of the behavior between the business environment and the various stakeholders. Subjective uncertainty arises due to the short-sightedness of the policymakers since everyone perceives things differently and this affects the systems and subsystems of Industry 4.0 in terms of storage, processing and acquisition. Structural uncertainty is the binary way of defining the cause and effect relationship between legal, technological, social and economic environments but the future happenings cannot be determined based on the present since there are huge changes in all the environments on a regular basis (Magruk 2016). Therefore the uncertainty component possesses a major downfall in the decision-making process of Industry 4.0 and the only way out is to use the fuzzy component. The usage of the fuzzy components in decision making will help in keeping options open for the uncertain situations that will arise due to evolution in technology, process or mentality of people. This will lead to the processes having a buffer between themselves whereby the modification component may fit in forming in eventuality a system whereby there are multiple-choice options for every user and all will form differentiated usable products.

4.2 REVIEW OF LITERATURE

The papers were reviewed keeping in mind four different applications of Industry 4.0. The first set of papers used MCDM methods to find out the solution to the problem which occurred while transitioning to Industry 4.0. Wang et al. 2016 stressed the 4 most important aspects of a company with respect to production instruction system, Veza et al. 2015 used the concept of Industry 4.0 for the problem of partner selection based on technology capacity, Erdogan et al. 2018 studied the best strategy to be selected for implementing Industry 4.0, Ramos et al. 2020 did a comparison of the new system with the legacy systems of the Industry 4.0 projects, Sachdeva et al. 2019 used the concept of Industry 4.0 in supplier selection, Medić et al. 2019 helped in determining the appropriate digital technologies to be used in the manufacturing industries, Raj et al. 2020 analyzed the implementation barriers of Industry 4.0 and Priya and Malhotra 2020 spoke about a handover scheme and smart network interface selection with respect to 5G communication. The conclusion which can be drawn is that either the application is applied to a specific part of the production environment or there is a limited framework under which the applications are applied.

The second set of papers studied Industry 4.0 as well as took into consideration its preferences so as to extend the structure of the problem when compared to the first set. Forstner and Dümmler 2014 and Chang and Wu 2016 studied the concept of Industry 4.0 and its benefits, Faller and Feldmüller 2015 looked at the same study but concentrated on the small and medium-sized enterprises, Schuh et al. 2014 analyzed the relationship between network structures and Industry 4.0. After the cumulative analysis of the studies the conclusion drawn is that Industry 4.0 integrates the different requirements of both the strategic and operational fields which consisted of technologies like smart machines with sensors as proposed by Alexopoulos et al. 2016, big data analysis studied by Raschinger et al. 2016, simulation by Pan et al. 2015, Internet of Things used by Stemmler et al. 2014; Wende and Kiradjiev 2014; Nukala et al. 2016; Greinke et al. 2016; Yoon et al. 2019, horizontal and vertical system integration by Brinkmeier and Kalbreyer 2016, cloud computing by Liu and Xu 2017, cyber security by Giannetti and Ransing (2016) and augmented reality by Greinke et al. (2016).

The third set of papers investigated the implementation process of Industry 4.0 and its application in different areas from the industry. Simon et al. (2018) stated that improvement in the mass customization model would lead to a control of production lines. The observations from the previous studies show that improvement in mass customization can be done by calling for large scale system integration as proposed by Qiu et al. (2016), by taking into consideration the rising demand for industrial automation systems which Bangemann et al. (2016) said would cause well-organized integration of the tasks and would meet client's demands and specifications as told by Binner (2014). Schlechtendahl et al. (2015) opined that these subproblems led to the transformation of the previous production systems into Industry 4.0 and Sarvari et al. (2018) add on saying that this also propelled a searching process for the company's management to smooth the progress of the planning and implementation process. Schumacher (2016) articulate that multi-perspective dimensions for the transition are introduced after considering the problems and the source from which they have arisen.

The last set of papers looked at the possible transition risks and the probable negative outcomes which could crop up due to transitioning into Industry 4.0. Condry and Nelson 2016 spoke about the security risks which would arise due to unauthorized access of an intruder who would then change the system settings and sabotage it and Corallo et al. 2020 also researched the cybersecurity risks and their impending negative outcomes. Konieczek et al. 2016 yielded that the current Internet of Things modus operandi does not have the capability of inter-device communication in real time. Hecklau et al. 2016 spoke about the risk of human resources and Kazancoglu and Ozkan-Ozen 2018 talked about the recruitment process risks. Badri et al. 2018 handled the occupational health and safety risks which arose due to Industry 4.0.

The Fuzzy Set Theory is the best way to handle the vagueness and uncertainties in MCDM. He et al. (2017, 2019) vouched for the versatility of fuzzy logic. A new extension of Fuzzy Set Theory was developed by Atanassov (1986) which is called Intuitionistic fuzzy set theory. This theory includes an extra degree called the degree of non-membership which models vagueness and uncertainties at independent levels. Intuitionistic set theory has been applied in day-to-day problems by Seker (2020); Karaşan and Kahraman (2019); Karasan (2019); Rouyendegh et al. (2020); Rani et al. (2020). Since the selection of the best strategy for transitioning to Industry 4.0 partakes the evaluation of both qualitative as well as quantitative data hence fuzzy set theory is best used to handle such an uncertain environment.

4.3 INDUSTRY 4.0 BARRIERS

Major changes in the organizational composition and method disclose various barriers to Industry 4.0. One of the first barriers to Industry 4.0 is the need for high investment (Engelbertink and Woudstra 2017; Glass et al. 2018; Zhou et al. 2015; Colotla et al. 2016; Geissbauer et al. 2014; Kamble et al. 2018; Aggarwal et al. 2019; Karadayi-Usta 2019; Moktadir et al. 2018; Vaidya et al. 2018). Since there is a lack of clarity in defining return on investment it leads to a failure in attracting high investments (Luthra and Mangla 2018). The unclear benefits earned for the investments in Industry 4.0 is due to lack of adaptability among organizations (Geissbauer et al. 2014). Organizations accepting Industry 4.0 is only possible if there is a clear understanding of its strategic importance. There needs to be dedicated management that conducts knowledge management programs for the employees (Luthra and Mangla 2018). In the absence of such programs there will be turmoil and the lack of management support will slow the transformation (Glass et al. 2018). Virtual organizations using Industry 4.0 do not have a legal existence unless the laws have strict data protection clauses. The ongoing unclear legal situation leads to unclear state of the external data (Geissbauer et al. 2014; Kamble et al. 2018; Aggarwal et al. 2019). Industry 4.0 uses horizontal integration in which the value-creating network is formed by integrating stakeholders which leads to the requirements of protocols and data collection and data protection (Türkeş et al. 2019). Industry 4.0 says that there is a requirement of reference guideline or standards (Kamble et al. 2018). The lack of standards is a barrier to Industry 4.0 (Glass et al. 2018; Kamble et al. 2018; Luthra and Mangla 2018; Türkeş et al. 2019; Stentoft et al. 2019; Chen 2017). Industry 4.0 is set to have a massive change in the expectations from the workforce due to new technological processes and machines being used in place of traditional ones (Kazancoglu and Ozkan-Ozen 2018) and so companies should consider strategic methods for human resources (Stachová et al. 2019). The barriers related to the workforce are lack of skilled and qualified individuals as employees (Glass et al. 2018; Colotla et al. 2016; Geissbauer et al. 2014; Kamble et al. 2018; Karadayi-Usta 2019; Stentoft et al. 2019; Tupa et al. 2017; Müller et al. 2018) and requirements for advanced training and education (Engelbertink and Woudstra 2017; Karadayi-Usta 2019; Türkeş et al. 2019; Stentoft et al. 2019). Cyber security is another major barrier to Industry 4.0 since these processes lead to sharing of a large amount of data (Aggarwal et al. 2019). A high reliance on data security and inadequate data management is a quick recipe for disaster (Engelbertink and Woudstra 2017; Glass et al. 2018; Zhou et al., 2015; Geissbauer et al. 2014; Moktadir et al. 2018; Vaidya et al. 2018; Luthra and Mangla 2018; Stentoft et al. 2019; Tupa et al. 2017; Schröder (2016). The need for monitoring and controlling the dynamic processes in Industry 4.0 environment reveals the significance of intelligent equipment and the creation of network environment (Zhou et al. 2015; Chen 2017). Matured data analytic techniques are needed in Industry 4.0 so that the companies have the ability to analyze the volumes of manufacturing business-related, specific and technological data (Vaidya et al. 2018). Intelligent decision-making system and negotiation mechanism is required for the infusion of autonomous intelligent decision-making AI based self-learning and adaptable system which will reinforce the knowledge of experience and expertise (Vaidya et al. 2018). Modular and flexible smart device is needed since it is a flexible distributed and smart system which enables grouping, regrouping and working together of devices integrated with technology (Vaidya et al. 2018). Low maturity levels and integration of desired technologies are required since they are low-cost manufactured devices that can be easily integrated with the software, data and hardware (Glass et al. 2018; Moktadir et al. 2018). Very high complexity is a barrier to Industry 4.0 since it has highly complex physical and technological aspects (Glass et al. 2018; Moktadir et al. 2018). There is poor compatibility of current solutions and devices or retrofitting with the required ones which is also a barrier (Kamble et al. 2018; Veile et al. 2019). Missing partners and funding support like financial institutions is a barrier to Industry 4.0 (Glass et al. 2018). In terms of funding, tax benefits, well-defined regulations, education and training government support is missing which is a barrier (Glass et al. 2018). Employment disruption, possible job loss, re-skilling and training puts an unwanted strain on manpower which is one of the barriers to Industry 4.0 (Glass et al. 2018; Kamble et al. 2018).

In Table 4.1, a summary of the Industry 4.0 barriers is presented.

TABLE 4.1
Summary of Industry 4.0 Barriers

1	Lack of knowledge about Industry 4.0	Stentoft et al. (2019); Geissbauer et al. (2014); Colotla et al. (2016); Türkeş et al. (2019); Kamble et al. (2018); Glass et al. (2018); Luthra and Mangla (2018)
2	Matured data analytic techniques	Vaidya et al. 2018
3	Unclear legal situation and laws concerning use of external data	Geissbauer et al. (2014); Kamble et al. (2018); Aggarwal et al. (2019)
4	Intelligent decision-making system and negotiation mechanism	Vaidya et al. 2018
5	Lack of standards	Glass et al. (2018); Stentoft et al. (2019); Türkeş et al. (2019); Geissbauer et al. (2014); Luthra and Mangla (2018); Kamble et al. 2018; Chen 2017
6	Modular and flexible smart devices	Vaidya et al. 2018
7	Requirements of intelligent equipment and construction of network environment	Zhou et al. (2015); Chen (2017); Glass et al. (2018); Kamble et al. (2018)
8	Lack of understanding of the strategic importance of Industry 4.0	Glass et al. (2018); Stentoft et al. (2019); Türkeş et al. (2019)
9	Low maturity level and integration of required technologies	Glass et al. (2018); Moktadir et al. (2018)
10	Lack of clarity in defining return on investment	Geissbauer et al. (2014); Luthra and Mangla (2018)

(Continued)

TABLE 4.1 (Continued)

11	Required continued education and training of employees	Stentoft et al. 2019; Engelbertink and Woudstra (2017); Türkeş et al. (2019); Karadayi-Usta (2019)
12	Lack of skilled and qualified workforce for adaptation to Industry 4.0 technologies	Glass et al. (2018); Tupa et al. (2017); Colotla et al. (2016); Kamble et al. (2018); Moktadir et al. (2018); Geissbauer et al. (2014); Karadayi-Usta (2019); Stentoft et al., 2019
13	Very high complexity	Glass et al. (2018); Moktadir et al. (2018)
14	Poor compatibility of current solutions/ devices or retrofitting	Kamble et al. (2018); Veile et al. (2019)
15	Required high investments	Glass et al. (2018); Engelbertink and Woudstra (2017); Zhou et al. (2015); Geissbauer et al. (2014); Colotla et al. (2016); Kamble et al. (2018); Karadayi-Usta (2019); Aggarwal et al. (2019); Moktadir et al. (2018); Kamble et al. 2018; Vaidya et al. (2018)
16	Missing partners and funding support	Glass et al. (2018)
17	Unwarranted strain to manpower	Glass et al. (2018); Kamble et al. (2018)
18	Missing government support	Glass et al. (2018)
19	Lack of management support for Industry 4.0 transformation	Glass et al. (2018); Geissbauer et al. (2014); Luthra and Mangla (2018); Aggarwal et al. (2019); Kamble et al., (2018)
20	High dependency on data security due to sensitivity and vulnerability of data and insufficient data management	Glass et al. (2018); Stentoft et al. (2019); Engelbertink and Woudstra (2017); Tupa et al. (2017); Zhou et al. (2015); Schroder, 2017; Geissbauer et al. (2014); Luthra and Mangla (2018); Aggarwal et al. (2019); Kamble et al. (2018); Moktadir et al. 2018; Vaidya et al. (2018)

4.4 CONCLUSION

Industry 4.0 will shake the economies of India and China where cheap labor will no longer be an additional plus. The surfacing and accessibility of newer technologies will bring the entire industrial world to the same playing field (Kumar et al. (2020). The speed at which the development is happening is what is so shocking since it brings with it a hurricane of problems. In order to stay in the market, the businesses will have to reinvent themselves by transforming their processes, installations and practices in accordance with Industry 4.0 technologies. On the other hand, re-skilling of existing manpower and recruitment of manpower having the new set of skills will prove to be a mammoth task for the companies. Moreover, in the uncertain environment, we live in Industry 4.0 will not be the last technological progress but it will open up the world to more innovative technologies. A classic example of this is given by the Japanese (Petrillo et al. 2018) who have started the discussion on Industry 5.0 when the rest of the world is still grappling to get hold of Industry 4.0. This will lead to the emergence of a new technology that will again set the wheels turning on understanding, re-skilling, recruiting. Industry 4.0 will need to be adopted by the industries due to the rate of technological development, rigorous competition, the lightning speed of technology spread and the pursuit of nations wanting to show up first. The industries in most of the developing countries are still in force with Industry 2.0 and Industry 3.0 and even though it will take time to leap to Industry 4.0, it will slowly but surely be done.

REFERENCES

Aggarwal, A., Gupta, S., & Ojha, M.K. (2019). Evaluation of key challenges to industry 4.0 in Indian context: a DEMATEL approach. In *Advances in Industrial and Production Engineering* (pp. 387–396). Springer, Singapore.

Alexopoulos, K., Makris, S., Xanthakis, V., Sipsas, K., & Chryssolouris, G. (2016). A concept for context-aware computing in manufacturing: the white goods case. *International Journal of Computer Integrated Manufacturing*, 29(8), 839–849.

Atanassov, K.T. Intuitionistic fuzzy sets, Fuzzy Sets Syst20 (1986), 87–96. *Google Scholar Google Scholar Digital Library Digital Library.*

Atzori, L., Iera, A., & Morabito, G. (2010). The internet of things: a survey. *Computer Networks*, 54(15), 2787–2805.

Badri, A., Boudreau-Trudel, B., & Souissi, A.S. (2018). Occupational health and safety in the industry 4.0 era: a cause for major concern?. *Safety Science*, 109, 403–411.

Bandyopadhyay, D., & Sen, J. (2011). Internet of things: applications and challenges in technology and standardization. *Wireless Personal Communications*, 58(1), 49–69.

Bangemann, T., Riedl, M., Thron, M., & Diedrich, C. (2016). Integration of classical components into industrial cyber–physical systems. *Proceedings of the IEEE*, 104(5), 947–959.

Binner, H.F. (2014). Industry 4.0 determines the working world of the future. *E &I Electrical Engineering and Information Technology*, 131(7), 230–236.

Brinkmeier, M., & Kalbreyer, D. (2016, October). A case study of physical computing in computer science education. In *Proceedings of the 11th Workshop in Primary and Secondary Computing Education* (pp. 54–59).

Chang, W.Y., & Wu, S.J. (2016, July). Investigated information data of CNC machine tool for established productivity of industry 4.0. In *2016 5th IIAI International Congress on Advanced Applied Informatics (IIAI-AAI)* (pp. 1088–1092). IEEE.

Chen, Y. (2017). Integrated and intelligent manufacturing: perspectives and enablers. Engineering, 3, 588–595.

Colotla, I., Fæste, A., Heidemann, A., Winther, A., Andersen, P.H., Duvold, T., & Hansen, M. (2016). Winning the Industry 4.0 race: How ready are Danish manufacturers.

Condry, M.W., & Nelson, C.B. (2016). Using smart edge IoT devices for safer, rapid response with industry IoT control operations. *Proceedings of the IEEE*, 104(5), 938–946.

Corallo, A., Lazoi, M., & Lezzi, M. (2020). Cybersecurity in the context of industry 4.0: a structured classification of critical assets and business impacts. *Computers in Industry*, 114, 103165.

Cuong, B.C., & Kreinovich, V. (2014). Picture fuzzy sets. *Journal of Computer Science and Cybernetics*, 30(4), 409–420.

ElMaraghy, H., & ElMaraghy, W. (2016). Smart adaptable assembly systems. *Procedia CIRP*, 44(4–13), 127–128.

Engelbertink, D.G.L., & Woudstra, S. (2017). *Managing the influences and risks of Industry 4.0* (Bachelor's thesis, University of Twente).

Erdogan, M., Ozkan, B., Karasan, A., & Kaya, I. (2018). Selecting the best strategy for industry 4.0 applications with a case study. In *Industrial engineering in the industry 4.0 era* (pp. 109–119). Springer, Cham.

Faller, C., & Feldmüller, D. (2015). Industry 4.0 learning factory for regional SMEs. *Procedia Cirp, 32*, 88–91.

Forstner, L., & Dümmler, M. (2014). Integrierte Wertschöpfungsnetzwerke–Chancen und Potenziale durch Industrie 4.0. *e & i Elektrotechnik und Informationstechnik, 131*(7), 199–201.

Fournier-Viger, P., Faghihi, U., Nkambou, R., & Nguifo, E.M. (2012). CMRules: mining sequential rules common to several sequences. *Knowledge-Based Systems, 25*(1), 63–76.

Geissbauer, R., Schrauf, S., Koch, V., & Kuge, S. (2014). Industrie 4.0–Chancen und Herausforderungen der viertenindustriellen Revolution. *PricewaterhouseCoopers (PWC), 227*(S 13), 343–358.

Giannetti, C., & Ransing, R.S. (2016). Risk based uncertainty quantification to improve robustness of manufacturing operations. *Computers & Industrial Engineering, 101*, 70–80.

Glass, R., Meissner, A., Gebauer, C., Stürmer, S., & Metternich, J. (2018). Identifying the barriers to Industrie 4.0. *Procedia Cirp, 72*, 985–988.

Greinke, B., Guetl, N., Wittmann, D., Pflug, C., Schubert, J., Helmut, V., ... & Joost, G. (2016, September). Interactive workwear: smart maintenance jacket. In *Proceedings of the 2016 ACM International Joint Conference on Pervasive and Ubiquitous Computing: Adjunct* (pp. 470–475).

He, Y., Zhu, C., He, Z., Gu, C., & Cui, J. (2017). Big data oriented root cause identification approach based on Axiomatic domain mapping and weighted association rule mining for product infant failure. *Computers & Industrial Engineering, 109*, 253–265.

He, Z., He, Y., Liu, F., & Zhao, Y. (2019). Big data-oriented product infant failure intelligent root cause identification using associated tree and fuzzy DEA. *IEEE Access, 7*, 34687–34698.

Hecklau, F., Galeitzke, M., Flachs, S., & Kohl, H. (2016). Holistic approach for human resource management in Industry 4.0. *Procedia Cirp, 54*(1), 1–6.

Hermann, M., Pentek, T., & Otto, B. (2016, January). Design principles for industrie 4.0 scenarios. In *2016 49th Hawaii international conference on system sciences (HICSS)* (pp. 3928–3937). IEEE.

Kagermann, H., Helbig, J., Hellinger, A., & Wahlster, W. (2013). *Recommendations for implementing the strategic initiative INDUSTRIE 4.0: Securing the future of German manufacturing industry; final report of the Industrie 4.0 Working Group*. Forschungsunion.

Kamble, S.S., Gunasekaran, A., & Sharma, R. (2018). Analysis of the driving and dependence power of barriers to adopt industry 4.0 in Indian manufacturing industry. *Computers in Industry, 101*, 107–119.

Karadayi-Usta, S. (2019). An interpretive structural analysis for industry 4.0 adoption challenges. *IEEE Transactions on Engineering Management, 67*, 973–978.

Karasan, A. (2019). A novel hesitant intuitionistic fuzzy linguistic AHP method and its application to prioritization of investment alternatives. *International Journal of the Analytic Hierarchy Process, 11*(1), 127–142.

Karaşan, A., & Kahraman, C. (2019). A novel intuitionistic fuzzy DEMATEL–ANP–TOPSIS integrated methodology for freight village location selection. *Journal of Intelligent & Fuzzy Systems, 36*(2), 1335–1352.

Kazancoglu, Y., & Ozkan-Ozen, YD. (2018). Analyzing Workforce 4.0 in the Fourth Industrial Revolution and proposing a road map from operations management perspective with fuzzy DEMATEL. *Journal of Enterprise Information Management, 31*(6), 897–907.

Keung, K.L., Lee, C.K.M., Ng, K.K.H., & Yeung, C.K. (2018, December). Smart city application and analysis: Real-time urban drainage monitoring by iot sensors: A case study of Hong Kong. In *2018 IEEE International Conference on Industrial Engineering and Engineering Management (IEEM)* (pp. 521–525). IEEE.

Konieczek, B., Rethfeldt, M., Golatowski, F., & Timmermann, D. (2016, May). A distributed time server for the real-time extension of coap. In *2016 IEEE 19th International Symposium on Real-Time Distributed Computing (ISORC)* (pp. 84–91). IEEE.

Kumar, S., Suhaib, M., & Asjad, M. (2020). Industry 4.0: complex, disruptive, but inevitable. *Management and Production Engineering Review, 11*(1), 43–51.

Lasi, H., Fettke, P., Kemper, H.G., Feld, T., & Hoffmann, M. (2014). Industry 4.0. Bus Inf SystEng 6 (4): 239–242.

Lee, C.K.M., Cao, Y., & Ng, K.H. (2017). Big data analytics for predictive maintenance strategies. In *Supply Chain Management in the Big Data Era* (pp. 50–74). IGI Global.

Lee, C.K.M., Lv, Y., Ng, K.K.H., Ho, W., & Choy, K.L. (2018). Design and application of Internet of things-based warehouse management system for smart logistics. *International Journal of Production Research, 56*(8), 2753–2768.

Lee, C.K.M., Zhang, S.Z., & Ng, K.K.H. (2017). Development of an industrial Internet of things suite for smart factory towards re-industrialization. *Advances in manufacturing, 5*(4), 335–343.

Lee, C.K., Keung, K.L., Ng, K.K.H., & Lai, D.C. (2018, December). Simulation-based multiple automated guided vehicles considering charging and collision-free requirements in automatic warehouse. In *2018 IEEE International Conference on Industrial Engineering and Engineering Management (IEEM)* (pp. 1376–1380). IEEE.

Liu, Y., & Xu, X. (2017). Industry 4.0 and cloud manufacturing: A comparative analysis. *Journal of Manufacturing Science and Engineering, 139*(3), 034701.

Lu, S., Xu, C., Zhong, R.Y., & Wang, L. (2018). A passive RFID tag-based locating and navigating approach for automated guided vehicle. *Computers & Industrial Engineering, 125,* 628–636.

Luthra, S., & Mangla, S.K. (2018). Evaluating challenges to Industry 4.0 initiatives for supply chain sustainability in emerging economies. *Process Safety and Environmental Protection, 117,* 168–179.

Luthra, S., & Mangla, S.K. (2018). When strategies matter: adoption of sustainable supply chain management practices in an emerging economy's context. *Resources, Conservation and Recycling, 138,* 194–206.

Magruk, A. (2016). Uncertainty in the sphere of the industry 4.0–potential areas to research. *Business, Management and Education, 14*(2), 275–291.

Medić, N., Anišić, Z., Lalić, B., Marjanović, U., & Brezočnik, M. (2019). Hybrid fuzzy multi-attribute decision making model for evaluation of advanced digital technologies in manufacturing: Industry 4.0 perspective. *Advances in Production Engineering & Management, 14*(4), 483–493.

Moktadir, M.A., Ali, S.M., Kusi-Sarpong, S., & Shaikh, M.A.A. (2018). Assessing challenges for implementing Industry 4.0: Implications for process safety and environmental protection. *Process Safety and Environmental Protection, 117,* 730–741.

Mosterman, P.J., & Zander, J. (2016). Industry 4.0 as a cyber-physical system study. *Software & Systems Modeling, 15*(1), 17–29.

Müller, J.M., Kiel, D., & Voigt, K.I. (2018). What drives the implementation of Industry 4.0? The role of opportunities and challenges in the context of sustainability. *Sustainability, 10*(1), 247.

Nukala, R., Panduru, K., Shields, A., Riordan, D., Doody, P., & Walsh, J. (2016, June). Internet of Things: a review from 'Farm to Fork'. In *2016 27th Irish Signals and Systems Conference (ISSC)* (pp. 1–6). IEEE.

Oesterreich, T.D., &Teuteberg, F. (2016). Understanding the implications of digitisation and automation in the context of Industry 4.0: A triangulation approach and elements of a research agenda for the construction industry. *Computers in industry*, *83*, 121–139.

Oztaysi, B., Onar, S.C., Kahraman, C., & Yavuz, M. (2017). Multi-criteria alternative-fuel technology selection using interval-valued intuitionistic fuzzy sets. *Transportation Research Part D: Transport and Environment*, *53*, 128–148.

Pan, M., Sikorski, J., Kastner, C.A., Akroyd, J., Mosbach, S., Lau, R., & Kraft, M. (2015). Applying industry 4.0 to the Jurong Island eco-industrial park. *Energy Procedia*, *75*, 1536–1541.

Petrillo, A., De Felice, F., Cioffi, R., & Zomparelli, F. (2018). Fourth industrial revolution: current practices, challenges, and opportunities. *Digital Transformation in Smart Manufacturing*, 1–20.

Porter, M.E., & Heppelmann, J.E. (2014). How smart, connected products are transforming competition. *Harvard Business Review*, *92*(11), 64–88.

Priya, B., & Malhotra, J. (2020). 5GAuNetS: an autonomous 5G network selection framework for Industry 4.0. *Soft Computing*, *24*(13), 9507–9523.

Qin, J., Liu, Y., & Grosvenor, R. (2016). A categorical framework of manufacturing for industry 4.0 and beyond. *Procedia cirp*, *52*, 173–178.

Qiu, Z., Guo, Z., Guo, S., Qiu, L., Wang, X., Liu, S., & Liu, C. (2016, May). IoTI: Internet of things instruments reconstruction model design. In *2016 IEEE International Instrumentation and Measurement Technology Conference Proceedings* (pp. 1–6). IEEE.

Raj, A., Dwivedi, G., Sharma, A., de Sousa Jabbour, A.B.L., & Rajak, S. (2020). Barriers to the adoption of industry 4.0 technologies in the manufacturing sector: An inter-country comparative perspective. *International Journal of Production Economics*, *224*, 107546.

Ramos, L., Loures, E., Deschamps, F., & Venâncio, A. (2020). Systems evaluation methodology to attend the digital projects requirements for industry 4.0. *International Journal of Computer Integrated Manufacturing*, *33*(4), 398–410.

Rani, P., Mishra, A.R., & Pardasani, K.R. (2020). A novel WASPAS approach for multi-criteria physician selection problem with intuitionistic fuzzy type-2 sets. *Soft Computing*, *24*(3), 2355–2367.

Raschinger, M., Kipouridis, O., & Gunthner, W.A. (2016, May). A service-oriented cloud application for a collaborative tool management system. In *2016 International Conference on Industrial Engineering, Management Science and Application (ICIMSA)* (pp. 1–5). IEEE.

Rouyendegh, B.D., Yildizbasi, A., & Üstünyer, P. (2020). Intuitionistic fuzzy TOPSIS method for green supplier selection problem. *Soft Computing*, *24*(3), 2215–2228.

Rüßmann, M., Lorenz, M., Gerbert, P., Waldner, M., Justus, J., Engel, P., & Harnisch, M. (2015). Industry 4.0: the future of productivity and growth in manufacturing industries. *Boston Consulting Group*, *9*(1), 54–89.

Sachdeva, N., Shrivastava, A.K., & Chauhan, A. (2019). Modeling supplier selection in the era of Industry 4.0. *Benchmarking: An International Journal*. https://doi.org/10.1108/BIJ-12-2018-0441

Sarvari, P.A., Ustundag, A., Cevikcan, E., Kaya, I., & Cebi, S. (2018). Technology roadmap for Industry 4.0. In *Industry 4.0: Managing the digital transformation* (pp. 95–103). Springer, Cham.

Schläpfer, R.C., Koch, M., & Merkofer, P. (2015). Industry 4.0 challenges and solutions for the digital transformation and use of exponential technologies (pp. 1–12), Deloitte, Zurique.

Schlechtendahl, J., Keinert, M., Kretschmer, F., Lechler, A., & Verl, A. (2015). Making existing production systems Industry 4.0-ready. *Production Engineering*, *9*(1), 143–148.

Schröder (2016). The challenges of industry 4.0 for small and medium-sized enterprises. *Friedrich-Ebert-Stiftung: Bonn, Germany.*

Schuh, G., Potente, T., Varandani, R., & Schmitz, T. (2014). Global Footprint Design based on genetic algorithms–An "Industry 4.0" perspective. *CIRP Annals*, *63*(1), 433–436.

Schumacher, A., Erol, S., & Sihn, W. (2016). A maturity model for assessing Industry 4.0 readiness and maturity of manufacturing enterprises. *Procedia Cirp*, *52*(1), 161–166.

Segovia, V.R., & Theorin, A. (2012). History of Control History of PLC and DCS. University of Lund.

Seker, S. (2020). A novel interval-valued intuitionistic trapezoidal fuzzy combinative distance-based assessment (CODAS) method. *Soft Computing*, *24*(3), 2287–2300.

Simon, J., Trojanova, M., Zbihlej, J., & Sarosi, J. (2018). Mass customization model in food industry using industry 4.0 standard with fuzzy-based multi-criteria decision making methodology. *Advances in Mechanical Engineering*, *10*(3), 1687814018766776.

Stachová, K., Papula, J., Stacho, Z., & Kohnová, L. (2019). External partnerships in employee education and development as the key to facing industry 4.0 challenges. *Sustainability*, *11*(2), 345.

Stemmler, S., Reiter, M., & Abel, D. (2014). Model predictive control as a module for autonomously running complex plastics production processes. *International Polymer Science and Technology*, *41*(12), 1–6.

Stentoft, J., Jensen, K.W., Philipsen, K., & Haug, A. (2019, January). Drivers and barriers for Industry 4.0 readiness and practice: a SME perspective with empirical evidence. In *Proceedings of the 52nd Hawaii International Conference on System Sciences.*

Stork, A. (2015). Visual computing challenges of advanced manufacturing and industrie 4.0 [guest editors' introduction]. *IEEE computer graphics and applications*, *35*(2), 21–25.

Tooranloo, H.S., & sadat Ayatollah, A. (2016). A model for failure mode and effects analysis based on intuitionistic fuzzy approach. *Applied soft computing*, *49*, 238–247.

Tupa, J., Simota, J., & Steiner, F. (2017). Aspects of risk management implementation for Industry 4.0. *Procedia Manufacturing*, *11*, 1223–1230.

Türkeş, M.C., Oncioiu, I., Aslam, H.D., Marin-Pantelescu, A., Topor, D.I., & Căpuşneanu, S. (2019). Drivers and barriers in using industry 4.0: a perspective of SMEs in Romania. *Processes*, *7*(3), 153.

Vaidya, S., Ambad, P., & Bhosle, S. (2018). Industry 4.0–a glimpse. *Procedia Manufacturing*, *20*, 233–238.

Veile, J.W., Kiel, D., Müller, J.M., & Voigt, K.I. (2019). Lessons learned from Industry 4.0 implementation in the German manufacturing industry. *Journal of Manufacturing Technology Management*, 31(5), 977–997.

Veza, I., Mladineo, M., & Gjeldum, N. (2015). Managing innovative production network of smart factories. *IFAC-PapersOnLine*, *48*(3), 555–560.

Wang, L.E., Liu, H.C., & Quan, M.Y. (2016). Evaluating the risk of failure modes with a hybrid MCDM model under interval-valued intuitionistic fuzzy environments. *Computers & Industrial Engineering*, *102*, 175–185.

Wang, Y., & Shi, Y. (2020). Measuring the service quality of urban rail transit based on interval-valued intuitionistic fuzzy model. *KSCE Journal of Civil Engineering*, *24*(2), 647–656.

Wende, J., & Kiradjiev, P. (2014). An implementation of lot size 1 according to Industry 4.0 principles. *E &I Electrical Engineering and Information Technology*, *131*(7), 202–206.

Womak, J., Jones, D.T., & Roos, D. (1990). The machine that changed the world. New York: Rawson Associates.

Yoon, S., Um, J., Suh, S.H., Stroud, I., & Yoon, J.S. (2019). Smart Factory Information Service Bus (SIBUS) for manufacturing application: requirement, architecture and implementation. *Journal of Intelligent Manufacturing*, *30*(1), 363–382.

Zadeh, L.A. (1965). Fuzzy sets. *Information and Control*, *8*(3), 338–353.

Zheng, P., Lin, Y., Chen, C.H., & Xu, X. (2019). Smart, connected open architecture product: an IT-driven co-creation paradigm with lifecycle personalization concerns. *International Journal of Production Research*, *57*(8), 2571–2584.

Zheng, P., Sang, Z., Zhong, R. Y., Liu, Y., Liu, C., Mubarok, K., ... & Xu, X. (2018). Smart manufacturing systems for Industry 4.0: Conceptual framework, scenarios, and future perspectives. *Frontiers of Mechanical Engineering*, *13*(2), 137–150.

Zheng, P., Xu, X., & Chen, C.H. (2020). A data-driven cyber-physical approach for personalised smart, connected product co-development in a cloud-based environment. *Journal of Intelligent Manufacturing*, *31*(1), 3–18.

Zhong, R.Y., Xu, C., Chen, C., & Huang, G.Q. (2017). Big data analytics for physical internet-based intelligent manufacturing shop floors. *International Journal of Production Research*, *55*(9), 2610–2621.

Zhou, K., Liu, T., & Zhou, L. (2015, August). Industry 4.0: towards future industrial opportunities and challenges. In *2015 12th International conference on fuzzy systems and knowledge discovery (FSKD)* (pp. 2147–2152). IEEE.

Zimmermann, H.J. (1991). Introduction to fuzzy sets. In *Fuzzy Set Theory—and Its Applications* (pp. 1–7). Springer, Dordrecht.

5 Consistency of Aggregation Function-Based m-Polar Fuzzy Digraphs in Group Decision Making

Azadeh Zahedi Khameneh[1], Adem Kilicman[1, 2] and Fadzilah Md Ali[1, 2]

[1]Institute for Mathematical Research, Universiti Putra Malaysia, 43400 UPM Serdang, Selangor, Malaysia
[2]Institute for Mathematical Research and Department of Mathematics, Universiti Putra Malaysia, 43400 UPM Serdang, Selangor, Malaysia

5.1 INTRODUCTION

Pairwise comparison of alternatives is the starting point for data analysis in decision situations, where the final aim is to rank alternatives from the best to the worst and choose the optimum solution. The comparison information is usually expressed as fuzzy preferences (Zadeh 1971; Tanino 1988; Orlovsky 1978); reciprocal or multiplicative preferences (Satty and others 1980); or linguistic preferences (Chiclana, Herrera, and Herrera-Viedma 2002; Bordogna, Fedrizzi, and Pasi 1997) over the set of alternatives by decision-makers where the consistency of these preferences, that has direct effect on making a reliable decision, should be addressed.

Decision situations are mostly multi-person rather than individual problem. In a group decision-making process, the final action is taken by the mentor or head of the group after collecting decision makers' preferences over the set of possible alternatives and combining these different judgments into a single one. Therefore, providing a suitable consensus tool and checking the consistency of final preference relation are two main tasks that should be handled in group decision-making problems. Because of the conflict between different decision-makers, arisen in most cases, reaching a consensus as a unanimous and total agreement of all decision-makers is naturally impossible. Accordingly, in group decision making with fuzzy information different consensus methods, such as fuzzy majority rules (Yan and Ma 2015; Kacprzyk, Fedrizzi, and Nurmi 1992) and aggregation functions (Dubois and

Prade 2004; Beliakov, Calvo, and James 2014; Beliakov, James, and Wilkin 2017) are developed to merge preferences of decision-makers. The most important problem in the aggregation of preferences is to consider the consistency of collective priority based on the group view. In the context of fuzzy preference relations, consistency property is associated with the concept of fuzzy transitivity (Herrera-Viedma et al. 2004; Peneva and Popchev 2007). Fuzzy graph theory (Rosenfeld 1975) is also applied to visualize the transitivity of (strictly) fuzzy preference relations between finite alternatives or states by using fuzzy directed graphs, or fuzzy digraph in brief, in which fuzzy edges show the fuzzy preference relations among nodes.

Studies on fuzzy transitivity were initiated by Zadeh (Lotfi Asker Zadeh 1971), known as $max - min$ transitivity. Tanino (Tanino 1984, 1988) proposed several types of transitivity, usually known as stochastic transitivity. Switalski (Switalski 2001) presented two weaker types of transitivity known as α-transitivity, where $\alpha \in [0, 1]$, and group transitivity. Herrera et al. (Herrera-Viedma et al. 2004) developed additive multiplicative transitivity property for fuzzy preferences. Dudziak (Dudziak 2013) generalized the concept of $max - min$ transitivity by using any t-norms T and t-conorms S instead of minimum and maximum operators to define the new concepts of T-transitive and negatively S-transitive. The assumptions of t-norm for T and t-conorm for S were then replaced, respectively, by fuzzy conjunction C: $[0, 1]^2 \rightarrow [0, 1]$ and fuzzy disjunction D: $[0, 1]^2 \rightarrow [0, 1]$ in (Bentkowska and Król 2016) to propose more general transitivity of fuzzy relations. Moreover, in the process of group decision making, checking the aggregating tool conditions for preservation the transitivity property of initial fuzzy relations is a crucial task that is considered by different researchers (García-Lapresta and Llamazares 2000; Peneva and Popchev 2003; Drewniak and Dudziak 2007; Bentkowska 2018).

5.1.1 PROBLEM DESCRIPTION

Let $V = \{v_1, v_2, \cdots, v_n\}$, where $n \geq 2$, be a finite set of n alternatives/states/objects. Suppose that there is a comparison relation between these n objects described as a fuzzy preference relation (FprR in brief) P: $V \times V \rightarrow [0, 1]$ such that the value $P(v_i, v_j) = P(v_i v_j) = p_{ij}$ denotes the preference degree of v_i over v_j. The fuzzy relation P can be also shown by an $n \times n$ additive reciprocal matrix $P = [p_{ij}]_{n \times n}$, such that $p_{ij} + p_{ji} = 1$ where $p_{ij} > 0.5$ means v_i is preferred to v_j (denoted by $v_i \succ v_j$) and $p_{ij} = 0.5$ shows there is no difference between v_i and v_j (denoted by $v_i \sim v$) (Tanino 1984). Using fuzzy graph theory, the transitive matrix P can be visualized as a fuzzy digraph where the crisp nodes show the alternatives v_i ($1 \leq i \leq n$) and the weighted arrow from v_i to v_j represents how much v_i is preferred to v_j. However, in many cases, the alternatives are also described as fuzzy nodes, not crisp ones. The membership degrees of them may show how much each of the alternatives has power/authority in the group or how much each of them owns the given parameters/features. However, in the sense of Rosenfeld (Rosenfeld 1975), a fuzzy (di)graph with both fuzzy nodes and fuzzy edges is not represented, necessarily, as a reciprocal square matrix.

Multi-polar or multi-index information, arisen from multi-source or multi-parameter data, is a common issue in group decision-making problems. In many cases, objects may have positive or negative influences on each other; or they may have relationships in different directions based on different features of a given property. By extending the range of fuzzy sets from $[0, 1]$ into the $[0, 1]^m$, the concepts of m-polar fuzzy sets (Chen et al. 2014) and m-polar fuzzy graphs (Akram 2013, 2011; Ghorai and Pal 2016; Samanta and Pal 2012; Singh 2018) were developed to cope with this issue. In order to have a reliable ordering of alternatives based on the given fuzzy preference relations by each decision-maker, the consistency of these initial m-polar fuzzy relations as well as the consistency of the aggregated data, resulting from the consensus phase, must be checked by the mentor/head of the decision-makers group. However, because of some reasons, such as lack of knowledge of decision-makers; unfit aggregation function; lack of unique definition for transitivity; the strong condition for transitivity, reaching to consistency is difficult or impossible. In fuzzy logic, the transitivity property of m-polar fuzzy edges/relations in a graph is checked based on membership degrees of the edges between any three nodes, where the membership value/weight of each edge at any direction depends on the minimum grade among the membership degrees of corresponding nodes at the same direction. Two natural questions arise here that (I) how we can measure the strength of m-polar fuzzy relationship between each pair of nodes v_i and v_j based on the membership degrees of both not only the minimum one and (II) how we can aggregate them such that the transitivity of m-polar fuzzy edges/relations is preserved during the consensus phase.

To answer these questions, in this work, we develop the concept of m-polar fuzzy relation ψ on the m-polar fuzzy subset ϕ of V by using any conjunction rather than the minimum. We also propose a new class of transitivity for m-polar fuzzy relations in an aggregation function-based framework. Based on the type of given aggregation function, different types of m-polar transitivity conditions are obtained. A method of three steps, including (1) representing the strict m-polar fuzzy information by an m-polar fuzzy digraph; (2) combining the obtained digraphs by using aggregation functions in order to get a collective m-polar fuzzy digraph; and (3) deriving a final judgment based on the resultant m-polar fuzzy digraph, is proposed to analyze the strict m-polar fuzzy comparison relations which are called m-polar fuzzy preference. By using the concept of **a**-level (di)graph, the obtained m-polar fuzzy output is converted into a crisp one to complete the selection phase.

5.2 FUZZY ORDERING THEORY

Traditionally, binary relations, especially orders, are applied to explain comparison information or preferences over different objects. By adding membership degree to this Boolean information, relations are presented in the fuzzy logic-based framework, called fuzzy relations, which are more suitable to express real-world situations.

Definition 5.2.1: (Zadeh 1971) *A fuzzy binary relation R from U to V is a fuzzy subset of $U \times V$ characterized by the membership function $R: U \times V \to [0, 1]$ where for each pair $(u, v) \in U \times V$ the value $R(u, v)$ shows the strength of the relation between u and v.*

Various properties of fuzzy relations including reflexivity (i.e. $R(v, v) = 1$; $\forall v \in V$), symmetry (i.e. $R(u, v) = R(v, u)$; $\forall u, v \in V$), antisymmetry (i.e. $R(u, v) > 0 \Rightarrow R(v, u) = 0$; $\forall u, v \in V$ such that $u \neq v$), and transitivity (i.e. $R(u, w) \geq max_v[min(R(u, v), R(v, w)); v \in V]$; $\forall u, v, w \in V$) were also introduced. Note that, there is not any unique formula in the mathematics community for expressing these definitions, in comparison with the corresponding crisp concepts. Accordingly, the fuzzy relation R is called:

- similarity relation if it is reflexive, symmetric and transitive;
- fuzzy ordering if it is reflexive;
- fuzzy preordering if it is reflexive and transitive;
- fuzzy partial ordering or fuzzy weak preference ordering if it is reflexive, antisymmetric and transitive;
- fuzzy strict preference ordering if it is antisymmetric and transitive.

Tanino (Tanino 1984) interpreted the membership grade of $R(u, v)$ as the degree of preference u over v rather than the strength of relationship between them. Moreover, to show the consistency of fuzzy preference ordering different types of transitivity were proposed as below. The fuzzy relation R is called:

- weak transitive if $\forall u, v, w \in V$: $(R(u, v) \geq 0.5, R(v, w) \geq 0.5) \Rightarrow R(u, w) \geq 0.5$;
- *min*-transitive if $\forall u, v, w \in V$: $min(R(u, v), R(v, w)) \leq R(u, w)$;
- *max*-transitive if $\forall u, v, w \in V$: $max(R(u, v), R(v, w)) \leq R(u, w)$;
- restricted *min*-transitive if $\forall u, v, w \in V$: $(R(u, v) \geq 0.5, R(v, w) \geq 0.5) \Rightarrow min(R(u, v), R(v, w)) \leq R(u, w)$;
- restricted *max*-transitive if $\forall u, v, w \in V$: $(R(u, v) \geq 0.5, R(v, w) \geq 0.5) \Rightarrow max(R(u, v), R(v, w)) \leq R(u, w)$;
- additive transitive if $\forall u, v, w \in V$: $R(u, w) = R(u, v) + R(v, w) - 0.5$.

5.2.1 Aggregation of Fuzzy Orderings

Aggregation functions theory has been widely applied in group decision making, where we need to combine and summarize a list of input data into a single output to reach consensus and take the final action (Zahedi Khameneh and Kilicman 2019; Zahedi Khameneh and Kilicman 2020). In decision making, inputs explain the assessment values of decision-makers over the objects under consideration. However, these assessments are sometimes expressed as comparison information between objects/options, characterized by fuzzy relations. The combining process of n fuzzy relations $R_1, ..., R_n$ in a group decision making prolem involves an n-ary function F, known as aggregation function, that assigns to the given fuzzy relations $R_1, ..., R_n$ a new fuzzy relation $R_F = F(R_1, ..., R_n)$ which is called the aggregated relation.

Definition 5.2.2: *An aggregation function of dimension $n \in \mathbb{N}$ is an n-ary function $A^{(n)}$: $[0, 1]^n \to [0, 1]$ satisfying*

1: $A(x) = x$, for $n = 1$ and any $x \in [0, 1]$;

2: $A^{(n)}(x_1, \cdots, x_n) \leq A^{(n)}(y_1, \cdots, y_n)$ if $(x_1, \cdots, x_n) \leq (y_1, \cdots, y_n)$;

3: $A^{(n)}(0, 0, \cdots, 0) = 0$ and $A^{(n)}(1, 1, \cdots, 1) = 1$.

Note that, if condition (1) in Definition 5.2.2 is fulfilled for the n-ary function A and all $(x, \cdots, x) \in [0, 1]^n$, i.e. $A^{(n)}(x, \cdots, x) = x$ for all $x \in [0, 1]$; then A is called an idempotent aggregation function. The aggregation function A is called conjunctive when $A^{(n)}(x_1, \cdots, x_n) \leq min(x_1, \cdots, x_n)$; disjunctive if $A^{(n)}(x_1, \cdots, x_n) \geq max(x_1, \cdots, x_n)$; and average whenever $min(x_1, \cdots, x_n) \leq A^{(n)}(x_1, \cdots, x_n) \leq max(x_1, \cdots, x_n)$. Clearly, the averaging aggregation functions are idempotent. For any two aggregation functions A, B, we say A dominates B, denoted by $A \gg B$, if the following inequality holds:

$$A^{(m)}(B^{(n)}(x_{11}, \cdots, x_{1n}), \cdots, B^{(n)}(x_{m1}, \cdots, x_{mn}))$$
$$\geq B^{(n)}(A^{(m)}(x_{11}, \cdots, x_{m1}), \cdots, A^{(m)}(x_{1n}, \cdots, x_{mn}))$$

where $X = [x_{ik}]_{m \times n}$ is an arbitrary $m \times n$ matrix.

Definition 5.2.3: A binary operation $T: [0, 1]^2 \to [0, 1]$ is called a triangular norm or t-norm if it is symmetric, associative, non-decreasing function and satisfies the boundary condition $T(x, 1) = x$, $\forall x \in [0, 1]$. A binary operation $S: [0, 1]^2 \to [0, 1]$ is called a triangular conorm or t-conorm if it is symmetric, associative, non-decreasing function and satisfies the boundary condition $S(x, 0) = x$, $\forall x \in [0, 1]$.

Example 5.2.4: $T_M(x, y) = min(x, y)$, $T_P(x, y) = xy$ and $T_L(x, y) = max(x + y - 1, 0)$ are some examples for t-norms. On the other hand, operators $S_M(x, y) = max(x, y)$, $S_P(x, y) = x + y - xy$ and $S_L(x, y) = min(x + y, 1)$ are t-conorms.

Note that, the operators t-norms and t-conorms are well-known examples of conjunctive and disjunctive aggregation functions, respectively.

5.2.2 FUZZY GRAPHS

The first appearance of terminology "fuzzy graph" backs to the Rosenfeld (Rosenfeld 1975) work. He first generalized the concept of fuzzy relation R over the non-fuzzy set V into the concept of fuzzy relation ψ over a fuzzy subset ϕ of V by inequity $\psi(u, v) \leq min(\phi(u), \phi(v))$. Then, he defined the concept of fuzzy graph as below.

Definition 5.2.5: A 3-tuple $G = (V, \phi, \psi)$ where $\phi: V \to [0, 1]$ and $\psi: V \times V \to [0, 1]$ are fuzzy sets on V and V^2, respectively, such that $\psi(uv) \leq min\{\phi(u), \phi(v)\}$ for all $u, v \in V$ is called a fuzzy graph (FG in brief) where ψ is a symmetric fuzzy relation on V.

G is called fuzzy digraph (or FdiG in brief) if ψ is not symmetric. The fuzzy graph $H = (V, \sigma, \mu)$ is a fuzzy subgraph of $G = (V, \phi, \psi)$ if for all $u, v \in V$: $\sigma(v) \le \phi(v)$ and $\mu(uv) \le \psi(uv)$. Based on the concept of α-level set in Zadeh's fuzzy set theory (Zadeh 1978), here we can also define α-level graph of $G = (V, \phi, \psi)$ for any $\alpha \in (0, 1]$ that gives us a crisp graph $G_\alpha = (V_\alpha, E_\alpha)$ where $V_\alpha = \{v \in V: \phi(v) \ge \alpha\}$ and $E_\alpha = \{uv \in V^2: \psi(uv) \ge \alpha\}$.

5.2.3 M-POLAR FUZZY GRAPHS

Multi-polar information is a common issue in many real-world problems, where data usually comes from m different sources. Since the standard format of fuzzy sets cannot model such situations, the concept of m-polar fuzzy set (m-PFS in brief), that is presented by a mapping $f: U \to [0, 1]^m$ where $m \in \mathbb{N}$ and $(0, ...,0)$ and $(1, ...,1)$ are the least and the greatest elements, was introduced in (Chen et al. 2014). By applying m-polar fuzzy sets to the theory of fuzzy graphs, a new concept of m-polar fuzzy graph is defined to describe the fuzzy relations among several objects in different directions.

Definition 5.2.6: (Singh 2018) *An m-polar fuzzy graph (shortly m-PFG) is defined as a 3-tuple $G = (V, \phi, \psi)$ where $\phi: V \to [0, 1]^m$ (an m-polar fuzzy set on V) and $\psi: V \times V \to [0, 1]^m$ (an m-polar fuzzy set on V^2) such that $\pi_s \circ \psi(uv) \le min\{\pi_s \circ \phi(u), \pi_s \circ \phi(v)\}$ for all $u, v \in V$ and $s = 1, 2, \cdots, m$; where $\pi_s: [0, 1]^m \to [0, 1]$ is the mapping of the s-th projection.*

An m-polar fuzzy graph $H = (V, \sigma, \mu)$ is a subgraph of m-polar fuzzy graph $G = (V, \phi, \psi)$ if for all $u, v \in V$ and $s = 1, 2, \cdots, m$: $\pi_s \circ \sigma(v) \le \pi_s \circ \phi(v)$ and $\pi_s \circ \mu(uv) \le \pi_s \circ \psi(uv)$. The underlying crisp graph $G_0 = (V_0, E_0)$ of the m-polar fuzzy graph $G = (V, \phi, \psi)$ is defined by vertex set $V_0 = \{v \in V: \pi_s \circ \phi(v) > 0; 1 \le s \le m\}$ and edge set $E_0 = \{(u, v) \in V^2: \pi_s \circ \psi(uv) > 0; 1 \le s \le m\}$. The m-polar fuzzy graph $G = (V, \phi, \psi)$ is called strong if $\pi_s \circ \psi(uv) = min\{\pi_s \circ \phi(u), \pi_s \circ \phi(v)\}$ for all $uv \in E_0$, and it is called complete m-PFG if the equation is held for all $u, v \in V$.

5.3 CONJUNCTION-BASED FUZZY RELATIONS

The initial step to propose a more general definition of m-polar fuzzy (di)graph is to generalize the concept of m-polar fuzzy relation over an m-polar fuzzy set. The following simple example is developed to show why this change gives a more suitable tool to model certain situations. Let $V = \{v_1, v_2, v_3\}$ and $E = \{v_1v_2, v_1v_3, v_2v_3\}$ show a digraph, modeling people behavior in a group known as influence graph, where nodes indicate the power of each person and edges present the influence of a person on another. The authority grade of each person in the group can be measured based on experience; persuading; legitimizing; exchanging idea and capitulating, that causes to get a five-polar fuzzy influence graph. If the fuzzy subset ϕ of V is defined by $\phi(v_1) = (0.3, 0.5, 0.5, 0.3, 0.2)$, $\phi(v_2) = (0.4, 0.6, 0.5, 0.5, 0.3)$ and $\phi(v_3) = (0.6, 0.5, 0.6, 0.7, 0.4)$. And the five-polar fuzzy relation ψ is defined by $\pi_s \circ \psi(v_i v_j) = min \{\pi_s \circ \phi(v_i), \pi_s \circ \phi(v_j)\}$. Then for instance, $\psi(v_1 v_2) = (0.3, 0.5, 0.5, 0.3, 0.2)$ that means the power/ authority of person v_2 in the group does not play any role in determining the level of relationship between v_1 and v_2. However, if we use product operator rather than minimum, then $\psi(v_1 v_2)$ is obtained based on the authority grades of v_1 and v_2, both.

By developing the conjunctive operator minimum to any conjunctive aggregation function C, a generalization for the definition of m-polar fuzzy binary relation on an m-polar fuzzy set is obtained as below. It should be mentioned that non-conjunctive operators cannot be used because of failing the complementary property of m-polar fuzzy graph.

Definition 5.3.1: *Let $\phi: V \to [0, 1]^m$ be an m-polar fuzzy subset of a set V and $\psi: V \times V \to [0, 1]^m$ be an m-polar fuzzy relation on V. If $C: \cup_{n \in \mathbb{N}}[0, 1]^n \to [0, 1]$ is a conjunctive aggregation function, then the m-polar fuzzy relation ψ satisfying in the following inequality*

$$\pi_s \circ \psi(uv) \leq C^{(2)}(\pi_s \circ \phi(u), \pi_s \circ \phi(v)): \forall\ u, v \in V \qquad (5.1)$$

for all $s = 1, 2, \cdots, m$; is called an m-polar fuzzy relation on the m-polar fuzzy subset ϕ w.r.t conjunction C or m-P C-FR in brief.

The vector $\psi(uv)$ represents strength of the existing relation between u and v in m different directions. If

$$\pi_s \circ \psi(uv) = C^{(2)}(\pi_s \circ \phi(u), \pi_s \circ \phi(v)): \forall\ u, v \in V \qquad (5.2)$$

for all $s = 1, 2, \cdots, m$; then the m-PC-FR ψ on ϕ is said to be strong.

Example 5.3.2: *Let $\phi: V \to [0, 1]^2$ be a given 2-polar fuzzy set on a set V and $C: [0, 1]^2 \to [0, 1]$ be the t-norm T_P, i.e. $C(x, y) = x \cdot y$. Define $\psi: V^2 \to [0, 1]^2$ by*

$$\pi_1 \circ \psi(uv) = \begin{cases} \pi_1 \circ \phi(u) + \pi_1 \circ \phi(v) - 1 & \pi_1 \circ \phi(u) + \pi_1 \circ \phi(v) > 1 \\ \pi_1 \circ \phi(u) \cdot \pi_1 \circ \phi(v) & else \end{cases}$$

and

$$\pi_2 \circ \psi(uv) = \begin{cases} 0 & min\{\pi_2 \circ \phi(u), \pi_2 \circ \phi(v)\} = 0 \\ \dfrac{\pi_2 \circ \phi(u) \cdot \pi_2 \circ \phi(v)}{1 + max(\pi_2 \circ \phi(u), \pi_2 \circ \phi(v))} & else \end{cases}$$

Then, ψ is a 2-PT$_P$-FR, consequently, 2-Pmin-FR on ϕ but it is not a 2-PT$_L$-FR.

For any conjunctive aggregation operator C, the m-PC-FR ψ on the m-PFS ϕ is also an m-polar min-fuzzy relation on ϕ in the traditional sense. However, the converse is not true in general.

Proposition 5.3.3: *Let C_1, C_2 be two conjunctive aggregation functions such that $C_1 \leq C_2$. If ψ is an m-PC_1-FR on the m-PFS ϕ, then it is also an m-PFR on ϕ w.r.t C_2.*

Proof. It is clear since we have $\pi_s \circ \psi(uv) \leq C_1^{(2)}(\pi_s \circ \phi(u), \pi_s \circ \phi(v)) \leq C_2^{(2)}$ $(\pi_s \circ \phi(u), \pi_s \circ \phi(v))$ for all $s = 1, \cdots, m$.

Definition 5.3.4: *Let ψ be an m-PC-FR on an m-polar fuzzy subset ϕ of V. If the m-tuple $a = (a_1, \cdots, a_m) \in (0, 1]^m$ is a given threshold vector on the membership degrees, then $\psi_a = \{(u, v) \in V^2 : \pi_s \circ \psi(uv) \geq a_s; s = 1, 2, \cdots, m\}$ is a non-fuzzy (crisp) binary relation on V that is called a-level relation generated by ψ.*

Clearly, for any two given threshold vectors $\mathbf{a}, \mathbf{b} \in (0, 1]^m$ such that $\mathbf{a} = (a_1, \cdots, a_m)$, $\mathbf{b} = (b_1, \cdots, b_m)$ and $a_s \geq b_s$ for all $1 \leq s \leq m$, we have $\psi_{\mathbf{a}} \subseteq \psi_{\mathbf{b}}$.

In the sequence, the concepts of reflexivity, symmetry and transitivity are developed for m-PC-FR ψ. Specially transitivity is defined in any aggregation-based framework rather than using the fixed aggregation operator minimum.

Definition 5.3.5: *Let ψ be a m-PC-FR on an m-polar fuzzy subset ϕ of V. If $\pi_s \circ \psi(vv) = \pi_s \circ \phi(v)$ for all $v \in V$ and $s = 1, 2, \cdots, m$; then ψ is called m-polar reflexive on ϕ.*

Proposition 5.3.6: *The m-PC-FR ψ on ϕ is reflexive if $C^{(2)}(x, x) = x$ for all $x \in Re_{\pi_s \circ \phi} = \{x \in [0, 1] : \exists v \in V; \pi_s \circ \phi(v) = x\}$ and any $s = 1, \cdots, m$.*

Proof. Let ψ be an m-polar reflexive fuzzy relation on the m-polar fuzzy set ϕ w.r.t C. For any $s = 1, \cdots, m$; suppose there exists $x_s \in Re_{\pi_s \circ \phi} \subseteq [0, 1]$ such that $C^{(2)}(x_s, x_s) \neq x_s$. This means that $C^{(2)}(x_s, x_s) < x_s$, followed from conjunction property of C. Take $v \in V$ where $\pi_s \circ \phi(v) = x_s$. Then $x_s = \pi_s \circ \phi(v) = \pi_s \circ \psi(vv) \leq C^{(2)}(\pi_s \circ \phi(v), \pi_s \circ \phi(v)) < x_s$ since ψ is reflexive on ϕ. That implies a contradiction. Thus, $C^{(2)}(x_s, x_s) = x_s$.

Example 5.3.7: *Let $V = \{v_1, v_2, v_3\}$ and $C: [0, 1]^2 \rightarrow [0, 1]$ be a conjunctive aggregation operator given by $C(x, y) = \frac{1}{2} min\{x, y\}$. Define $\phi: V \rightarrow [0, 1]^2$ by $\phi(v_1) = \left(\frac{1}{2}, \frac{1}{3}\right)$, $\phi(v_2) = \left(\frac{1}{3}, \frac{1}{4}\right)$ and $\phi(v_3) = \left(\frac{1}{4}, \frac{1}{5}\right)$; and $\psi: V^2 \rightarrow [0, 1]^2$ by*

$$\psi(uv) = \begin{cases} \left(\frac{1}{2}, \frac{1}{3}\right) & \text{if } u = v = v_1 \\ \left(\frac{1}{3}, \frac{1}{4}\right) & \text{if } u = v = v_2 \\ \left(\frac{1}{4}, \frac{1}{5}\right) & \text{if } u = v = v_3 \\ \left(\frac{1}{8}, \frac{1}{7}\right) & \text{else.} \end{cases}$$

then ψ is not a 2-P C-FR on ϕ since

$$\frac{1}{2} = \pi_1 \circ \psi (v_1 v_1) \nleq C (\pi_1 \circ \phi (v_1), \pi_1 \circ \phi (v_1)) = \frac{1}{4}$$

$$\frac{1}{3} = \pi_1 \circ \psi (v_2 v_2) \nleq C (\pi_1 \circ \phi (v_2), \pi_1 \circ \phi (v_2)) = \frac{1}{6}$$

$$\frac{1}{4} = \pi_1 \circ \psi (v_3 v_3) \nleq C (\pi_1 \circ \phi (v_3), \pi_1 \circ \phi (v_3)) = \frac{1}{8}$$

and

$$\frac{1}{3} = \pi_2 \circ \psi (v_1 v_1) \nleq C (\pi_2 \circ \phi (v_1), \pi_2 \circ \phi (v_1)) = \frac{1}{6}$$

$$\frac{1}{4} = \pi_2 \circ \psi (v_2 v_2) \nleq C (\pi_2 \circ \phi (v_2), \pi_2 \circ \phi (v_2)) = \frac{1}{8}$$

$$\frac{1}{5} = \pi_2 \circ \psi (v_3 v_3) \nleq C (\pi_2 \circ \phi (v_3), \pi_2 \circ \phi (v_3)) = \frac{1}{10}$$

Accordingly, it cannot be considered as a 2-polar reflexive fuzzy relation on ϕ w.r.t C while $\pi_s \circ \psi (v_i v_i) = \pi_s \circ \phi (v_i)$ for all $s = 1, 2$ and $i = 1, 2, 3$. If we define

$$C(x, y) = \begin{cases} \frac{1}{2} min \{x, y\} & x \neq y \\ min \{x, y\} & else. \end{cases}$$

Then, ψ is a 2-polar reflexive fuzzy relation on ϕ w.r.t C.

Proposition 5.3.8: The m-polar fuzzy relation ψ on $V \subseteq X$ is reflexive iff it is reflexive over the m-polar fuzzy subset $\chi_V : X \rightarrow [0, 1]^m$ of V, which assigns to each $v \in V$ the m-tuple $(1, \cdots , 1)$ and to each $v \in X - V$ the m-tuple $(0, \cdots ,0)$.

Proof. Take $v \in V$. Then, $\pi_s \circ \psi (vv) = \pi_s \circ \chi_V (v) = 1$ for any $1 \leq s \leq m$.

Definition 5.3.9: Let ψ be an m-PC-FR on an m-polar fuzzy subset ϕ of V.

- If for any $s = 1, 2, \cdots ,m$; $\pi_s \circ \psi (uv) = \pi_s \circ \psi (vu)$ for all $u, v \in V$, then ψ is called m-polar fuzzy symmetric on ϕ.
- ψ is called m-polar fuzzy C-antisymmetric on ϕ if $C^{(2)} (\pi_s \circ \psi (uv), \pi_s \circ \psi (vu)) = 0$ for any $s = 1, 2, \cdots ,m$ and $u, v \in V$ where $u \neq v$.

Proposition 5.3.10: If ψ is a symmetric (antisymmetric) m-PC-FR on ϕ where C is a conjunction operator (without zero divisors), then for every threshold vector $a \in (0, 1]^m$ the crisp binary relation ψ_a is symmetric (antisymmetric) on V.

Proof. Take $a = (a_1, \cdots, a_s, \cdots, a_m) \in (0, 1]^m$. First, suppose that ψ be an m-polar symmetric fuzzy relation on ϕ w.r.t C. Take $(u, v) \in \psi_a$, then $\pi_s \circ \psi(vu) = \pi_s \circ \psi(uv) \geq a_s$ for any $1 \leq s \leq m$. Therefore $(v, u) \in \psi_a$, meaning that ψ_a is symmetric on V. Now, let ψ be an m-polar antisymmetric fuzzy relation on ϕ w.r.t C. Take $(u, v) \in \psi_a$ which meaning that $\pi_s \circ \psi(uv) \geq a_s > 0$ for all $1 \leq s \leq m$. By assumption $C^{(2)}(\pi_s \circ \psi(uv), \pi_s \circ \psi(vu)) = 0$ we have $\pi_s \circ \psi(vu) = 0$. Thus $(v, u) \notin \psi_a$ that means ψ_a is antisymmetric on V.

Proposition 5.3.11: *Let ψ be a strong m-PC-FR on ϕ. The relation ψ is symmetric on ϕ iff the conjunctive aggregation operator C is symmetric.*

Proof. Suppose that ψ is a strong m-PC-FR on ϕ, meaning that $\pi_s \circ \psi(uv) = C^{(2)}(\pi_s \circ \phi(u), \pi_s \circ \phi(v))$ for all $s = 1, \cdots, m$ and $u, v \in V$. Then, the equality $\pi_s \circ \psi(uv) = \pi_s \circ \psi(vu)$ is followed from the symmetry condition of C. The converse is clear.

Corollary 5.3.12: If ψ is a strong m-polar fuzzy relation on ϕ w.r.t t-norm T, then ψ is symmetric m-PT-FR on ϕ.

Proposition 5.3.13: *Let ψ be a symmetric m-PC$_1$-FR on ϕ and $C_1 \leq C_2$. Then it is a symmetric m-PC$_2$-FR on ϕ.*

Corollary 5.3.14: Let C be an arbitrary conjunction. If ψ is a symmetric m-PC-FR on ϕ, then it is symmetric on ϕ w.r.t any t-norm T.

Example 5.3.15: *Let $V = \{v_1, v_2, v_3\}$. Suppose $\phi: V \to [0, 1]^2$ and $\psi: V^2 \to [0, 1]^2$ be 2-polar fuzzy sets on V and V^2, respectively. If for any $i, j = 1, 2, 3$; we define $\pi_s \circ \psi(v_i v_j) = T_L(\pi_s \circ \phi(v_i), \pi_s \circ \phi(v_j)) = max(\pi_s \circ \phi(v_i) + \pi_s \circ \phi(v_j) - 1, 0)$ for all $s = 1, 2$. Then ψ is a symmetric 2-polar fuzzy relation on ϕ w.r.t t-norms T_L and T_P, consequently w.r.t minimum operator.*

Definition 5.3.16: Let ψ be an m-PC-FR on a fuzzy subset ϕ of V. Let $A: \cup_{n \in \mathbb{N}}[0, 1]^n \to [0, 1]$ be an arbitrary aggregation function. The m-polar fuzzy relation ψ is said to be A-transitive on ϕ if

$$A^{(2)}(\pi_s \circ \psi(uv), \pi_s \circ \psi(vw)) \leq \pi_s \circ \psi(uw): \forall u, v, w \in V \qquad (5.3)$$

for any $s = 1, 2, \cdots, m$.

Proposition 5.3.17: *Let ψ be an m-PC-FR on an m-polar fuzzy subset ϕ of V and A be an aggregation function.*

1: *If A is conjunctive, then min-transitivity implies A-transitivity.*
2: *If A is disjunctive, then A-transitivity implies max-transitivity.*
3: *If A is an average or alternatively idempotent aggregation function, then A-transitivity implies min-transitivity and max-transitivity implies A-transitivity.*

Proof. Let ψ be an *m-PC-FR* on an *m*-polar fuzzy subset ϕ of V. Suppose that ψ be *min*-transitive and A is conjunctive. Then for any $u, v, w \in V$: $A^{(2)}(\pi_s \circ \psi(uv), \pi_s \circ \psi(vw)) \leq min(\pi_s \circ \psi(uv), \pi_s \circ \psi(vw)) \leq \pi_s \circ \psi(uw)$ which means ψ is *A*-transitive. Other parts are obtained similarly.

Corollary 5.3.18: Let ψ be an *m-P C FR* on ϕ. Then *min*-transitivity of ψ implies *C*-transitivity.

Example 5.3.19: *Let* $V = \{v_1, v_2, v_3\}$. *If* $\phi: V \to [0, 1]^3$ *is a 3-polar fuzzy subset of V given by the constant membership function* $\phi(v_i) = \left(\frac{1}{2}, \frac{1}{3}, \frac{5}{6}\right)$ *for* $i = 1, 2, 3;$ *and* $\psi: V \times V \to [0, 1]^3$ *is a 3-polar fuzzy relation on V given by* $\psi(v_1v_2) = \left(\frac{1}{2}, \frac{1}{4}, \frac{1}{6}\right)$, $\psi(v_2v_3) = \left(\frac{1}{2}, \frac{1}{3}, \frac{2}{7}\right)$ *and* $\psi(v_1v_3) = \left(\frac{1}{4}, \frac{1}{5}, \frac{1}{2}\right)$. *Then clearly* ψ *is a 3-P min-FR on* ϕ. *However it does not verify min-transitivity condition since for instance*

$$\frac{1}{4} = \pi_1 \circ \psi(v_1v_3) \ngeq min(\pi_1 \circ \psi(v_1v_2), \pi_1 \circ \psi(v_2v_3)) = \frac{1}{2}$$

But, if we consider the product t-norm $A: =T_P: =A = \Pi$, *then* ψ *is* T_P-*transitive fuzzy relation on* ϕ. *That is a weaker condition than min-transitive.*

Proposition 5.3.20: *Let* ψ *be an m-PC-FR on* ϕ. *If it is* A_1-*transitive then it is transitive fuzzy relation on* ϕ *w.r.t* $A_2 \leq A_1$.

Proof. Let $A_2 \leq A_1$. Then $A_2^{(2)}(\pi_s \circ \psi(uv), \pi_s \circ \psi(vw)) \leq A_1^{(2)}(\pi_s \circ \psi(uv), \pi_s \circ \psi(vw)) \leq \pi_s \circ \psi(uw)$ for all $u, v, w \in V$ and $s = 1, 2, \cdots, m$.

Proposition 5.3.21: *Let* ψ *be an m-PC-FR on an m-polar fuzzy subset* ϕ *of V. Suppose that A is a conjunctive aggregation function. Then* ψ *is A-transitive if for every vector* $\boldsymbol{a} \in (0, 1]^m$ *the relations* $\psi_{\boldsymbol{a}}$ *are a nested sequence of distinct transitive relations on V.*

Proof. Take $u, v, w \in V$. Suppose that $\psi(uv) = \boldsymbol{a}$ and $\psi(vw) = \boldsymbol{b}$ where $\boldsymbol{a} = (a_1, \cdots, a_m) \in [0, 1]^m$ and $\boldsymbol{b} = (b_1, \cdots, b_m) \in [0, 1]^m$. Put $\boldsymbol{m} = inf\{\boldsymbol{a}, \boldsymbol{b}\}$ such that $\boldsymbol{m} = (min(a_1, b_1), \cdots, min(a_m, b_m))$. Then equivalently $(u, v) \in \psi_{\boldsymbol{m}}$ and $(v, w) \in \psi_{\boldsymbol{m}}$. By the transitivity of $\psi_{\boldsymbol{m}}$ we have $\psi(uw) \geq \boldsymbol{m}$, thus $\pi_s \circ \psi(uw) \geq min(\pi_s \circ \psi(uv), \pi_s \circ \psi(vw))$. The conjunction behavior of A implies $\pi_s \circ \psi(uw) \geq A^{(2)}(\pi_s \circ \psi(uv), \pi_s \circ \psi(vw))$ that means ψ is A-transitive.

Proposition 5.3.22: *Let* ψ *be an m-PC-FR on an m-polar fuzzy subset* ϕ *of V and A be a disjunctive or average aggregation function. If* ψ *is a A-transitive. Then for any choice* $\boldsymbol{a} \in (0, 1]^m$, *the non-fuzzy relation* $\psi_{\boldsymbol{a}}$ *is transitive on V.*

Proof. Take $a \in (0, 1]^m$ where $a = (a_1, \cdots, a_m)$ and $u, v, w \in V$. Suppose that $(u, v), (v, w) \in \psi_a$. By the A-transitivity of ψ and for any $s = 1, \cdots, m$; we have $a_s \leq A^{(2)}(a_s, a_s) \leq A^{(2)}(\pi_s \circ \psi(uv), \pi_s \circ \psi(vw)) \leq \pi_s \circ \psi(uw)$ since A is a disjunctive aggregation function. Thus, we have $(u, w) \in \psi_a$.

Corollary 5.3.23: Let ψ be an m-PC-FR on an m-polar fuzzy subset ϕ of V and A be an aggregation function. If A has the annihilator element $a \in [0, 1]$ then for the specific value $a = (a, \cdots, a) \in [0, 1]^m$, ψ_a is transitive on V.

Note that the similar result will be held if $A^{(2)}(x, x) = x$.

Example 5.3.24: Let ψ be an m-PC-FR on an m-polar fuzzy subset ϕ which is transitive w.r.t minimum operator. The underlying crisp relation ψ_0 is a transitive relation on V.

Definition 5.3.25: Let $A, C: \bigcup_{n \in \mathbb{N}} [0, 1]^n \to [0, 1]$ be two aggregation operators where C is conjunctive that has no zero divisors. The $m - PC - FR\psi$ on an m-polar fuzzy subset ϕ of the set V is said m-PC-FprR w.r.t A if it is C-antisymmetric and A-transitive.

Example 5.3.26: Let $V = \{v_1, v_2, v_3\}$ and $\phi: V \to [0, 1]^2$ is the 2-polar fuzzy subset on V given by $\phi(v_1) = \left(\frac{1}{2}, \frac{1}{4}\right)$, $\phi(v_2) = \left(\frac{2}{3}, \frac{1}{3}\right)$ and $\phi(v_3) = \left(\frac{3}{4}, \frac{6}{7}\right)$. If for any $i \neq j$ and $s = 1, 2$; the 2-polar fuzzy relation $\psi: V \times V \to [0, 1]^2$ is defined by

$$\pi_s \circ \psi(v_i, v_j) = \begin{cases} max \{\pi_s \circ \phi(v_i) + \pi_s \circ \phi(v_j) - 1, 0\} & \pi_s \circ \phi(v_i) - \pi_s \circ \phi(v_j) > 0 \\ 0 & else. \end{cases}$$

Then ψ is a 2-Pmin-FprR on ϕ w.r.t operators T_P and minimum.

Theorem 5.3.27: Let A, C be two aggregation operators where C is a conjunction without zero divisors and A is averaging or disjunction. If ψ is an m-P C-FprR on an m-PFS ϕ w.r.t A, then for any threshold vector $a \in (0, 1]^m$ the non-fuzzy reation ψ_a is a preference order on V.

Proof. It is obtained by Propositions 5.3.10 and 5.3.22.

Proposition 5.3.28: If $A_2 \leq A_1$ are two aggregation functions and ψ is an m-P C-FprR on an m-PFS ϕ w.r.t A_1, then it is also an m-polar fuzzy preference order on ϕ w.r.t A_2.

Proof. It is clear since for any $1 \leq s \leq m$; we have $A_2^{(2)}(\pi_s \circ \psi(uv), \pi_s \circ \psi(vw)) \leq A_1^{(2)}(\pi_s \circ \psi(uv), \pi_s \circ \psi(vw)) \leq \pi_s \circ \psi(uw)$ where $u, v, w \in V$.

5.4 CONJUNCTION-BASED FRAMEWORK FOR M-POLAR FUZZY GRAPHS

This section is devoted to the main conribution of this study, which is concerning the generalization of m-polar fuzzy graphs based on conjunctive aggregation operators or m-PC-FG in brief. It is worth mentioning that the results do not hold for any arbitrary aggregation function.

Definition 5.4.1: Let $V = \{v_1, \ldots, v_m\}$ be a set of nodes/vertices and $C: \bigcup_{n \in \mathbb{N}}[0, 1]^n \to [0, 1]$ be an extended conjunctive aggregation function. Suppose that $\phi: V \to [0, 1]^m$ and $\psi: V \times V \to [0, 1]^m$ be the m-polar fuzzy subsets of V and V^2, respectively, that show the m-polar fuzzy vertices and m-polar fuzzy edges. The 3-tuple $G^C = (V, \phi, \psi)$ where ψ is an m-PC-FR on ϕ, i.e.

$$\pi_s \circ \psi(v_i v_j) \leq C^{(2)}(\pi_s \circ \phi(v_i), \pi_s \circ \phi(v_j)): \forall v_i, v_j \in V \qquad (5.4)$$

for all $s = 1, 2, \cdots, m$, is called an m-polar fuzzy graph w.r.t conjunction C or m-PC-FG in brief.

Example 5.4.2: Let $V = \{v_1, v_2, v_3\}$ be a set of vertices and ϕ be a 2-polar fuzzy subset on V. Let $C: = \prod$ be the multiplication operator. If for any $i \neq j$ and $s = 1, 2;$ the 2-polar fuzzy relation $\psi: V \times V \to [0.1]^2$ is defined by $\pi_s \circ \psi(v_i v_j) = \frac{\pi_s \circ \phi(v_i) \cdot \pi_s \circ \phi(v_j)}{2}$ if $|\pi_s \circ \phi(v_i) - \pi_s \circ \phi(v_j)| > 0.5$ and otherwise $\pi_s \circ \psi(v_i v_j) = \pi_s \circ \phi(v_i) \cdot \pi_s \circ \phi(v_j)$. Then clearly $G^{\prod} = (V, \phi, \psi)$ is a 2-polar FG on V w.r.t multiplication operator $\prod$.

For instance, if $\phi: V \to [0, 1]^2$ is given by $\phi(v_1) = \left(\frac{1}{4}, \frac{1}{3}\right)$, $\phi(v_2) = \left(\frac{1}{2}, \frac{8}{9}\right)$ and $\phi(v_3) = \left(\frac{4}{5}, \frac{7}{9}\right)$. Then the 2-polar fuzzy relation ψ of 2-P C-FG $G^{\prod}$ is defined by the following matrix

$$
\psi = \begin{array}{c} \\ v_1 \\ v_2 \\ v_3 \end{array}
\begin{array}{ccc} v_1 & v_2 & v_3 \\ \end{array}
\left[
\begin{array}{ccc}
- & \left(\frac{1}{8}, \frac{4}{27}\right) & \left(\frac{1}{10}, \frac{7}{27}\right) \\
\left(\frac{1}{8}, \frac{4}{27}\right) & - & \left(\frac{2}{5}, \frac{56}{81}\right) \\
\left(\frac{1}{10}, \frac{7}{27}\right) & \left(\frac{2}{5}, \frac{56}{81}\right) & -
\end{array}
\right]
$$

that is shown in Figure 5.1.

Definition 5.4.3: The m-PC-FG $H^C = (U, \nu, \mu)$ is called a subgraph of $G^C = (V, \phi, \psi)$ (or m-PC-FsubG in brief), shown by $H^C \subseteq G^C$, if $U \subseteq V$, $\pi_s \circ \nu(u) \leq \pi_s \circ \phi(u)$ and $\pi_s \circ \mu(uv) \leq \pi_s \circ \psi(uv)$ for all $u, v \in U$ and $s = 1, \cdots, m$.

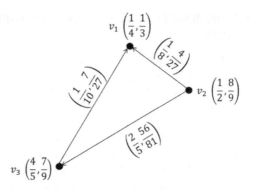

FIGURE 5.1 2-polar fuzzy graph G^{Π}.

Note that, the graph G^C is known as supergraph of H^C w.r.t conjunctive aggregation operator C or briefly m-PC-FsupG.

Example 5.4.4: *Consider the 2-PC-FG G^{Π} given inExample 5.4.2. If we define $\mu: V \times V \to [0, 1]^2$ by $\pi_s \circ \mu(v_i v_j) = (\pi_s \circ v(v_i) \cdot \pi_s \circ v(v_j))^{\frac{1}{2}}$ for s = 1, 2 where $v = \phi$, then clearly $H^{\Pi} = (V, v, \mu)$ is a 2-polar fuzzy subgraph of $G^{\Pi} = (V, \phi, \psi)$ w.r.t multiplication operator Π.*

Proposition 5.4.5: *Suppose that C_1 and C_2 be two conjunctive aggregation functions such that $C_1 \leq C_2$. If $G^{C_1} = (V, \phi, \psi)$ is an m-polar fuzzy graph w.r.t C_1, then (V, ϕ, ψ) is also an m-polar fuzzy graph w.r.t C_2.*

Proof. Take $u, v \in V$. Clearly, $\pi_s \circ \psi(uv) \leq C_1^{(2)} (\pi_s \circ \phi(u), \pi_s \circ \phi(v)) \leq C_2^{(2)} (\pi_s \circ \phi(u), \pi_s \circ \phi(v))$ for any s = 1, 2, $\cdots$,m.

Proposition 5.4.6: *Let C_1 and C_2 be two conjunctive aggregation functions such that $C_1 \leq C_2$. The m-PC$_1$-FG $G^{C_1} = (V, \phi, \psi)$ is a subgraph of the strong m-PC$_2$-FG $H^{C_2} = (U, v, \mu)$ if $V \subseteq U$ and $\phi \leq v$.*

Proof. Take $uv \in V \times V$, then $\pi_s \circ \psi(uv) \leq C_1^{(2)} (\phi(u), \phi(v)) \leq C_2^{(2)} (v(u), v(v)) = \mu(uv)$.

Corollary 5.4.7: *According to Proposition 5.4.6, the m-polar fuzzy graph w.r.t minimum operator is the super graph of any m-PC-FG.*

Proposition 5.4.8: *Let $G^C = (V, \phi, \psi)$ be an m-PC-FG on ϕ. If $a = (a_1, \cdots ,a_m) \in [0, 1]^m$ is a given threshold vector on membership degrees, then $G_a^C = (V_a^\phi, E_a^\psi)$ defined by*

$$V_a^\phi = \{v \in V: a_s \leq \pi_s \circ \phi(v); 1 \leq s \leq m\} \tag{5.5}$$

$$E_a^\psi = \{uv \in V \times V: a_s \leq \pi_s \circ \psi(uv); \ 1 \leq s \leq m\} \tag{5.6}$$

is a crisp graph on V called **a**-level graph of G^C.

Proof. Let $G^C = (V, \phi, \psi)$ be an m-PC-FG on ϕ. Consider the structure $G_a^C = (V_a^\phi, E_a^\psi)$ defined by Eq. (5.5) and Eq. (5.6). If $uv \in E_a^\psi$ is an arbitrary arch in G_a^C, then clearly $a_s \leq \pi_s \circ \phi(u)$ and $a_s \leq \pi_s \circ \phi(v)$ that means the ending points u and v are in V_a^ϕ. This means G_a^C is a crisp graph on V.

Definition 5.4.9: *Let $G^{C,A} = (V, \phi, \psi)$ be an m-PC-FG on V where ψ presents an m-PC-FprR on ϕ w.r.t aggregation function A. Then we call $G^{C,A}$ the m-PC-FprG on V w.r.t A.*

Note that, the m-PC-FprG $G^{C,A}$ is in fact an m-polar fuzzy digraph where the m-polar fuzzy edge $\psi(v_i v_j)$ presents an m-polar fuzzy preference relationship from m-polar fuzzy node $\phi(v_i)$ over $\phi(v_j)$ such that

$$C^{(2)}(\pi_s \circ \phi(v_i), \pi_s \circ \phi(v_j)) \geq \pi_s \circ \psi(v_i v_j): \forall \ v_i, v_j \in V \tag{5.7}$$

$$C^{(2)}(\pi_s \circ \psi(v_i v_j), \pi_s \circ \psi(v_j v_i)) = 0: \forall \ v_i, v_j \in V \tag{5.8}$$

$$A^{(2)}(\pi_s \circ \psi(v_i v_j), \pi_s \circ \psi(v_j v_l)) \leq \pi_s \circ \psi(v_i v_l): \forall \ v_i, v_j, v_l \in V \tag{5.9}$$

Example 5.4.10: *ReconsiderExample 5.4.2where $V = \{v_1, v_2, v_3\}$ and $\phi: V \rightarrow [0, 1]^2$ is the 2-polar fuzzy subset on V given by $\phi(v_1) = \left(\frac{1}{4}, \frac{1}{3}\right)$, $\phi(v_2) = \left(\frac{1}{2}, \frac{8}{9}\right)$ and $\phi(v_3) = \left(\frac{4}{5}, \frac{7}{9}\right)$. If for any $i \neq j$ and $s = 1, 2$; the 2-polar fuzzy relation $\psi: V \times V \rightarrow [0, 1]^2$ is defined by $\pi_s \circ \psi(v_i v_j) = \frac{\pi_s \circ \phi(v_i) \cdot \pi_s \circ \phi(v_j)}{2}$ if $\pi_s \circ \phi(v_i) - \pi_s \circ \phi(v_j) > 0.5$; $\pi_s \circ \psi(v_i v_j) = \pi_s \circ \phi(v_i) \cdot \pi_s \circ \phi(v_j)$ if $0 < \pi_s \circ \phi(v_i) - \pi_s \circ \phi(v_j) \leq 0.5$; and otherwise $\pi_s \circ \psi(v_i v_j) = 0$. Then $G^{\Pi, T_L} = (V, \phi, \psi)$ is a 2-polar fuzzy preference graph on V w.r.t operators Π, T_L (see Figure 5.2), shown by the following matrix*

$$\psi = \begin{array}{c} \\ v_1 \\ v_2 \\ v_3 \end{array} \begin{array}{ccc} v_1 & v_2 & v_3 \end{array} \\ \begin{bmatrix} - & (0, 0) & (0, 0) \\ \left(\frac{1}{8}, \frac{4}{27}\right) & - & \left(0, \frac{56}{81}\right) \\ \left(\frac{1}{10}, \frac{7}{27}\right) & \left(\frac{2}{5}, 0\right) & - \end{bmatrix}$$

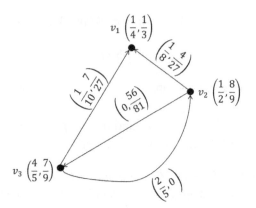

FIGURE 5.2 2-polar fuzzy digraphs G^{Π, T_L}.

Proposition 5.4.11: *Let $G^{C,A} = (V, \phi, \psi)$ be an m-PC-FprG on V w.r.t aggregation operator A. Then, for any choice $a \in (0, 1]^m$ the a-level graph $G_a^C = (V_a^\phi, E_a^\psi)$ presents a preference graph on V if A is disjunctive or average operator and C has no zero divisors.*

Proof. It is obtained easily by Propositions 5.3.10 and 5.3.22.

5.4.1 Preservation of A-Transitivity for Aggregated Fuzzy Relation

As already mentioned above, in order to have a consistent choice in a decision-making problem, preserving transitivity during the consensus process is required. In this section, the relationship between properties of aggregation functions and preserving the A-transitivity during the consensus process is discussed.

Theorem 5.4.12: *Let $\{G_k^C = (V, \phi_k, \psi_k): k = 1, \cdots, K\}$ be a sequence of K number of m-PC-FG on V. Let $B: \cup_{n \in \mathbb{N}} [0, 1]^n \to [0, 1]$ be an extended aggregation function. Then the aggregation of m-PC-FGs $G_1^C, \cdots, G_K^C$ by operator B, defined by $G_B^C = (V, B(\phi_k)_{k=1}^K, B(\psi_k)_{k=1}^K)$, is also an m-P C-FG if $B \ll C$.*

Proof. Let $\{G_k^C = (V, \phi_k, \psi_k): k = 1, \cdots, K\}$ be a set of m-PC-FGs where C is conjunctive. Take the aggregation function B such that $B \ll C$. Then for any $s = 1, \cdots, m$ and $v_i, v_j \in V$;

$$\pi_s \circ B(\psi_k)_{k=1}^K (v_i v_j) = B(\pi_s \circ \psi_1 (v_i v_j), \cdots, \pi_s \circ \psi_K (v_i v_j))$$

$$\leq B(C^{(2)} (\pi_s \circ \phi_1 (v_i), \pi_s \circ \phi_1 (v_j)), \cdots, C^{(2)} (\pi_s \circ \phi_K (v_i), \pi_s \circ \phi_K (v_j)))$$

$$\leq C^{(2)} (B(\pi_s \circ \phi_1 (v_i), \cdots, \pi_s \circ \phi_K (v_i)), B(\pi_s \circ \phi_1 (v_j), \cdots, \pi_s \circ \phi_K (v_j)))$$

$$= C^{(2)} (\pi_s \circ B(\phi_k)_{k=1}^K(v_i), \pi_s \circ B(\phi_k)_{k=1}^K(v_j))$$

This completes the proof.

Theorem 5.4.13: Let $\{G_k^{C,A} = (V, \phi_k, \psi_k): k = 1, \cdots, K\}$ be a sequence of m-PC-FprG on the set V w.r.t aggregation operator A. Then the structure $G_B^{C,A} = (V, B(\phi_k)_{k=1}^K, B(\psi_k)_{k=1}^K)$, is also an m-PC-FprG on V w.r.t A if $A \ll B \ll C$.

Proof. It is only needed to show that the aggregation operator B preserves A-transitivity of m-polar fuzzy edges $B(\psi_k)_{k=1}^K$ in $G_B^{C,A}$ where $\psi_1, \cdots, \psi_K$ are m-polar A-transitive relations on m-polar fuzzy subsets $\phi_1, \cdots, \phi_K$ of the set V. For any $1 \le s \le m$ and $v_i, v_j, v_l \in V$ we have

$$A^{(2)} (\pi_s \circ B(\psi_k)_{k=1}^K(v_i v_j), \pi_s \circ B(\psi_k)_{k=1}^K(v_j v_l)) = A^{(2)} (B(\pi_s \circ \psi_1(v_i v_j), \cdots, \pi_s \circ \psi_K(v_i v_j)),$$
$$B(\pi_s \circ \psi_1(v_j v_l), \cdots, \pi_s \circ \psi_K(v_j v_l)))$$

$$\le B(A^{(2)} (\pi_s \circ \psi_1(v_i v_j), \pi_s \circ \psi_1(v_j v_l)), \cdots, A^{(2)} (\pi_s \circ \psi_K(v_i v_j), \pi_s \circ \psi_K(v_j v_l)))$$

$$\le B(\pi_s \circ \psi_1(v_i v_l), \cdots, \pi_s \circ \psi_K(v_i v_l)) = \pi_s \circ B(\psi_k)_{k=1}^K(v_i v_l)$$

This completes the proof.

Example 5.4.15: Let $G_1^{min} = (V, \phi_1, \psi_1), \cdots, G_K^{min} = (V, \phi_K, \psi_K)$ be a sequence of 3-Pmin-FprG on the set V w.r.t t-norm $T_L(x, y) = max(x + y - 1, 0)$. The aggregated 3-P min-FprG $G_{AM}^{min} = (V, AM(\phi_k)_{k=1}^K, AM(\psi_k)_{k=1}^K)$ by aggregation function mean value AM is also a 3-Pmin-FprG on V w.r.t T_L since $T_L \ll AM \ll Min$.

5.4.2 PROPOSED ALGORITHM

Let K decision-makers provide their strict preferences over the set of alternatives $V = \{v_1, v_2, \cdots, v_n\}$ by the m-polar fuzzy relations. A mentor/expert or decision analyst then assesses this information to make the final decision accepting by the group. In this section, using graph theory, an algorithm is presented to develop a consistence method for judging and ranking alternatives in group decision-making problems. We first define a preference matrix over the set V by using the non-fuzzy relation $\psi_a = \{(v_i, v_j) \in V^2: \pi_s \circ \psi(v_i v_j) \ge a_s; \forall s; 1 \le s \le m\}$ where $\mathbf{a} = (a_1, \cdots, a_m) \in (0, 1]^m$ is a threshold vector.

Suppose that $\mathbf{a} \in (0, 1]^m$ is given. The preference matrix $P_\mathbf{a} = [p_{\mathbf{a}_{ij}}]_{n \times n}$ of an m-polar fuzzy relation $\Psi = [\psi_{ij}]_{n \times n}$ is defined on V as

$$p_{\mathbf{a}_{ij}} = \begin{cases} 1 & \pi_s \circ \psi(v_i v_j) \geq a_s \\ 0 & otherwise \end{cases} \tag{5.10}$$

where $s = 1, \cdots, m$; and each entry ψ_{ij} of the $n \times n$ matrix Ψ is in fact the m-tuple vector $(\psi_{ij}^{(1)}, \cdots, \psi_{ij}^{(m)}) = (\pi_1 \circ \psi(v_i v_j), \cdots, \pi_m \circ \psi(v_i v_j))$.

The implied relationships in matrix $P_\mathbf{a}$ can be denoted by a digraph $G_\mathbf{a}$ whose nodes show the alternatives of the set V and whose edges denote a preference relation between them. The $p_{\mathbf{a}_{ij}} = 1$ shows there is a directed edge from v_i to v_j in $G_\mathbf{a}$ meaning that v_i is preferred to v_j. Clearly, the matrix $P_\mathbf{a}$ is additive reciprocal and transitive.

Theorem 5.4.16: *The matrix P_a, defined byEq. (5.10). represents a strict preference relation if C is a conjunction without zero divisors and A is an averaging or disjunction operator.*

Proof. It is obtained by Proposition 5.4.11.

Accordingly, the following algorithm is designed to obtain a final consistence solution by aggregating K different m-polar fuzzy preference graphs.

Algorithm

Input: $\quad\quad n$ = Size of alternative set V;

m = Size of feature set S;

K = Size of decision makers set D;

Threshold vector $\mathbf{a} \in (0, 1]^m$;

Aggregation functions A, B, C such that $A \ll B \ll C$;

Matrices $\Phi_k = \left[\phi_{k_i} \right]_{1 \times n} = \left[\left(\phi_{k_i}^{(s)} \right)_{1 \times m} \right]_{1 \times n}$ for $k = 1, 2, \cdots, K$ where

$\phi_{k_i} = \phi_k(v_i) = (\pi_1 \circ \phi_k(v_i), \cdots, \pi_m \circ \phi_k(v_i))$ and $\phi_{k_i}^{(s)} = \pi_s \circ \phi_k(v_i)$;

Matrices $\Psi_k = \left[\psi_{k_{ij}} \right]_{n \times n} = \left[\left(\psi_{k_{ij}}^{(s)} \right)_{1 \times m} \right]_{n \times n}$ for $k = 1, 2, \cdots, K$ where

$\psi_{k_{ij}} = \psi_k(v_i v_j) = (\pi_1 \circ \psi_k(v_i v_j), \cdots, \pi_m \circ \psi_k(v_i vj))$ and $\psi_{k_{ij}}^{(s)} = \pi_s \circ \psi_k(v_i v_j)$;

such that:

$\pi_s \circ \psi_k(v_i v_j) \leq C^{(2)}(\pi_s \circ \phi_k(v_i), \pi_s \circ \phi_k(v_j))$

$C^{(2)}(\pi_s \circ \psi_k(v_i v_j), \pi_s \circ \psi_k(v_j v_i)) = 0$

$\pi_s \circ \psi_k(v_i v_l) \geq A^{(2)}(\pi_s \circ \psi_k(v_i v_j), \pi_s \circ \psi_k(v_j v_l))$

for all $1 \leq i, j, l \leq n$.

Begin: $\quad$ Step 1. Compute matrices $B(\Phi_k)$ and $B(\Psi_k)$ to obtain the aggregated matrix $G_B^{C,A}$. (See Theorems 5.4.12 and 5.4.13).

Step 2. Establish preference matrix P_a from $G_B^{C,A}$ by Eq. (5.10).

Step 3. Rank all alternatives of V based on the obtained priority in Step 2.

Step 4. Find the best and the worst objects.

Output: A digraph to show the final preference on alternatives.

End

5.4.3 NUMERICAL EXAMPLE

Here, a numerical example is provided to illustrate the proposed method in the above algorithm.

Example 5.4.17: *Suppose three decision makers d_1, d_2 and d_3 evaluate the alternative set $V = \{v_1, v_2, v_3, v_4\}$ based on two attributes by 2-polar fuzzy sets (matrices Φ_1, Φ_2, Φ_3) as below:*

$$\Phi_1 = [(0.5, 0.9) \quad (0.4, 0.3) \quad (0.1, 0.5) \quad (0.2, 0.6)]$$

$$\Phi_2 = [(0.6, 0.4) \quad (0.2, 0.55) \quad (0.6, 0.3) \quad (0.35, 0.7)]$$

$$\Phi_3 = [(0.7, 0.6) \quad (0.9, 0.5) \quad (0.3, 0.3) \quad (0.8, 0.6)]$$

The three 2-polar min-FprR w.r.t operator T_L on each of the 2-PFS Φ_1, Φ_2, Φ_3 are given by them as matrices Ψ_1, Ψ_2, Ψ_3:

$$\Psi_1 = \begin{bmatrix} - & (0.2, 0.27) & (0.05, 0.5) & (0, 0) \\ (0, 0) & - & (0, 0) & (0, 0) \\ (0, 0) & (0.04, 0.15) & - & (0, 0) \\ (0.1, 0.54) & (0.08, 0.18) & (0.02, 0.3) & - \end{bmatrix}$$

$$\Psi_2 = \begin{bmatrix} - & (0, 0) & (0.6, 0.12) & (0.3, 0.4) \\ (0.2, 0.35) & - & (0.1, 0.17) & (0.07, 0.5) \\ (0, 0) & (0, 0) & - & (0.21, 0.3) \\ (0, 0) & (0, 0) & (0, 0) & - \end{bmatrix}$$

$$\Psi_3 = \begin{bmatrix} - & (0.7, 0.5) & (0, 0) & (0.56, 0.6) \\ (0, 0) & - & (0, 0) & (0.8, 0.5) \\ (0.21, 0.15) & (0.27, 0.2) & - & (0.25, 0.2) \\ (0, 0) & (0, 0) & (0, 0) & - \end{bmatrix}$$

TABLE 5.1

Overall Ranking on the Set V

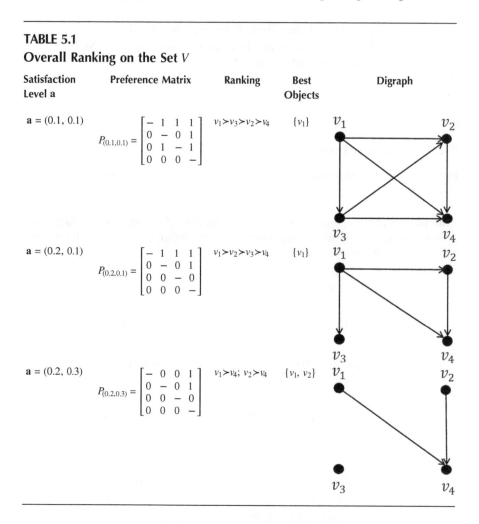

Satisfaction Level a	Preference Matrix	Ranking	Best Objects	Digraph
$a = (0.1, 0.1)$	$P_{(0.1,0.1)} = \begin{bmatrix} - & 1 & 1 & 1 \\ 0 & - & 0 & 1 \\ 0 & 1 & - & 1 \\ 0 & 0 & 0 & - \end{bmatrix}$	$v_1 > v_3 > v_2 > v_4$	$\{v_1\}$	
$a = (0.2, 0.1)$	$P_{(0.2,0.1)} = \begin{bmatrix} - & 1 & 1 & 1 \\ 0 & - & 0 & 1 \\ 0 & 0 & - & 0 \\ 0 & 0 & 0 & - \end{bmatrix}$	$v_1 > v_2 > v_3 > v_4$	$\{v_1\}$	
$a = (0.2, 0.3)$	$P_{(0.2,0.3)} = \begin{bmatrix} - & 0 & 0 & 1 \\ 0 & - & 0 & 1 \\ 0 & 0 & - & 0 \\ 0 & 0 & 0 & - \end{bmatrix}$	$v_1 > v_4;\ v_2 > v_4$	$\{v_1, v_2\}$	

Now, let the aggregation function arithmetic mean, i.e. AM, is applied by the mentor of the decision makers to combine these different judgments and obtain the collective view. ByTheorem 5.4.13, the aggregated 2-polar fuzzy graph $G_{AM}^{min,T_L} = (V,\ AM\,(\Phi_k)_{k=1}^3,\ AM\,(\Psi_k)_{k=1}^3)$, whose edges present the 2-polar fuzzy T_L-preference relations on $AM\,(\Phi_k)_{k=1}^3$, is computed as the following:

$$AM\,(\Phi_k)_{k=1}^3 = [(0.6, 0.63)\ (0.5, 0.45)\ (0.33, 0.36)\ (0.45, 0.63)]$$

and

$$AM\,(\Psi_k)_{k=1}^3 = \begin{bmatrix} - & (0.3, 0.256) & (0.216, 0.206) & (0.288, 0.33) \\ (0.06, 0.116) & - & (0.03, 0.056) & (0.29, 0.33) \\ (0.07, 0.05) & (0.103, 0.116) & - & (0.153, 0.16) \\ (0.13, 0.072) & (0.026, 0.06) & (0.006, 0.1) & - \end{bmatrix}$$

Next, by Eq. (5.10) the preference matrices P_a for different vetors $\boldsymbol{a} = (0.1, 0.1)$, $\boldsymbol{a} = (0.2, 0.1)$ *and* $\boldsymbol{a} = (0.2, 0.3)$ *are calculated as shown in Table 5.1, where for each case, the corresponding preference relation on V, consequently a digraph on V is derived.*

It is concluded that the alternative v_1 is the best option among these three options.

5.5 CONCLUSION

A generalization of the concept of fuzzy relation on a fuzzy set is presented for m-polar fuzzy sets in a conjunction-based framework. In situations where the membership degrees of any pair of points affect the level or strength of the relation between them, the proposed approach is applied to fuzzy graph theory for considering a new definition of m-polar fuzzy graph. Since digraphs offer a reliable way to have a consistent choice in decision-making problems, first m-polar fuzzy antisymmetric w.r.t conjunctive aggregation functions and m-polar fuzzy transitivity w.r.t arbitrary aggregation functions are discussed. It is proved this new type of transitivity gives a weaker condition than min-transitivity and max-transitivity in the traditional sense. Then, m-polar fuzzy preference relation is defined based on this new framework. By combining fuzzy digraph theory and m-polar fuzzy preference relations, the m-polar fuzzy preference graph is used to model decision-making processes. In order to reach the selection phase in group decision-making problems, the collective m-polar fuzzy preference relation is first obtained by applying aggregation functions. The domination property of the aggregation operators should be addressed for preserving the transitivity while having zero element but not zero divisors for aggregation functions helps us to preserve the antisymmetric property. Using matrix technique for the resultant m-polar fuzzy preference graph and converting it into a crisp value by using **a**-level graph, a consistent approach is proposed for ranking data. Moreover, a numerical example shows the computational process of the proposed procedure.

ACKNOWLEDGMENT

This study was supported by the Fundamental Research Grants, Ref. NO.: FRGS/1/2019/STG06/UPM/02/6, awarded by the Malaysia Ministry of Higher Education.

REFERENCES

Akram, M. (2011). Bipolar fuzzy graphs. *Information Sciences*, *181*(24), 5548–5564. https://doi.org/10.1016/j.ins.2011.07.037
Akram, M. (2013). Bipolar fuzzy graphs with applications. *Knowledge-Based Systems*, *39*, 1–8. https://doi.org/10.1016/j.knosys.2012.08.022
Beliakov, G., Calvo, T., & James S. (2014). Consensus measures constructed from aggregation functions and fuzzy implications. *Knowledge-Based Systems*, *55*, 1–8. https://doi.org/10.1016/j.knosys.2013.07.002
Beliakov, G., James S., & Wilkin, T. (2017). Aggregation and consensus for preference relations based on fuzzy partial orders. *Fuzzy Optimization and Decision Making*, *16*(4), 409–428. https://doi.org/10.1007/s10700-016-9258-4

Bentkowska, U. (2018). Aggregation of diverse types of fuzzy orders for decision making problems. *Information Sciences*, *424*, 317–336. https://doi.org/10.1016/j.ins.2017.1 0.002.

Bentkowska, U., & Król, A. (2016). Preservation of fuzzy relation properties based on fuzzy conjunctions and disjunctions during aggregation process. *Fuzzy Sets and Systems*, *291*, 98–113. https://doi.org/10.1016/j.fss.2015.06.001

Bordogna, G., Fedrizzi, M., & Pasi, G. (1997). A linguistic modeling of consensus in group decision making based on OWA operators. *IEEE Transactions on Systems, Man, and Cybernetics*, *27*(1), 126–133.

Chen, J., Li, S., Ma, S., & Wang, X. (2014). m-Polar fuzzy sets: an extension of bipolar fuzzy sets. *Scientific World Journal*, *2014*, 416530. https://doi.org/10.1155/2014/416530

Chiclana, F., Herrera, F., & Herrera-Viedma, E. (2002). The ordered weighted geometric operator: properties and application in MCDM problems. In Bouchon-Meunier B., Gutierrez-Rios J., Magdalena L., Yager R.R. (eds.) *Technologies for Constructing Intelligent Systems 2. Studies in Fuzziness and Soft Computing*, vol 90. Physica, Heidelberg. 173–183. https://doi.org/10.1007/978-3-7908-1796-6_14

Drewniak, J., & Dudziak, U. (2007). Preservation of properties of fuzzy relations during aggregation processes. *Kybernetika*, *43*(2), 115–132.

Dubois, D., & Prade, H. (2004). On the use of aggregation operations in information fusion processes. *Fuzzy Sets and Systems*, *142*(1), 143–161. https://doi.org/10.1016/j.fss.2003 .10.038

Dudziak, U. (2013). Preservation of t-Norm and t-Conorm based properties of fuzzy relations during aggregation process. *8th Conference of the European Society for Fuzzy Logic and Technology, EUSFLAT 2013 - Advances in Intelligent Systems Research*, *32* (Eusflat): 376–383. https://doi.org/10.2991/eusflat.2013.59

García-Lapresta, J.L., & Llamazares, B. (2000). Aggregation of fuzzy preferences: some rules of the mean. *Social Choice and Welfare*, *17*(4), 673–690. https://doi.org/10.1007/ s003550000048

Ghorai, G., & Pal, M. (2016). Some properties of m-polar fuzzy graphs. *Pacific Science Review A: Natural Science and Engineering*, *18*(1), 38–46. https://doi.org/10.1016/ j.psra.2016.06.004

Herrera-Viedma, E., Herrera, F., Chiclana, F., & Luque, M. (2004). Some issues on consistency of fuzzy preference relations. *European Journal of Operational Research*, *154*(1), 98–109. https://doi.org/10.1016/S0377-2217(02)00725-7

Kacprzyk, J., Fedrizzi, M., & Nurmi, H. (1992). Group decision making and consensus under fuzzy preferences and fuzzy majority. *Fuzzy Sets and Systems*, *49*(1), 21–31. https:// doi.org/10.1016/0165-0114(92)90107-F

Orlovsky, S.A. (1978). Decision-making with a fuzzy preference relation. *Fuzzy Sets and Systems*, *1*(3), 155–167.

Peneva, V., & Popchev, I. (2003). Properties of the aggregation operators related with fuzzy relations. *Fuzzy Sets and Systems*, *139*(3), 615–633. https://doi.org/10.1016/S0165- 0114(03)00141-6

Peneva, V., & Popchev, I. (2007). Aggregation of fuzzy preference relations to multicriteria decision making. *Fuzzy Optimization and Decision Making*, *6*(4), 351–365. https:// doi.org/10.1007/s10700-007-9018-6

Rosenfeld, A. (1975). Fuzzy graphs. In: *Fuzzy Sets and Their Applications to Cognitive and Decision Processes*. Academic Press. 77–95. https://doi.org/10.1016/b978-0-12-7752 60-0.50008–6

Samanta, S., & Pal, M. (2012). Bipolar fuzzy hypergraphs. *International Journal of Fuzzy Logic Systems*, 2 (1), 17–28. https://doi.org/10.5121/ijfls.2012.2103

Saminger, S., Mesiar, R., & Bodenhofer, U. (2002). Domination of aggregation operators and preservation of transitivity. *International Journal of Uncertainty, Fuzziness and Knowledge-Based Systems*, *10* (December), 11–35. https://doi.org/10.1142/s02184885 02001806

Satty, T.L., et al. (1980). *The Analytic Hierarchy Process.* McGraw-Hill New York, New York.

Singh, P.K. (2018). m-Polar Fuzzy Graph Representation of Concept Lattice. *Engineering Applications of Artificial Intelligence*, *67*, 52–62. https://doi.org/10.1016/J.ENGAPPAI.2 017.09.011

Switalski, Z. (2001). Transitivity of fuzzy preference relations—an empirical study. *Fuzzy Sets and Systems*, *118* (3), 503–508. https://doi.org/10.1016/S0165-0114(98)00287-5.

Tanino, T. (1984). Fuzzy preference orderings in group decision making. *Fuzzy Sets and Systems*, *12*(2), 117–131. https://doi.org/10.1016/0165-0114(84)90032-0

Tanino, T. (1988). Fuzzy preference relations in group decision making. In Kacprzyk J., Roubens M. (eds.) *Non-Conventional Preference Relations in Decision Making. Lecture Notes in Economics and Mathematical Systems.* Vol. 301. Springer Berlin Heidelberg. http://www.spatial.maine.edu/~worboys/Sie565/papers/aggregation operators.pdf

Yan, H.B., & Ma, T. (2015). A group decision-making approach to uncertain quality function deployment based on fuzzy preference relation and fuzzy majority. *European Journal of Operational Research*, *241*(3), 815–829. https://doi.org/10.1016/j.ejor.2014.09.017

Zadeh, L.A. (1978). Fuzzy sets theory. *Fuzzy Sets and Systems*, *1*(1), 3–28.

Zadeh, L.A. (1971). Similarity relations and fuzzy orderings. *Information Sciences*, *3*(2), 177–200. https://doi.org/10.1016/S0020-0255(71)80005-1.

Zahedi Khameneh, A., & Kilicman, A. (2019). A fuzzy majority-based construction method for composed aggregation functions by using combination operator. *Information Sciences*, *505*, 367–387. https://doi.org/10.1016/j.ins.2019.07.090.

Zahedi Khameneh, A., & Kilicman, A. (2020). Some construction methods of aggregation operators in decision-making problems: an overview. *Symmetry*, *12*(5), 694. https://doi.org/10.3390/SYM12050694

6 Path Programming Problems in Fuzzy Environment

Madineh Farnam[1] *and Majid darehmiraki*[2]
[1]Department of Electrical Engineering, Shohadaye Hoveizeh Campus of Technology, Shahid Chamran, University of Ahvaz, Dasht-e Azadegan, Khuzestan, Iran
[2]Department of Mathematics, Behbahan Khatam Alanbia University of Technology, Behbahan, Khuzestan, Iran

6.1 INTRODUCTION

One of the main problems considered in networks is the discussion of the shortest path, so that the main goal is to find the shortest path between the two points in the network. Among the important applications of this type of problem in communication and social networks, especially the transportation system, design of water and gas supply lines, electricity distribution system, post office, etc. Due to the practical context of this problem and the fair and economic development of infrastructure, it provides adequate access to various resources for all, and as a result, public growth and welfare is improved. Therefore, in this research, we are looking for an efficient way to solve this type of problem. At first glance, practical goals may seem a little different, but in all these types of problems, the general goal is to find a way to transfer flow or goods from origin to destination. The lowest cost for this transfer. Due to the special structure of this type of problem, various techniques have been proposed to solve them in researches.

Often in the real world, the function of the objective and the parameters in the problem may not be precisely defined. In cases where accurate and complete knowledge of costs is not available, classical mathematics will not be able to model and solve problems. One of the most important ways to express uncertainty is to define fuzzy problem parameters in a way that makes it possible to express cost coefficients with linguistic variables. For example, instead of assigning a definite numerical edge length such as 4, we can consider a number between 3 and 5, which can be an interval fuzzy number, acceptable. One of the most important advantages of such a display is that the decision-maker's mental inference can be considered effective in formulating the problem. Of course, numbers such as each edge can be considered from various other types of fuzzy numbers, such as triangular fuzzy numbers, trapezoids, and so on (Darehmiraki 2019, 2020).

Dubois (Dubois 1980) has been the pioneer in presenting the problem of the fuzzy shortest path in the network, in which the cost of each edge was considered as the fuzzy number. They developed the concepts of plural, maximum, and neuter, and used Floyd's and Ford's algorithm to solve the problem. But since, for example, the minimum of a few fuzzy numbers is not necessarily one of those numbers, the lowest cost may not be corresponding to any path from origin to destination, and this was one of the major drawbacks of their algorithm. Later, a developed algorithm based on recurring dynamic programming was proposed by Klein (Klein 1991).

Chuang and Kung (Chuang and Kung 2006) first found the shortest fuzzy length in a network to find the shortest fuzzy path in a network whose arc lengths corresponded to the fuzzy sets. Then, using a fuzzy similarity measure, they found the degree of similarity between the shortest fuzzy length and each of the lengths of the available paths. Keshavarz and Khorram in (Keshavarz and Khorram 2009) considering the costs in the form of interval fuzzy numbers and inspired by the allocation model presented in (Lin and Wen 2004), after formulating the problem, they proposed a bi-level algorithm to find the lowest cost and the shortest path, which, despite the accuracy of the solution, required a high volume of computations. Mahdavi et al. (Mahdavi et al. 2009) to find the shortest chain in a fuzzy graph, apply dynamic programming method. Mukerje (Mukherjee 2015) proposed fuzzy programming to solve fuzzy shortest path problem by converting the single objective fuzzy linear programming in to crisp multi objective programming. By introducing new extensions of fuzzy numbers several algorithms developed for further compliance with these generalizations, for instance, in 2018, a method of hybrid neutrosophic multiple criteria group decision making is established by Basset et al for project selection (Abdel-Basset et al. 2018). Dey et al. (Dey et al. 2016) stated a method based on genetic algorithm for finding the SP from source node to sink node in a network with interval type-2 fuzzy arcs. An extended version of Dijkstra's algorithm was developed by Broumi (Broumi et al 2016). In 2020, Zedam et al. (Zedam et al. 2020) analysis some developments in fuzzy graph theory and state an approach in shortest path problem based on T-Spherical fuzzy data.

In this chapter, we intend to provide an improved analysis to find the lowest cost and the shortest path corresponding to that by using the concept of parametric paths and highest reliability. Let us illustrate the efficiency of the solutions compared to the model presented in previous works by paths analysis.

For this purpose, the other parts of this study are arranged as follows:

Section 2: Most of the prerequisites and concepts required in the field of graph theory, network, and especially Dijkstra's algorithm is given.

Section 3: The formulation of the FSPP problem is given using Bellman and Zade's decision theory and considering the imperativeness of highest reliability. Another approach presented by interval-valued arithmetic. After solving an example with two methods, discussion and analysis paths for evaluation the convincing solution are given.

Section 4: We present the SP problem in hesitant fuzzy environment and develop the previous methods in this problem.

Section 5: The results of this study and suggestions for future research are presented.

6.2 PRELIMINARIES

According to the requirements of the following sections, some of the definitions and concepts required and the formulation of the problem are given as follows [12].

Definition 6.2.1: A network consists of a set of elements called nodes, all or some of which are connected by one or more edges. Each connected junction is assigned a number between nodes j and i, such as c_{ij}, which generally represents distance, time, cost, capacity, safety, and so on. A network can be represented by $G(N, E, C)$ in which N represents the nodes with the numbers n, E represents the set of edges at which a current can be established and C involves the all c_{ij}'s. The display as a ordered pair (i, j) represents an edge in which i and $j \in N$ are present. Often the source node is displayed with s and the sink node is displayed with t.

If the flow direction in each of the edges is clear, we call the network directional, and if we have more than one edge between the two nodes, we say that the network has multiple edges.

Definition 6.2.2: An ordered set of edges is an interconnected path from vertex i to vertex j such as $\{(i, p), (p, q), ..., (t, u), (u, j)\}$ where each node in it except the first and last nodes are the endpoints for only two edges in the set. In the path i to j, which we display with p_{ij}. The sum of all the c_{ij}'s corresponding to the edges on a path shows the value of that path. If the path is such that $i = j$, that is, the points at the beginning and end of the path coincide, we call this loop.

As mentioned, one of the most useful current problems in the network is the SP problem, which can be considered as an integer programming problem with binary variables as follows:

$$min \sum_{(i,j)\in E} c_{ij}x_{ij} \tag{6.1a}$$

$$\sum_{\{j|(i,j)\in E\}} x_{ij} - \sum_{\{j|(j,i)\in E\}} x_{ji} = \begin{cases} 1 & i = s \\ 0 & i \neq s, t \ (i = 1, 2, \cdots, n) \\ -1 & i = t \end{cases} \tag{6.1b}$$

$$x_{ij} \in \{0, 1\} \quad for \ (i, j)\in E. \tag{6.1c}$$

The relation (6.1a) shows the objective function of the problem, which is the flow rate in the network. The constraints presented in relations (6.1b) represent the flow in each node, and the category relations (6.1c) are related to the decision variables in the network, in which $x_{ij} = 1$ means the presence of the edge (i, j) in the network and $x_{ij} = 0$ means that there is no similar edge in the network. There are some efficient algorithms to find SP in the network (Lin et al. 2020). The most well-known algorithm has been existed to find the SP is Dijkstra's Algorithm. This algorithm is designed to find the SP between the source and the sink nodes in a network without any negative cost for each edge, but automatically takes the SPs tree from the source node to the other nodes. The procedure of this efficient Algorithm can summarize as follows:

ALGORITHM 1   (DIJKSTRA'S ALGORITHM)

Input: Network $G = (N, E, C)$ where $c_{ij}'s$ are real the costs.

Initialization Step: Consider X_N and d_i as a collection of the selected nodes where belongs N and the distance travelled from the source node respectively.

In the beginning assume $X_N = \{1\}$, $d_1 = 0$

Main stage:

Step 1: Let $\bar{X}_N = N - X$ and consider all of the edges from:

$$(X_N, \bar{X}_N) = \{ (i, j) | i \epsilon X_N, j \epsilon \bar{X}_N \}.$$

Step 2: For all edges defined in step1 from the main stage, get $d_i + c_{ij}$ and set:

$$d_p + c_{pq} = \min \{ d_i + c_{ij} | (i, j) \epsilon (X_N, \bar{X}_N) \}.$$

Step 3: Set $d_q = d_p + c_{pq}$ and add node q to X_N. Then return to step 1 from the main stage and iterate this procedure $n - 1$ times.

Output: The optimal tree of the SPs from the source node to other nodes.

6.3   THE SHORTEST PATH (SP) PROBLEM IN FUZZY ENVIRONMENT

To make the SP problem more compatible with real-world problems, instead of assigning c_{ij} to each edge, the decision maker may assign a number as $\tilde{c}_{ij} = [l_{ij}, u_{ij}]$, which represents a range of fuzzy numbers, in which l_{ij} the lowest cost of flow the edge (i, j) from node i to j with the least reliability and u_{ij} the highest cost of flow the edge (i, j) from node i to j with the highest reliability or an interval-valued fuzzy number [4,13]. We intend to solve the SP problem by these two attitudes.

6.3.1   FIRST APPROACH: THE FUZZY SHORTEST PATH (FSP) PROBLEM BY RELIABILITY

As we mentioned, since the cost of transmission can be affected by various factors such as quality, safety, inflation, etc. The effect of such cases can be interpreted

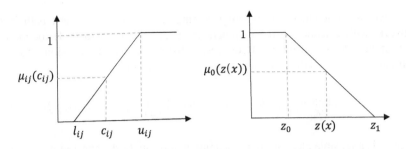

FIGURE 6.1 a) $\tilde{c}_{ij}$ membership function. b) $\tilde{z}$ membership function.

with the term reliability. This means that the higher cost of crossing an edge, the more confident we are. Of course, this is true as long as it reaches its highest level, which is one. This means that any increase in cost will not lead to greater reliability. To ensure the correctness of the choice of interval fuzzy numbers by the decision maker without losing anything from the whole problem, it can be assumed that $u_{ij} > l_{ij} > 0$. The degree of reliability, such as the cost of c_{ij}, which is related to the edge (i, j) is equal to $0 \leq \mu_{ij} \leq 1$. According to this method of expressing the cost for each edge, the membership function like it, which is a decreasing linear uniform function (Figure 6.1-a), can be expressed as follows.

$$\mu_{ij}(c_{ij}) = \begin{cases} 1 & c_{ij} \geq u_{ij}, \ x_{ij} = 1 \\ \frac{c_{ij} - l_{ij}}{u_{ij} - l_{ij}} & l_{ij} \leq c_{ij} \leq u_{ij}, \ x_{ij} = 1 \\ 0 & otherwise \end{cases} \tag{6.2}$$

If we display the total cost of the path from the beginning to the end of the node as an interval fuzzy number such as $\tilde{z}$ with the symbol $z = [z_0, z_1]$. Where z_0 is the lowest total cost and z_1 is the highest total cost, we should be able to make the right choice for these values. By introducing $X = \{x | x$ satisfy constraints $(6.1 - b), (6.1 - c)\}$ the values of z_0 and z_1 are obtained by solving the following sub-problems.

$$z_0 = \min_{x \in X} \sum_{(i,j) \in E} l_{ij} x_{ij} \tag{6.3a}$$

$$z_1 = \max_{x \in X} \sum_{(i,j) \in E} u_{ij} x_{ij} \tag{6.3b}$$

Therefore, the fuzzy membership function for the total cost of z, which is a uniform decreasing and linear function (Figure 6.1-b) can be presented in the following form:

$$\mu_0(z(x)) = \begin{cases} 1 & z(x) \leq z_0 \\ \frac{z_1 - z(x)}{z_1 - z_0} & z_0 \leq z(x) \leq z_1 \\ 0 & otherwise \end{cases} \tag{6.4}$$

To solve the problem of fuzzy programming related to the shortest path in the network, with considering the membership functions (6.2) and (6.4) for the cost each of the edges and the total cost respectively, we use the decision criteria of Bellman and Zadeh (Bellman and Zadeh 1970) as follows:

$$\max \left(\min_{x \varepsilon X}(\mu_{ij}(c_{ij}), \mu_0(z(x))) \right) = \max \left(\min_{x_{ij}=1}(\mu_{ij}(c_{ij}), \mu_0(\tilde{z})) \right), \tag{6.5}$$

where x is a feasible element in X, meaning that it satisfy the constraints (6.1b) and (6.1c), and $x_{ij} = 1$ represents the edges selected to be in the shortest path. Therefore, form (6.5) can be written as follows:

$$\max \left(\min_{x_{ij}=1}(\mu_{ij}(c_{ij}), \mu_0(z(x))) \right), \tag{6.6a}$$

$$\sum_{\{j|(i,j)\varepsilon E\}} x_{ij} - \sum_{\{j|(j,i)\varepsilon E\}} x_{ji} = \begin{cases} 1 & i = s \\ 0 & i \neq s, t \ (i = 1, 2, \cdots, n), \\ -1 & i = t \end{cases} \tag{6.6b}$$

$$x_{ij} \varepsilon \{0, 1\} \quad for(i, j)\varepsilon E \tag{6.6c}$$

We recall in the SP problem the main purpose is to find a path with the minimum total cost (the cost of a directed path is equal to sum of the arc value in the SP). This model not only determine the SP problem with the minimum total cost but also, shows the highest reliability from such path. Now consider membership functions (6.2) and (6.4), if the minimum of λ-cut of each $\tilde{c}_{ij}$ expresses $c_{ij}{}^{\lambda}$ then, $\sum_{(i,j)\varepsilon E} c_{ij}{}^{\lambda} x_{ij}$ denotes the total cost of the SP from source node to the end node. After solving, this is clear that λ is the highest reliability of each arc in the SP. Therefore, based on what has been discussed and with the placement of relations (6.2) and (6.4) the model (6.6) can be formulated as follows:

$$\max \ \lambda \tag{6.7a}$$

$$\lambda \, x_{ij} \leq \frac{c_{ij}{}^{\lambda} - l_{ij}}{u_{ij} - l_{ij}} x_{ij} \quad for \ (i, j) \in E, \tag{6.7b}$$

$$\lambda \leq \frac{z_1 - \sum_{(i,j)\varepsilon E} c_{ij}{}^{\lambda} x_{ij}}{z_1 - z_0}, \tag{6.7c}$$

$$0 \leq \lambda \leq 1, \tag{6.7d}$$

$$c_{ij}{}^{\lambda} x_{ij} \leq u_{ij} x_{ij} \quad for \ (i, j) \in E, \tag{6.7e}$$

$$\sum_{\{j|(i,j)\epsilon E\}} x_{ij} - \sum_{\{j|(j,i)\epsilon E\}} x_{ji} = \begin{cases} 1 & i = s \\ 0 & i \neq s, t \ (i = 1, 2, \cdots, n), \\ -1 & i = t \end{cases} \tag{6.7f}$$

$$x_{ij} \epsilon \{0, 1\} \quad \text{for } (i, j) \epsilon E. \tag{6.7g}$$

Because in this model, in addition to x_{ij}, the parameters c_{ij}^λ and λ are also decision variables for the problem, it is the mixed nonlinear integer programming. The optimal solution to this problem is $(\lambda^*, X^*, C^{\lambda*})$ where $C^{\lambda*} = \{c_{ij}^{\lambda*}|(i, j)\epsilon E\}$ and $X^* = \{x_{ij}^*|(i, j)\epsilon E\}$. Methods for solving this type of problem can be found in [15].

For convenience, let $\bar{E} = \{(i, j)|(i, j) \in E, x_{ij} = 1\}$ be a special feasible solution x of (6.6) so we have:

$$\max \quad \lambda \tag{6.8a}$$

$$\lambda \leq \frac{c_{ij}^\lambda - l_{ij}}{u_{ij} - l_{ij}} \quad \text{for } (i, j) \in \bar{E}, \tag{6.8b}$$

$$\lambda \leq \frac{z_1 - \sum_{(i,j)\epsilon\bar{E}} c_{ij}^\lambda}{z_1 - z_0}, \tag{6.8c}$$

$$0 \leq \lambda \leq 1, \tag{6.8d}$$

$$c_{ij}^\lambda \leq u_{ij} \quad \text{for } (i, j) \in \bar{E}. \tag{6.8e}$$

If assume $w_{ij} = u_{ij} - c_{ij}^\lambda$, then (6.8) is equivalent:

$$\max \quad \lambda \tag{6.9a}$$

$$\lambda \leq \frac{u_{ij} - l_{ij} - w_{ij}}{u_{ij} - l_{ij}} \quad \text{for } (i, j) \in \bar{E}, \tag{6.9b}$$

$$\lambda \leq \frac{z_1 - \sum_{(i,j)\epsilon\bar{E}} (u_{ij} - w_{ij})}{z_1 - z_0}, \tag{6.9c}$$

$$w_{ij}, \ \lambda \geq 0 \quad \text{for } (i, j) \in \bar{E}. \tag{6.9d}$$

Theorem 6.3.1.1: Let $\bar{E} = \{(i, j)|(i, j) \in E, x_{ij} = 1\}$, if x is a feasible solution of model (6.6), then (λ_x, w_{ij}) for $(i, j)\epsilon\bar{E}$ is the optimal solution of (6.9):

$$\lambda_x = \frac{z_1 - \Sigma_{(i,j)\epsilon\bar{E}}\,(u_{ij} - w_{ij})}{z_1 - z_0} = \frac{u_{ij} - l_{ij} - w_{ij}}{u_{ij} - l_{ij}} \quad for \quad (i,j) \epsilon \bar{E}. \qquad (6.10)$$

Therefore, optimal solution is unique.

Proof: See [4].

According to the equation (6.10) and previous content realize that $c_{ij}{}^\lambda$, can consider as $l_{ij} + (u_{ij} - l_{ij})\lambda$. So, if we solve the following parametric SP problem, obtain the optimal solution set $X^* \subseteq X$.

$$min \sum_{(i,j)\epsilon E} (l_{ij} + (u_{ij} - l_{ij})\lambda)x_{ij} \qquad (6.11a)$$

$$\sum_{\{j|(i,j)\epsilon E\}} x_{ij} - \sum_{\{j|(j,i)\epsilon E\}} x_{ji} = \begin{cases} 1 & i = s \\ 0 & i \neq s, t \ (i = 1, 2, \cdots, n), \\ -1 & i = t \end{cases} \qquad (6.11b)$$

$$x_{ij} \epsilon \{0, 1\} \quad for \quad (i, j) \epsilon E. \qquad (6.11c)$$

Then, the optimal λ for each $x \in X^*$ can be discovered by solving the following problem.

$$max \quad \lambda \qquad (6.12a)$$

$$\lambda = \frac{z_1 - \Sigma_{(i,j)\epsilon E}\,(l_{ij} + (u_{ij} - l_{ij})\lambda)x_{ij}}{z_1 - z_0}, \qquad (6.12b)$$

$$x \in X^*. \qquad (6.12c)$$

In fact, to find the solution for the main problem, we must first solve the minimum parametric cost with (6.11). Appropriate methods are provided for solving (6.11) in (Dempe 2002). But as it turns out, the solutions are in λ terms. This means that intervals as $[\lambda_1, \lambda_2] \subseteq [0, 1]$ can obtain, and for each interval $T(\lambda)$ defines the SP tree, which is optimal for all $\lambda\epsilon\,[\lambda_1, \lambda_2]$.

So, to find λ, need to solve the problem (6.12). For more efficiency due to the linearity of total cost changes in (6.12b) we have:

$$f(\lambda) = \lambda - \frac{z_1 - \Sigma_{(i,j)\epsilon E}\,c_{ij}{}^\lambda}{z_1 - z_0} = \lambda - \frac{z_1 - \Sigma_{(i,j)\epsilon\bar{E}}\,c_{ij}{}^\lambda}{z_1 - z_0} = \lambda - \frac{z_1 - \Sigma_{(i,j)\epsilon p(\lambda)}\,c_{ij}{}^\lambda}{z_1 - z_0},$$

$$(6.13)$$

where $p(\lambda)$ indicative the SP from node s to destination node t in $T(\lambda)$. For any interval $[\lambda_1, \lambda_2]$, if $f(\lambda_1)f(\lambda_2) \leq 0$, then comprehend $[\lambda_1, \lambda_2]$ contains the optimal value of λ, and $f(\lambda) = 0$ when λ is optimal.

For proposing algorithm 2, in the following, we summarize important notations:

$$c_{ij}^{\lambda} = l_{ij} + \delta_{ij}\lambda \quad where \quad \delta_{ij} = u_{ij} - l_{ij} \quad for \ all \ (i,j) \epsilon E:$$

$$the \ parametric \ cost \ of \ (i,j).$$

$$d_i^{\lambda}: distance \ label \ of \ node \ i \epsilon N.$$

$$d_i^{\delta}: distance \ label \ of \ node \ i \epsilon N \ related \ with \ costs \ \delta_{ij}.$$

$$\bar{c}_{ij}^{\lambda} = c_{ij}^{\lambda} + d_i^{\lambda} - d_i^{\lambda}: reduced \ cost \ of \ (i,j) which \ is \ related \ to \ c_{ij}^{\lambda}.$$

$$\bar{\delta}_{ij} = \delta_{ij} + d_i^{\delta} - d_j^{\delta}: reduced \ cost \ of \ (i,j) which \ is \ related \ to \ \delta_{ij}.$$

ALGORITHM 2   INPUT: NETWORK $G = (N, E, C^{\lambda})$ WHERE $C_{ij}^{\lambda} = l_{ij} + \delta_{ij}\lambda$.

Step 1: Assume $\lambda = 0$.

Step 2: Find SP problem on $G = (N, E, C^{\lambda})$ by Dijkstra's Algorithm, for any $i \epsilon N$ find d_i^{λ}, and determine the tree of the SPs, $T(\lambda)$.

Step 3: Determine d_i^{δ}, where is associated with costs δ_{ij} for any $i \epsilon N$.

Step 4: For any edge (k, l) that is not belong to $T(\lambda)$, after finding the reduced costs $\bar{C}_{ij}^{\lambda}$ and $\bar{\delta}_{ij}$, calculate λ_{kl} by:

$$\lambda_{kl} = \begin{cases} -\dfrac{\bar{C}_{kl}^{\lambda}}{\bar{\delta}_{kl}} & \bar{\delta}_{kl} < 0 \\ \infty & o.\,w \end{cases}$$

Step 5: Select $\bar{\lambda} = min\{\lambda_{kl} | (k,l) \notin T(\lambda)\} + \lambda$.

Step 6: For edge (p, q) which is a non-tree edge, if $\lambda_{pq} + \lambda = \bar{\lambda}$, determine an alternative tree of the SP at $\bar{\lambda}$ by adding edge (p, q) and deleting one edge entering node q and up to date the distance labels of $T(\bar{\lambda})$.

Step 7: If $f(\lambda).f(\bar{\lambda}) > 0$, return to step 3, otherwise go to step 8.

Step 8: let $\lambda* = \dfrac{\lambda f(\bar{\lambda}) - \bar{\lambda}f(\lambda)}{f(\bar{\lambda}) - f(\lambda)}$

Output: $\lambda*$ as an optimal value of λ and $T(\lambda*)$ is the optimal tree of the SPs.

Finally, in this part the algorithm 2 can be proposed as follows:
This algorithm designed to find the shortest path with highest reliability.

6.3.2   Second Approach: The Fuzzy Shortest Path (FSP) Problem by Interval-Valued Arithmetic

In this part, we will propose an ordering interval numbers which can be used in Dijkstra's Algorithm for finding the SP when the cost of every arc is corresponded with interval-valued fuzzy number [13]. In order to this aim, for any $(i, j) \in E$ the cost define:

$$\tilde{c}_{ij} = [l_{ij}, u_{ij}] = \{c_{ij} | l_{ij} \le c_{ij} \le u_{ij}\}, \tag{6.14}$$

or, in alternative symbolization, we have:

$$\tilde{c}_{ij} = \langle m(\tilde{c}_{ij}), w(\tilde{c}_{ij}) \rangle = \langle \frac{l_{ij} + u_{ij}}{2}, \frac{u_{ij} - l_{ij}}{2} \rangle, \tag{6.15}$$

where the $m(\tilde{c}_{ij})$ and $w(\tilde{c}_{ij})$ are the mid-point and half-width of the interval $\tilde{c}_{ij}$, respectively. Notice that if $l_{ij}, u_{ij} = \hat{c}_{ij}$, where $\hat{c}_{ij}$ is a real number, then $\tilde{c}_{ij} = [\hat{c}_{ij}, \hat{c}_{ij}]$. Alefeld and Herzberger [17] introduce some basic arithmetic notation.

Definition 6.3.2.1: If $a = [l_a, u_a]$ and $b = [l_b, u_b]$ are two interval-valued fuzzy number and α is scalar number, then:

1. $a \oplus b = [l_a + l_b, u_a + u_b]$ (symbol $\oplus$ is the extended addition)
2. $a \ominus b = [l_a - u_b, u_a - l_b]$ (symbol $\ominus$ is the extended subtraction)
3. $\alpha a = \alpha[l_a, u_a] = \begin{cases} [\alpha l_a, \alpha u_a], & \alpha \ge 0 \\ [\alpha u_a, \alpha l_a], & \alpha \le 0 \end{cases}$

Now, suppose that a and b are two interval-valued costs. we purpose to select the lower number.

Definition 6.3.2.2: Any pair of interval numbers, a and b, can be ordered as (a, b), hence:

1. if $m(a) \le m(b)$, $w(a) \le w(b)$, then $(a, b) \in s_1$,
2. if $m(a) \le m(b)$, $w(a) > w(b)$, then $(a, b) \in s_2$,

where s_1 and s_2 are two sets for classifying intervals. Therefore, in minimization problem, for $(a, b) \in s_1$, always a is the best selection, unless a and b are identical. Also for $(a, b) \in s_2$, there exist a fuzzy preference between a and b, in some situations which follows.

Definition 6.3.2.3: A set of intervals (a, y) exist in s_2 for any $a = [l_a, u_a]$, such that $y = [l_y, u_y] = (m(y), w(y))$ are defined as a variable interval. Hence as the rejection set of interval a, for any pair $(a, y) \in s_2$, a fuzzy set which are named a' defines:

$$a' = \{(a, y) | m(a) \leq m(y), \ w(a) > w(y)\},$$

with $\mu_{a'}(a, y)$ as a membership function:

$$\mu_{a'}(a, y) = \begin{cases} 1 & m(a) = m(y), \\ \max\left\{0, \ \frac{u_a - w(y) - m(y)}{u_a - w(y) - m(a)}\right\} & m(a) \leq m(y) \leq u_a - w(y), \quad (6.16) \\ 0 & o.\,w, \end{cases}$$

where $\mu_{a'} : s_2 \to [0, 1]$.

Various values of $\mu_{a'}$ can be interpreted as follows:

1. if $\mu_{a'} = 1$, then a is rejected.
2. if $\mu_{a'} = 0$, then a is accepted.
3. if $\mu_{a'} \in (0, 1)$, then various grades of rejection are introduced for a.

Let us to complete preference structure by definition $\mu_{y'}(a, y) = 1 - \mu_{a'}(a, y)$ for all y of $(a, y) \in s_2$ which as the complement of a' demonstrate the rejection of y in s_2.

Based on the algorithm 3, we can choose a preferred minimum in a set of intervals, so it can be used in step (2) of Dijkstra's algorithm.

ALGORITHM 3   ORDERING AND SELECTING THE PREFERRED MINIMUM AMONG k INTERVALS

Step 1: Rewrite the intervals as a new set; $\{a_1, a_2, \ldots, a_k\}$. (use of the both structure (6.14), (6.15)).

Step 2: Order intervals by ascending mid-points. If $m(a_i) = m(a_j)$ for some intervals where $i \neq j$ then order by ascending $w(a_i)$ and $w(a_j)$.

Step 3: Rename the ordered interval numbers in step2, as a new set; $\{y_1, y_2, \ldots, y_k\}$.

Step 4: Draw a square table with k rows and k columns that each array of cell (i, j) shows a preference relation (y_i, y_j). This table is called the fuzzy rejection table.

(Notice that rows and columns are related to ordered set in step3).

Step 5: In cell (i, j) of the fuzzy rejection table, according to the following instruction we assign memberships:

1. If $i = j$, set $\mu_{y_i'}(y_i, y_i) = 0.5$. (i.e. there is no differences between being rejected or accepted when an interval is compared with itself.)
2. If $i < j$, then;
   a. If $(u)_{y_i} \leq (l)_{y_j}$, then set $\mu_{y_i'}(y_i, y_j) = 0$

b. If $m(y_i) = m(y_j)$ and
$$\begin{cases} w(y_i) = w(y_j), & then\ set\ \mu_{y_i'}(y_i,\ y_j) = 0.5, \\ w(y_i) < w(y_j), & then\ set\ \mu_{y_i'}(y_i,\ y_j) = 0, \\ w(y_i) > w(y_j), & then\ set\ \mu_{y_i'}(y_i,\ y_j) = 1. \end{cases}$$

c. If $m(y_i) < m(y_j)$,

and
$$\begin{cases} w(y_i) \le w(y_j), & then\ set\ \mu_{y_i'}(y_i,\ y_j) = 0, \\ w(y_i) > w(y_j), & then\ compute:\ \mu_{y_i'} = max\left\{0,\ \frac{u_{y_i} - w(y_j) - m(y_j)}{u_{y_i} - w(y_j) - m(y_i)}\right\}. \end{cases}$$

3. if $i > j$, then set $\mu_{y_i'}(y_i,\ y_j) = 1 - \mu_{y_i'}(y_j,\ y_i)$.

Step 6: Add $(k + 1)$st column to the fuzzy rejection table that is completed in step 5 and repeat the following procedure until all intervals are ordered.

Iteration 1: Compute k row-sums for the k rows, then set the results in $(k + 1)$st column.

Iteration 2: Select the row that has the minimum row-sum, then label the corresponded interval number to the selected row.

Iteration 3: Delete the corresponding row as well as column from the table, then in the reminded table repeat the process in this step 6.

Step 7: Decode the selected labeled rows to y_i and a_i.

6.3.3 Numerical Example

In this section, a numerical example (Keshavarz and Khorram 2009) is given to illustrate the capability of the proposed algorithms (Sengupta and Pal 2006, Keshavarz and Khorram 2009).

Example 1: Consider the network of Figure 6.2. According to the decision of the decision maker, each arc is assigned an interval fuzzy number whose information is written in Table 6.1.

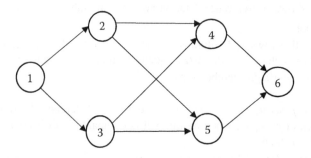

FIGURE 6.2 The network problem of Example 1.

TABLE 6.1

Arcs Information for Example 1

Arc (i, j)	(1, 2)	(1, 3)	(2, 4)	(2, 5)	(3, 4)	(3, 5)	(4, 6)	(5, 6)
Fuzzy cost $[l_{ij},\ u_{ij}]$	[4, 9]	[5, 8]	[3, 6]	[4, 8]	[3, 5]	[6, 7]	[4, 9]	[4, 6]

First approach:

According to the relation (6.3) we find $z_0 = 11$ and $z_1 = 24$. So the membership function of $z(x)$ can obtain. The information of the first iteration in the Algorithm 2 is presented in Table 6.2. For instance, we obtain $\delta_{12} = 5$, $\delta_{13} = 3$, $\delta_{24} = 3$, $\delta_{25} = 4$, $\delta_{34} = 2$, $\delta_{35} = 1$, $\delta_{46} = 5$, $\delta_{56} = 2$ by equation $\delta_{ij} = u_{ij} - l_{ij}$, which shown in the row that named d_i^δ in the Table 6.2. Due to (3, 4), (3, 5), (5, 6) are non-tree edges in the first iteration, by step (4) and (5) we determine:

$$\bar\lambda = min\left\{\frac{1}{3}, \frac{3}{5}, \frac{1}{2}\right\} + \lambda = \frac{1}{3},$$

Now we should update the distance labels in $T(\bar\lambda)$, notice that arcs (3, 4), (2, 4) represent the entering and leaving arcs for new SP tree respectively. As $f(\lambda)f(\bar\lambda) = f(0)f(\frac{1}{3}) = (-1)(-\frac{1}{3}) > 0$, return to step (3) and repeat the Algorithm. New results of the second iteration are provided in Table 6.3. Because (2, 4), (3, 5) and (5, 6) are non-tree edges in the second iteration, by step (4) and (5) we determine:

$$\bar\lambda = min\left\{\infty, \frac{4}{15}, \infty\right\} + \lambda = \frac{4}{15} + \frac{1}{3} = \frac{3}{5}$$

TABLE 6.2

Results of Algorithm 2 (Iteration 1)

$\lambda = 0$

Costs	Arc (i, j)	(1, 2)	(1, 3)	(2, 4)	(2, 5)	(3, 4)	(3, 5)	(4, 6)	(5, 6)
	c_{ij}^λ	4	5	3	4	3	6	4	4
Distance labels of node	Node i	1	2	3	4	5	6		
	d_i^λ	0	4	5	7	8	11		
	d_i^δ	0	5	3	8	9	13		
$T(\lambda)$	$1 \to 2 \to 4 \to 6$								
	$1 \to 2 \to 5$								
	$1 \to 3$								

TABLE 6.3

Results of Algorithm 2 (Iteration 2)

$\lambda = 1/3$

	Arc (i, j)	$(1, 2)$	$(1, 3)$	$(2, 4)$	$(2, 5)$	$(3, 4)$	$(3, 5)$	$(4, 6)$	$(5, 6)$
Costs	c_{ij}^{λ}	$\frac{17}{3}$	$\frac{18}{3}$	$\frac{12}{3}$	$\frac{16}{3}$	$\frac{11}{3}$	$\frac{19}{3}$	$\frac{17}{3}$	$\frac{14}{3}$
Distance labels of node	Node i	1	2	3	4	5	6		
	d_i^{λ}	0	$\frac{17}{3}$	$\frac{18}{3}$	$\frac{29}{3}$	$\frac{33}{3}$	$\frac{46}{3}$		
	d_i^{δ}	0	5	3	5	9	10		
$T(\lambda)$	$1 \rightarrow 3 \rightarrow 4 \rightarrow 6$								
	$1 \rightarrow 2 \rightarrow 5$								

Now we should update the distance labels in $T(\bar{\lambda})$, notice that arcs $(3, 5)$ and $(2, 5)$ represent the entering and leaving arcs for new SP tree respectively. As $f(\lambda)f(\bar{\lambda}) = f(\frac{1}{3})f(\frac{3}{5}) = (-\frac{1}{3})(\frac{9}{65}) < 0$, hence we go to step (8) and compute:

$$\lambda^* = \frac{\lambda f(\bar{\lambda}) - \bar{\lambda} f(\lambda)}{f(\bar{\lambda}) - f(\lambda)} = \frac{\frac{1}{3}(\frac{9}{65}) - \frac{3}{5}(-\frac{1}{3})}{(\frac{9}{65}) - (-\frac{1}{3})} = \frac{12}{23} \epsilon \left[\frac{1}{3}, \frac{3}{5}\right]$$

Table 6.4 shows the final results.

In this approach $\lambda^* = \frac{12}{23}$ is the optimal value of λ and the SP from node 1 to node 6 which is related to λ^* and has a highest reliability is:

TABLE 6.4

Results of Algorithm 2 (Iteration 3)

$\lambda = 3/5$

	Arc (i, j)	$(1, 2)$	$(1, 3)$	$(2, 4)$	$(2, 5)$	$(3, 4)$	$(3, 5)$	$(4, 6)$	$(5, 6)$
Costs	c_{ij}^{λ}	$\frac{35}{5}$	$\frac{34}{5}$	$\frac{24}{5}$	$\frac{32}{5}$	$\frac{21}{5}$	$\frac{33}{5}$	$\frac{35}{5}$	$\frac{26}{5}$
Distance labels of node	Node i	1	2	3	4	5	6		
	d_i^{λ}	0	$\frac{35}{5}$	$\frac{34}{5}$	$\frac{55}{5}$	$\frac{67}{5}$	$\frac{90}{5}$		
	d_i^{δ}	0	5	3	5	4	10		
$T(\lambda)$	$1 \rightarrow 3 \rightarrow 4 \rightarrow 6$								
	$1 \rightarrow 3 \rightarrow 5$								
	$1 \rightarrow 2$								

$$1 \rightarrow 3 \rightarrow 4 \rightarrow 6$$

hence, the total cost is:

$$d_6^{\lambda*} = c_{13}^{\lambda*} + c_{34}^{\lambda*} + c_{46}^{\lambda*} = \frac{34}{5} + \frac{21}{5} + \frac{35}{5} = 17.217391$$

We can repeat this procedure to find $T(\lambda)$, for other value of λ. (for any $\lambda \varepsilon [0, 1]$ we can correspond $T(\lambda)$).

Second approach:
Iteration 1: $d_1 = 0$, $X_N = \{1\}$ and $\bar{X}_N = \{2, 3, 4, 5, 6\}$

$$d_p + c_{pq} = min \begin{cases} d_1 \oplus c_{12} = 0 \oplus [4, 9] = [4, 9] = (6.5, 2.5) \\ d_1 \oplus c_{13} = 0 \oplus [5, 8] = [5, 8] = (6.5, 1.5) \end{cases}$$

We use algorithm 3 to find the lowest interval among the all.
$a_1 = [4, 9] = (6.5, 2.5)$, $a_2 = [5, 8] = (6.5, 1.5)$
Based on ascending mid-point or ascending half-width of the intervals when the mid-points are equal, we have:

$$a_2 = y_1, \quad a_1 = y_2$$

So, fuzzy rejection information can be as follows:

	y_1	y_2
y_1	s_1	s_2
y_2	s_1	

After assigning the memberships and computing the row-sums:

	y_1	y_2	
y_1	0.5	0	0.5
y_2	1	0.5	1.5

As we can observe, y_1 (interval a_1) the lower row-sum, so it can select as a smaller interval, edge (1, 3) labeled. The results of the rest repetitions with similar steps are as follows:
Iteration 2: $d_3 = [5, 8]$, $X_N = \{1, 3\}$ and $\bar{X}_N = \{2, 4, 5, 6\}$,

$$d_p + c_{pq} = min \{[4, 9], [8, 13], [11, 15]\} = [4, 9]$$

Selected edge: (1, 2).
Iteration 3: $d_2 = [4, 9]$, $X_N = \{1, 2, 3\}$ and $\bar{X}_N = \{4, 5, 6\}$,

$$d_p + c_{pq} = min \{[8, 13], [11, 15], [7, 15], [8, 17]\} = [8, 13].$$

Selected edge: (3, 4).
   Iteration 4: $d_4 = [8, 13]$, $X_N = \{1, 2, 3, 4\}$, and $\bar{X}_N = \{5, 6\}$,

$$d_p + c_{pq} = \min\{[11, 15], [8, 17], [12, 22]\} = [11, 15].$$

Selected edge: (3, 5).
   Iteration 5: $d_5 = [11, 15]$, $X_N = \{1, 2, 3, 4, 5\}$, $\bar{X}_N = \{6\}$,
   $d_p + c_{pq} = \min\{[12, 22], [15, 21]\} = [12, 22]$.
   Selected edge: (4, 6).
   According to the overhead iterations, $T(\lambda)$ is:

$$1 \rightarrow 3 \rightarrow 4 \rightarrow 6$$

$$1 \rightarrow 3 \rightarrow 5$$

$$1 \rightarrow 2$$

And minimum interval total cost corresponded with the SP is, $[12, 22]$ (in the iteration 5) which is equal to:

$$[5, 8] \oplus [3, 5] \oplus [4, 9] = [12, 22]$$

Paths Analysis:
   In the first approach, the SPs tree is obtained for each subinterval of $[0, 1]$, and based on stop condition optimal path that has a highest reliability is introduced. But in the second approach single path with interval total cost is represented that fortunately, this path is the same as the optimal path with highest reliability in the first approach. When the number of the non-dominated paths is a few, specially less than number of the nodes, we can consider Table 6.5, after defining the total parametric cost select the path that has a minimum lower bound, then find the intersection of this path with the next path, which actually has the second lower boundary among all the paths. So interval that is optimal for this path is found. (See Figure 6.3 that shows the total cost for any path). In the same way, we continue to define a path as the SP for any $\lambda \varepsilon [0, 1]$.

6.4   THE SHORTEST PATH (SP) PROBLEM IN HESITANT FUZZY ENVIRONMENT

In this section at first the model of the SP problem in hesitant fuzzy environment presented then due to the concept of hesitant fuzzy decision making for the proposed model, we develop two methods for solving this kind of problem.

6.4.1   MATHEMATICAL MODEL OF HESITANT FUZZY SHORTEST PATH (HFSP) PROBLEM

There are always different notions of uncertainty in the real world, moreover ambiguous situations often occur at various parts of the study, investigation and

TABLE 6.5
Paths Analysis for Example 1

Arc (i, j)	$(1, 2)$	$(1, 3)$	$(2, 4)$	$(2, 5)$	$(3, 4)$	$(3, 5)$	$(4, 6)$	$(5, 6)$
Fuzzy cost $[l_{ij}, u_{ij}]$	[4, 9]	[5, 8]	[3, 6]	[4, 8]	[3, 5]	[6, 7]	[4, 9]	[4, 6]
Parametric costs	$4 + 5.\lambda$	$5 + 3.\lambda$	$3 + 3.\lambda$	$4 + 4.\lambda$	$3 + 2.\lambda$	$6 + \lambda$	$4 + 5.\lambda$	$4 + 2.\lambda$

Paths analysis	paths	Parametric total costs	Non-dominated paths	Analysis variations of λ
	$p1: 1 \to 2 \to 4 \to 6$	$11 + 13.\lambda$	■	Optimal for: $\left[0, \frac{1}{3}\right]$
	$p2: 1 \to 2 \to 5 \to 6$	$12 + 11.\lambda$	–	–
	$p3: 1 \to 3 \to 4 \to 6$	$12 + 10.\lambda$	■	Optimal for: $\left[\frac{1}{3}, \frac{3}{4}\right]$
	$p4: 1 \to 3 \to 5 \to 6$	$15 + 6.\lambda$	■	Optimal for: $\left[\frac{3}{4}, 1\right]$

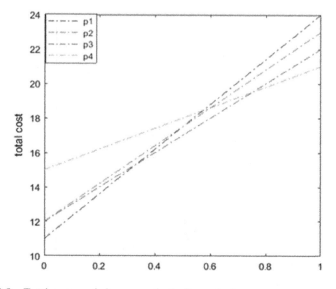

FIGURE 6.3 Total cost graph for any paths in Example 1.

process solving. In these cases, if the problem formulated and solved based crisp data we will not reach a convincing and satisfactory solution. So the optimal solution will not be selected correctly. As we know fuzzy logic try to replace inference techniques by the human brain in modeling. Specifically, in last decade a new extension of fuzzy logic introduced by Tora and Narukawa (Torra and Narukawa 2009). To clarify the significant role of this kind of sets, it is assumed that the network is managed with more than one decision-maker, therefore, has chosen various fuzzy costs for each arc. Due to the differences in sights, they comprehend it is not possible to assess a single evaluation to each arc lengths for formulation of such a problem. So in this part, we will introduce the mathematical formulation of the hesitant fuzzy shortest path problem. In the beginning consider an acyclic directed network with node set $N = \{1, 2, \ldots, n\}$, and also arc set $E = \{(i, j)|i, j \in N, \ i \neq j\}$ where $|E| = m$ each cost corrresponds to costs and are hesitant fuzzy set. It is necessary to review some important concepts and application operators in hesitant fuzzy sets. In the following, we gather some required definitions.

Definition 6.4.1.1: [19] Suppose X is a universal set, then a hesitant fuzzy set (HFS) $\widetilde{A}$ in X is a collection of the ordered pairs as follows:

$$\widetilde{A} = \left\{ \left(x, h_{\widetilde{A}}(x) \right) | x \in X \right\}, \tag{6.17}$$

where $h_{\widetilde{A}}(x): X \to P([0, 1])$ such that $P([0, 1])$ is the power set of $[0, 1]$. Most of the time, $h_{\widetilde{A}}(x)$ is named an HFE. Several basic operations on HFEs are proposed by (Torra 2010). Union and intersection are two important operators among them which can be defines as follows:

1. $h_1(x) \cup h_2(x) = \cup_{\gamma_1 \in h_1(x), \gamma_2 \in h_2(x)} max\{\gamma_1, \gamma_2\}$.
2. $h_1(x) \cap h_2(x) = \cup_{\gamma_1 \in h_1(x), \gamma_2 \in h_2(x)} min\{\gamma_1, \gamma_2\}$.

HFS may have constructed with a set of finite fuzzy sets that can represented by the following mathematical symbol:

$$\widetilde{A} = \{ (x, \tilde{h}_{\widetilde{A}}(x)) | x \in X \}, \tag{6.18}$$

where $\tilde{h}_{\widetilde{A}}(x) = \{\mu_{\widetilde{A}^1}(x), \mu_{\widetilde{A}^2}(x), ..., \mu_{\widetilde{A}^k}(x)\}$ for all $x \epsilon X$. The number of the HFEs in $\tilde{h}_{\widetilde{A}}$ are denoted by k.

If we have $\widetilde{A}_1 = \{ (x, \tilde{h}_{\widetilde{A}_1}(x)) | x \in X \}$ and $\widetilde{A}_2 = \{ (x, \tilde{h}_{\widetilde{A}_2}(x)) | x \in X \}$ as two HFSs, then the union and intersection operations on $\widetilde{A}_1$ and $\widetilde{A}_2$ are defined:

1. $\widetilde{A}_1 \cup \widetilde{A}_2 = \{ (x, (\tilde{h}_{\widetilde{A}_1}(x) \cup \tilde{h}_{\widetilde{A}_2}(x))) | x \in X \}$,
2. $\widetilde{A}_1 \cup \widetilde{A}_2 = \{ (x, (\tilde{h}_{\widetilde{A}_1}(x) \cap \tilde{h}_{\widetilde{A}_2}(x))) | x \in X \}$.

According to the above content, the hesitant fuzzy SP problem which having non-negative HFSs in the arc costs is proposed as follows:

$$min \sum_{(i,j) \in E} \tilde{c}_{ij} x_{ij} \tag{6.19a}$$

$$\sum_{\{j|(i,j) \in E\}} x_{ij} - \sum_{\{j|(j,i) \in E\}} x_{ji} = \begin{cases} 1 & i = s, \\ 0 & i \neq s, t \ (i = 1, 2, \cdots, n), \\ -1 & i = t, \end{cases} \tag{6.19b}$$

$$x_{ij} \epsilon \{0, 1\} \quad for \ (i, j) \epsilon E, \tag{6.19c}$$

where $\tilde{c}_{ij} = \{\tilde{c}_{ij}^1, \tilde{c}_{ij}^2, ..., \tilde{c}_{ij}^{k_{ij}}\}$ for all $(i, j) \epsilon E$, when k_{ij} is the number decision maker that record their attitudes for the cost of edge (i, j) or in equivalent form:

$$\tilde{c}_{ij} = \{ [l_{ij}^1, u_{ij}^1], [l_{ij}^1, u_{ij}^1], ..., [l_{ij}^{k_{ij}}, u_{ij}^{k_{ij}}] \} \quad for \ all \ (i, j) \epsilon E. \tag{6.20}$$

With the hesitant fuzzy membership function as follows:

$$\tilde{h}_{\tilde{c}_{ij}}(c_{ij}) = \{ \mu_{\tilde{c}_{ij}^1}(c_{ij}), \mu_{\tilde{c}_{ij}^2}(c_{ij}), ..., \mu_{\tilde{c}_{ij}^{k_{ij}}}(c_{ij}) \} \quad for \ all \ (i, j) \epsilon E \tag{6.21}$$

where

$$\mu_{\tilde{c}_{ij}{}^{k_{ij}}}(c_{ij}) = \begin{cases} 1 & c_{ij} \geq u_{ij}{}^{k_{ij}}, \; x_{ij} = 1, \\ \dfrac{c_{ij} - l_{ij}{}^{k_{ij}}}{u_{ij}{}^{k_{ij}} - l_{ij}{}^{k_{ij}}} & l_{ij}{}^{k_{ij}} \leq c_{ij} \leq u_{ij}{}^{k_{ij}}, \; x_{ij} = 1, \\ 0 & otherwise. \end{cases} \tag{6.22}$$

Thus the decision space which caused by hesitant fuzzy cost can be proposed by:

$$\tilde{c} = \bigcap_{(i,j) \in E} \tilde{c}_{ij}, \tag{6.23}$$

In feasible region with the hesitant fuzzy element:

$$\tilde{h}_{\tilde{c}}(c_{ij}) = \bigcup \{ \mu_{\tilde{c}_{ij}{}^{\gamma_{ij}}}(c_{ij}) \in \tilde{h}_{\tilde{c}_{ij}}(c_{ij}) \}_{(i,j) \in E}$$

$$= \min_{c_{ij}} \{ \mu_{\tilde{c}_{ij}{}^{\gamma_{ij}}}(c_{ij}) \}_{(i,j) \in E} = \left\{ \min_{c_{ij}} \{ \mu_{\tilde{c}_{ij}{}^{\gamma_{ij}{}^r}}(c_{ij}) \}_{(i,j) \in E} \right\}_{r=1}^{\tau}, \tag{6.24}$$

where $\tau = \Pi_{(i,j) \in E} \, k_{ij}$ and $\gamma_{ij} \in \{1, 2, ..., k_{ij}\}$. Since the members of $\tilde{h}_{\tilde{c}}(c_{ij})$ are a set of fuzzy numbers, we can suggest the following solution to each member of $\tilde{h}_{\tilde{c}}(c_{ij})$ by:

For each $r\epsilon \{1, 2, ..., \tau\}$, by introducing new variable λ^r, we suggest following parametric problem:

$$P^r: \; \min \; \Sigma_{(i,j) \in E} \, c_{ij} x_{ij}$$
$$s.\, t \quad \lambda^r \leq \min_{c_{ij}} \{ \mu_{\tilde{c}_{ij}{}^{\gamma_{ij}{}^r}}(c_{ij}) \} \; for \; (i,j) \epsilon E, \tag{6.25}$$
$$0 \leq \lambda^r \leq 1,$$
$$x \in X.$$

Or, in equivalent form:

$$P^r: \; \min \; \Sigma_{(i,j) \in E} \, c_{ij} x_{ij}$$
$$s.\, t \quad \lambda^r \leq \mu_{\tilde{c}_{ij}{}^{\gamma_{ij}{}^r}}(c_{ij}) \; for \; (i,j) \epsilon E, \tag{6.26}$$
$$0 \leq \lambda^r \leq 1,$$
$$x \in X.$$

And, since the membership functions are continuous and strictly monotonic (in intervals) we have:

$$P^r: \ min \ \Sigma_{(i,j)\in E} \ c_{ij} x_{ij}$$
$$s. \ t \quad \mu^{-1}_{\tilde{c}_{ij}\gamma_{ij}}(\lambda^r) \le c_{ij} \ for \quad (i,j)\epsilon E, \tag{6.27}$$
$$0 \le \lambda^r \le 1,$$
$$x \in X.$$

So, we can state:

$$P^r: \ min \ \Sigma_{(i,j)\in E} \ \mu^{-1}_{\tilde{c}_{ij}\gamma_{ij}}(\lambda^r) x_{ij}$$
$$s. \ t \quad 0 \le \lambda^r \le 1, \tag{6.28}$$
$$x \in X.$$

Hence, by solving r-th parametric problem we can find some intervals of λ^r (belong to $[0, 1]$) with corresponding c_{ij}'s.

6.4.2 First Approach: HFSP Problem by Reliability

In the previous section mentioned to find an optimal solution of (6.19), we should solve the parametric programming which was stated in (6.28) for each $r\epsilon\{1, 2, \ ...,\tau\}$, for the optimal hesitant path we should find:

$$x^* = \{x_{ij}^*|(i, j) \in E\},$$

where $x_{ij}^* = \{x_{ij}^1, x_{ij}^2, \ ... \ , x_{ij}^\tau\}$ and is corresponding to:

$$c^* = \{c_{ij}^*|(i, j) \in E\},$$

where $c_{ij}^* = \{c_{ij}^1, c_{ij}^2, \ ... \ , c_{ij}^\tau\}$, for any $\bar{\lambda}^* = [\lambda_1, \lambda_2] \subseteq [0, 1]$.

According to (3) we can find $[z_0^r, z_1^r]$ for any $r\epsilon\{1, 2, \ ..., \tau\}$, and propose membership function $z^r(x)$ by:

$$\mu_0^r(z(x)) = \begin{cases} 1 & z^r(x) \le z_0, \\ \frac{z_1 - z^r(x)}{z_1 - z_0} & z_0 \le z^r(x) \le z_1, \\ 0 & otherwise. \end{cases} \tag{6.29}$$

Based on Bellman and Zadeh's decision theory, to choose the best path that minimizes total cost when maximizes reliability, (28) may converted to:

$$(Problem)^r: \ max \ \{\min_{x_{ij}=1} \ \{\mu_{\tilde{c}_{ij}\gamma_{ij}^r}(c_{ij})\}, \mu_0^r(z(x))\} \tag{6.30}$$
$$s. \ t \quad x \in X,$$

where $r\epsilon\{1, 2, \ ..., \tau\}$. Thus the Algorithm 2 can perform τ times to find an optimal hesitant solution.

6.4.3 Second Approach: HFSP Problem by Interval-Valued Arithmetic

To extend the method mentioned in Section 6.3.2, Dijkstra's algorithm must run τ times using the interval sorting method described in the Algorithm 3 to find an optimal hesitant fuzzy solution.

6.4.4 Numerical Example

In this section, a numerical example is given to illustrate the new aspects of SP problem in hesitant fuzzy environment.

Example 2: Consider the network in Figure 6.2 of Example 1. For 3 edges, two decision makers did not have the same opinion based on their experiences, so the cost of these edges is established as hesitant fuzzy numbers (Table 6.6)

It is clear that we have 8 problems with following information:
p^1 with:

[4, 9] *for arc*(1, 2), [5, 8] *for arc*(1, 3), [3, 5] *for arc*(3, 4) *and other fuzzy arcs,*

which is an arcs information in Example 1.
p^2 with:

[4, 9] *for arc* (1, 2), (2, 7) *for arc* (1, 3), [3, 5] *for arc* (3, 4) *and other fuzzy arcs.*
p^3 with:

[4, 9] *for arc* (1, 2), [5, 8] *for arc* (1, 3), [5, 8] *for arc* (3, 4) *and other fuzzy arcs.*
p^4 with:

[4, 9] *for arc* (1, 2), (2, 7) *for arc* (1, 3), [5, 8] *for arc* (3, 4) *and other fuzzy arcs.*
p^5 with:

[5, 6] *for arc* (1, 2), [2, 7] *for arc* (1, 3), [5, 8] *for arc* (3, 4) *and other fuzzy arcs.*
p^6 with:

[5, 6] *for arc* (1, 2), [5, 8] *for arc* (1, 3), [5, 8] *for arc* (3, 4) *and other fuzzy arcs.*

TABLE 6.6
Arcs Information for Example 2

Arc (i, j)	Hesitant Fuzzy Cost $\{[l_{ij}^1, u_{ij}^1], [l_{ij}^2, u_{ij}^2]\}$
(1, 2)	$\{[4, 9], [5, 6]\}$
(1, 3)	$\{[5, 8], [2, 7]\}$
(2, 4)	$\{[3, 6]\}$
(2, 5)	$\{[4, 8]\}$
(3, 4)	$\{[3, 5], [5, 8]\}$
(3, 5)	$\{[6, 7]\}$
(4, 6)	$\{[4, 9]\}$
(5, 6)	$\{[4, 6]\}$

p^7 with:

$[5, 6]$ *for arc* $(1, 2)$, $[2, 7]$ *for arc* $(1, 3)$, $[4, 5]$ *for arc* $(3, 4)$ *and other fuzzy arcs.*
p^8 with:

$[5, 6]$ *for arc* $(1, 2)$, $[5, 8]$ *for arc* $(1, 3)$, $(4, 5)$ *for arc* $(3, 4)$ *and other fuzzy arcs.*

Results for solving of p^2 to p^8 by second approach are summarized in Table 6.7 as:
  Decision makers can provide an optimistic, pessimistic or close to the average cost of the interval from the results of solving the example using the interval ranking.
  Tables 6.8–6.14 shows paths analysis of p^1 to p^8 for example 2, as follows:

TABLE 6.7
Results of Solutions for Example 2 with Second Approach

p^r	Interval-valued fuzzy total cost	Optimal path
p^1	[12, 22]	$1 \rightarrow 3 \rightarrow 4 \rightarrow 6$
p^2	[9, 21]	$1 \rightarrow 3 \rightarrow 4 \rightarrow 6$
p^3	[12, 23]	$1 \rightarrow 2 \rightarrow 5 \rightarrow 6$
p^4	[12, 20]	$1 \rightarrow 3 \rightarrow 5 \rightarrow 6$
p^5	[12, 20]	$1 \rightarrow 3 \rightarrow 5 \rightarrow 6$
p^6	[13, 20]	$1 \rightarrow 2 \rightarrow 5 \rightarrow 6$
p^7	[12, 20]	$1 \rightarrow 3 \rightarrow 5 \rightarrow 6$
p^8	[13, 20]	$1 \rightarrow 2 \rightarrow 5 \rightarrow 6$

TABLE 6.8
Paths Analysis for p^2

Arc(i, j)	(1, 2)	(1, 3)	(2, 4)	(2, 5)	(3, 4)	(3, 5)	(4, 6)	(5, 6)
Fuzzy cost [l_{ij}, u_{ij}]	[4, 9]	[2, 7]	[3, 6]	[4, 8]	[3, 5]	[6, 7]	[4, 9]	[4, 6]
Parametric costs	$4 + 5.\lambda$	$2 + 5.\lambda$	$3 + 3.\lambda$	$4 + 4.\lambda$	$3 + 2.\lambda$	$6 + \lambda$	$4 + 5.\lambda$	$4 + 2.\lambda$

Paths analysis	paths	Parametric total costs	Select non-dominated paths	Analysis variations of λ
	$p1$: $1 \to 2 \to 4 \to 6$	$11 + 13.\lambda$	–	–
	$p2$: $1 \to 2 \to 5 \to 6$	$12 + 11.\lambda$	–	–
	$p3$: $1 \to 3 \to 4 \to 6$	$9 + 12.\lambda$	■	Optimal for: $\left[0, \frac{3}{4}\right]$
	$p4$: $1 \to 3 \to 5 \to 6$	$12 + 8.\lambda$	■	Optimal for: $\left[\frac{3}{4}, 1\right]$

TABLE 6.9
Paths Analysis for p^3

Arc (i, j)	(1, 2)	(1, 3)	(2, 4)	(2, 5)	(3, 4)	(3, 5)	(4, 6)	(5, 6)
Fuzzy cost $[l_{ij}, u_{ij}]$	[4, 9]	[5, 8]	[3, 6]	[4, 8]	[5, 8]	[6, 7]	[4, 9]	[4, 6]
Parametric costs	$4 + 5.\lambda$	$5 + 3.\lambda$	$3 + 3.\lambda$	$4 + 4.\lambda$	$5 + 3.\lambda$	$6 + \lambda$	$4 + 5.\lambda$	$4 + 2.\lambda$

Paths analysis	paths	Parametric total costs	Select non-dominated paths	Analysis variations of λ
	$p1: 1 \to 2 \to 4 \to 6$	$11 + 13.\lambda$	■	Optimal for: $\left[0, \frac{1}{2}\right]$
	$p2: 1 \to 2 \to 5 \to 6$	$12 + 11.\lambda$	■	Optimal for: $\left[\frac{1}{2}, \frac{3}{5}\right]$
	$p3: 1 \to 3 \to 4 \to 6$	$14 + 11.\lambda$	—	—
	$p4: 1 \to 3 \to 5 \to 6$	$15 + 6.\lambda$	■	Optimal for: $\left[\frac{3}{5}, 1\right]$

TABLE 6.10
Paths Analysis for p^4

Arc (i, j)	(1, 2)	(1, 3)	(2, 4)	(2, 5)	(3, 4)	(3, 5)	(4, 6)	(5, 6)
Fuzzy cost $[l_{ij},\ u_{ij}]$	[4, 9]	[2, 7]	[3, 6]	[4, 8]	[5, 8]	[6, 7]	[4, 9]	[4, 6]
Parametric costs	$4 + 5.\lambda$	$2 + 5.\lambda$	$3 + 3.\lambda$	$4 + 4.\lambda$	$5 + 3.\lambda$	$6 + \lambda$	$4 + 5.\lambda$	$4 + 2.\lambda$

Paths analysis	paths	Parametric total costs	Select non-dominated paths	Analysis variations of λ
	$p1: 1 \to 2 \to 4 \to 6$	$11 + 13.\lambda$	Equal with: $p3$	Optimal for: $\left[0,\ \frac{1}{5}\right]$
	$p2: 1 \to 2 \to 5 \to 6$	$12 + 11.\lambda$	–	
	$p3: 1 \to 3 \to 4 \to 6$	$11 + 13.\lambda$	Equal with: $p1$	Optimal for: $\left[0,\ \frac{1}{5}\right]$
	$p4: 1 \to 3 \to 5 \to 6$	$12 + 8.\lambda$	■	Optimal for: $\left[\frac{1}{5},\ 1\right]$

TABLE 6.11
Paths Analysis for p^5

Arc (i, j)	(1, 2)	(1, 3)	(2, 4)	(2, 5)	(3, 4)	(3, 5)	(4, 6)	(5, 6)
Fuzzy cost $[l_{ij}, u_{ij}]$	[5, 6]	[2, 7]	[3, 6]	[4, 8]	[5, 8]	[6, 7]	[4, 9]	[4, 6]
Parametric costs	$5 + 1.\lambda$	$2 + 5.\lambda$	$3 + 3.\lambda$	$4 + 4.\lambda$	$5 + 3.\lambda$	$6 + \lambda$	$4 + 5.\lambda$	$4 + 2.\lambda$

Paths analysis

paths	Parametric total costs	Select non-dominated paths	Analysis variations of λ
$p1$: $1 \to 2 \to 4 \to 6$	$12 + 9.\lambda$	–	–
$p2$: $1 \to 2 \to 5 \to 6$	$13 + 7.\lambda$	–	–
$p3$: $1 \to 3 \to 4 \to 6$	$11 + 13.\lambda$	∎	∎ Optimal for: $\left[0, \frac{1}{5}\right]$
$p4$: $1 \to 3 \to 5 \to 6$	$12 + 8.\lambda$	∎	Optimal for: $\left[\frac{1}{5}, 1\right]$

TABLE 6.12
Paths Analysis for p^6

Arc (i, j)	(1, 2)	(1, 3)	(2, 4)	(2, 5)	(3, 4)	(3, 5)	(4, 6)	(5, 6)
Fuzzy cost $[l_{ij}, u_{ij}]$	[5, 6]	[5, 8]	[3, 6]	[4, 8]	[5, 8]	[6, 7]	[4, 9]	[4, 6]
Parametric costs	$5 + \lambda$	$5 + 3.\lambda$	$3 + 3.\lambda$	$4 + 4.\lambda$	$5 + 3.\lambda$	$6 + \lambda$	$4 + 5.\lambda$	$4 + 2.\lambda$
Paths analysis	paths		Parametric total costs			Select non-dominated paths	Analysis variations of λ	
	$p1: 1 \to 2 \to 4 \to 6$		$12 + 9.\lambda$			■	Optimal for: $\left[0, \frac{1}{2}\right]$	
	$p2: 1 \to 2 \to 5 \to 6$		$13 + 7.\lambda$			■	Optimal for: $\left[\frac{1}{2}, 1\right]$	
	$p3: 1 \to 3 \to 4 \to 6$		$14 + 11.\lambda$			—	—	
	$p4: 1 \to 3 \to 5 \to 6$		$15 + 6.\lambda$			—	—	

TABLE 6.13
Paths Analysis for p^7

Arc (i, j)	(1, 2)	(1, 3)	(2, 4)	(2, 5)	(3, 4)	(3, 5)	(4, 6)	(5, 6)
Fuzzy cost $[l_{ij}, u_{ij}]$	[5, 6]	[2, 7]	[3, 6]	[4, 8]	[4, 5]	[6, 7]	[4, 9]	[4, 6]
Parametric costs	$5 + 1.\lambda$	$2 + 5.\lambda$	$3 + 3.\lambda$	$4 + 4.\lambda$	$4 + \lambda$	$6 + \lambda$	$4 + 5.\lambda$	$4 + 2.\lambda$
Paths analysis	paths		Parametric total costs			Select non-dominated paths		Analysis variations of λ
	$p1: 1 \rightarrow 2 \rightarrow 4 \rightarrow 6$		$12 + 9.\lambda$			–		–
	$p2: 1 \rightarrow 2 \rightarrow 5 \rightarrow 6$		$13 + 7.\lambda$			–		–
	$p3: 1 \rightarrow 3 \rightarrow 4 \rightarrow 6$		$11 + 10.\lambda$			■		Optimal for: $\left[0, \frac{2}{3}\right]$
	$p4: 1 \rightarrow 3 \rightarrow 5 \rightarrow 6$		$12 + 8.\lambda$			■		Optimal for: $\left[\frac{2}{3}, 1\right]$

TABLE 6.14
Paths Analysis for p^8

Arc (i, j)	(1, 2)	(1, 3)	(2, 4)	(2, 5)	(3, 4)	(3, 5)	(4, 6)	(5, 6)
Fuzzy cost $[l_{ij}, u_{ij}]$	[5, 6]	[5, 8]	[3, 6]	[4, 8]	[4, 5]	[6, 7]	[4, 9]	[4, 6]
Parametric costs	$5 + \lambda$	$5 + 3.\lambda$	$3 + 3.\lambda$	$4 + 4.\lambda$	$4 + 1.\lambda$	$6 + \lambda$	$4 + 5.\lambda$	$4 + 2.\lambda$

Paths analysis	paths	Parametric total costs	Select non-dominated paths	Analysis variations of λ
	$p1: 1 \to 2 \to 4 \to 6$	$12 + 9.\lambda$	■	Optimal for: $\left[0, \frac{1}{2}\right]$
	$p2: 1 \to 2 \to 5 \to 6$	$13 + 7.\lambda$	■	Optimal for: $\left[\frac{1}{2}, 1\right]$
	$p3: 1 \to 3 \to 4 \to 6$	$13 + 9.\lambda$	—	—
	$p4: 1 \to 3 \to 5 \to 6$	$15 + 6.\lambda$	—	—

6.5 CONCLUSION

The problem of the shortest path in the network is one of the attractive and practical problems in the field of graph theory. In this study, SP model develops to the hesitant fuzzy environment was presented two developed methods to find the shortest path in the network and the efficiency of its response to the model illustrated in an example using paths analysis. For future research in this field, the following may be of interest to researchers:

1. Development and more application of hesitant fuzzy sets for other issues related to networks.
2. Improving the speed and compute the complexity of the methods in a hesitant fuzzy environment.
3. Considering the multi-objective model for the network in a hesitant fuzzy environment.
4. Implementing the method in models with higher dimensions and especially solving them with combined, innovative and meta-innovative methods and comparing the answer with the developed methods presented in this research.

REFERENCES

Alefeld, G. & Herzberger, J. (2012). Introduction to interval computation. Academic Press, New York, 1983.

Abdel-Basset, M., Mohamed, M. & Chang, V. (2018). NMCDA: A framework for evaluating cloud computing services. Future Generation Computer Systems, 86, 12–29. https://doi.org/10.1016/j.future.2018.03.014

Bazaraa, M.S., Sherali, H.D. & Shetty, C.M. (2013). Nonlinear programming: theory and algorithms. John Wiley & Sons, New York.

Bellman, R.E. & Zadeh, L.A. (1970). Decision-making in a fuzzy environment. Management science, 17 (4), B-141. https://doi.org/10.1287/mnsc.17.4.B141

Broumi, S., Talea, M., Bakali, A. & Smarandache, F. (2016, December). Application of Dijkstra algorithm for solving interval valued neutrosophic shortest path problem. In 2016 IEEE symposium series on computational intelligence (SSCI), 1–6. https://doi.org/10.1109/SSCI.2016.7850151

Chuang, T.N. & Kung, J.Y. (2006). A new algorithm for the discrete fuzzy shortest path problem in a network. Applied Mathematics and Computation, 174 (1), 660–668.

Darehmiraki, M. (2020). A solution for the neutrosophic linear programming problem with a new ranking function. In Optimization Theory Based on Neutrosophic and Plithogenic Sets. Academic Press, 235–259, Elsevier.

Darehmiraki, M. (2019). A novel parametric ranking method for intuitionistic fuzzy numbers. Iranian Journal of Fuzzy Systems, 16 (1), 129–143. https://doi.org/10.22111/IJFS.2019.4489

Dempe, S. (2002). Foundations of bilevel programming. Springer Science & Business Media, Kluwer Academic, Dordrecht, The Netherlands.

Dey, A., Pal, A. & Pal, T. (2016). Interval type 2 fuzzy set in fuzzy shortest path problem. Mathematics, 4(4), p. 62. https://doi.org/10.3390/math4040062

Dubois, D.J. (1980). Fuzzy sets and systems: theory and applications (144). Academic press.

Keshavarz, E. & Khorram, E. (2009). A fuzzy shortest path with the highest reliability. Journal of Computational and Applied Mathematics, 230(1), pp.204–212. https://doi.org/10.1016/j.cam.2008.11.007

Klein, C.M. (1991). Fuzzy shortest paths. Fuzzy sets and systems, 39 (1), 27–41.

Lin, C.J. & Wen, U.P. (2004). A labeling algorithm for the fuzzy assignment problem. Fuzzy sets and systems, 142(3), pp. 373–391. https://doi.org/10.1016/S0165-0114(03)00017-4

Lin, L., Wu, C. & Ma, L. (2020). A genetic algorithm for the fuzzy shortest path problem in a fuzzy network. Complex & Intelligent Systems, 1–10. https://doi.org/10.1007/s40747-020-00195-8

Mahdavi, I., Nourifar, R., Heidarzade, A. & Amiri, N.M. (2009). A dynamic programming approach for finding shortest chains in a fuzzy network. Applied Soft Computing, 9(2), 503–511. https://doi.org/10.1016/j.asoc.2008.07.002

Mukherjee, S. (2015). Fuzzy programming technique for solving the shortest path problem on networks under triangular and trapezoidal fuzzy environment. International Journal of Mathematics in Operational Research, 7(5), pp.576–594. https://doi.org/10.1504/IJMOR.2015.071282

Sengupta, A. and Pal, T.K. (2006). Solving the shortest path problem with interval arcs. Fuzzy Optimization and Decision Making, 5(1), 71–89. https://doi.org/10.1007/s10700-005-4916-y

Torra, V. (2010). Hesitant fuzzy sets. International Journal of Intelligent Systems, 25 (6), 529–539. https://doi.org/10.1002/int.20418

Torra, V. & Narukawa, Y. (2009, August). On hesitant fuzzy sets and decision. In 2009 IEEE International Conference on Fuzzy Systems, 1378–1382. https://doi.org/10.1109/FUZZY.2009.5276884

Zedam, L., Jan, N., Rak, E., Mahmood, T. & Ullah, K. (2020). An Approach Towards Decision-Making and Shortest Path Problems Based on T-Spherical Fuzzy Information. https://doi.org/10.1007/s40815-020-00820-1.

7 Weather Forecast and Climate Prediction Using Soft Computing Methods

Morteza Pakdaman[1] *and Yashar Falamarzi*[2]

[1]Disasters and Climate Change Group, Climatological Research Institute (CRI), Atmospheric Science and Meteorological Research Center (ASMERC), Mashhad, Iran

[2]Climate Modelling and Prediction Group, Climatological Research Institute (CRI), Atmospheric Science and Meteorological Research Center (ASMERC), Mashhad, Iran

7.1 INTRODUCTION

Rapidly changing weather affects all aspects of our life. Agriculture, water resources, economy and transportation are example sectors that are very sensitive to climate and weather conditions. Thus, weather forecasts and climate predictions are required for future planning. Regarding this importance, several approaches have been developed. Nowadays, soft computing methods are also utilized successfully for weather forecast and climate prediction. For example, seasonal forecast of precipitation and temperature are made by using mathematical techniques as well as soft computing algorithms.

An important issue in the field of climatology and meteorology is the existence of uncertainty in the structure of the atmospheric phenomena. Although there are powerful dynamic systems and mathematical models for climate modeling, in all of these models, a very small change in the initial conditions can lead to different results in the final response of the system. Therefore, one of the important problems in meteorological models and also studies in this field is to pay attention to the existence of uncertainty. Therefore, the use of fuzzy logic in modeling atmospheric phenomena and dealing with issues in the field of climatology and meteorology, can be very useful. For example, fuzzy initial values (see Pakdaman et al. [2020]) or using fuzzy systems for prediction can be of interest. Another issue related to climatology is climate change (see Latif 2011). Due to the increase in the average temperature of the planet, there are many concerns about climate change. Scientists, on the other hand, consider different scenarios for predicting climate change, all of which are associated with uncertainty.

When studying climatic and meteorological models, the output of the models needs to be post-processed and studied. Usually, the output of meteorological and climatological models is big data. Obviously, analyzing this large amount of data is very difficult. This data is generated by models for different atmospheric levels at different times. Soft computing tools are a great tool for handling this huge amount of data.

In this chapter, some soft-computing methods and their usages in climatology will be discussed in detail. Section 7.2 is devoted to description of the applications of Artificial Neural Networks in climatology. Sections 7.3 and 7.4 describe the decision tree and support vector machines. Finally, Section 7.5 introduces the applications of fuzzy systems in climate prediction and climate forecast and Section 7.6 contains concluding remarks.

7.2 ARTIFICIAL NEURAL NETWORKS

This section contains two main sub-sections. First, we will introduce some important preliminaries of ANNs and then, some applications of ANNs in climate prediction and weather forecast will be introduced.

7.2.1 A CONCISE INTRODUCTION TO ANNs

Human brain looks like a complex, nonlinear and parallel computer. Attempts to copy human brain computing process have been performed a lot during the last decades. The most well-known type of these attempts is Artificial Neural Networks (ANNs). ANNs include a parallel network of connecting nods called neurons. Inter neuron connections which is called synapse link these neurons a to each other. Information related to the environment is stored in each synapse as its weight. Altering the weights using a learning algorithm constructs a learning process.

The unit of information and process of neural network is called neuron. Its structure is shown in Figure 7.1 and its mathematical form can be expressed as follows:

$$\vartheta = (\sum_{i=1}^{m} w_i x_i) - \theta = \overrightarrow{w} . \overrightarrow{x} - \theta = \tilde{w} . \tilde{x} \qquad (7.1)$$

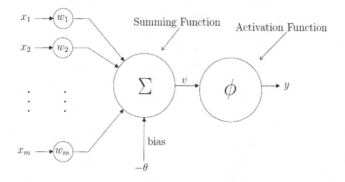

FIGURE 7.1   Typical scheme of a neuron.

where:

$$\tilde{w} = (-\theta, w_1, \ldots, w_m) \ and \ \tilde{x} = (1, x_1, \ldots, x_m) \tag{7.2}$$

and finally:

$$y = \phi(\vartheta) = \phi(\tilde{w}. \tilde{x}) \tag{7.3}$$

Activation function ($\phi(\vartheta)$) transfers the output of neurons to the main output. There are three popular different activation function types:

1. Threshold Function: This type of functions is based on McCulloch–Pitts model:

$$y = \phi(\vartheta) = \phi(\tilde{w}. \tilde{x}) \tag{7.4}$$

2. Piecewise Linear Function: This kind of activation functions takes one for the values above a specified threshold and zero for the values under it. The output follows a linear function for values between lower and upper threshold.

$$\phi(\vartheta) = \begin{cases} 1 & \vartheta \geq \frac{1}{2} \\ \vartheta & -\frac{1}{2} < \vartheta < \frac{1}{2} \\ 0 & \vartheta \leq -\frac{1}{2} \end{cases} \tag{7.5}$$

3. Sigmoid Function:

The most popular activation function in ANNs is the sigmoid function.

$$\phi(\vartheta) = \frac{1}{1 + e^{(-a\vartheta)}} \tag{7.6}$$

where: a is the slope parameter. When a limits to infinity, this function performs as a threshold function but it is continuously differentiable. For more details see (Bishop 2006).

ANNs can be divided into different groups in different ways. For example:

1. Single Layer Feed Forward
2. Multilayer Feed Forward
3. Recurrent

Multilayer feed forward networks contain one or more hidden layers. These hidden layers have neurons which perform only the computations. Each neuron in hidden

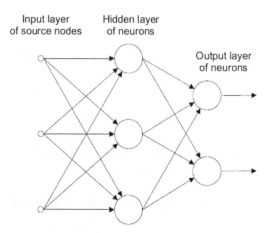

FIGURE 7.2 A typical structure of multi-layer feed forward neural network.

layers receives the outputs of the neurons in the previous layer. Figure 7.2 shows the structure of this network.

Recurrent network is similar to the multilayer feed forward network but it has at least a feed forward loop (Veitch 2005). In these loops the output can be fed back into its own input which is called self-fed back. In addition, the output can be fed back into one or more neurons in input or hidden layer. Figure 7.3 shows a simple structure of a recurrent network. For more details see (Hammer 2007).

As it was mentioned before, the synapse are the links between the neurons and each synapse has its own weight. These weights must be optimized utilizing a learning algorithm. These algorithms can be divided into two major groups namely supervised learning and unsupervised learning.

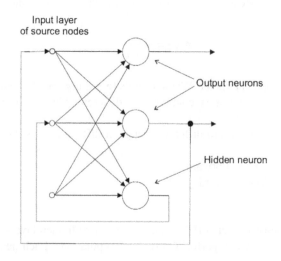

FIGURE 7.3 A typical structure of recurrent neural network.

The Perceptron is the simplest form of ANNs. It contains a single neuron and it is based on McCulloch–Pitts neuron theory. The activation function of this network is the threshold function and the outputs can be expressed as follows:

$$y = \phi(\overrightarrow{w} \cdot \overrightarrow{x}) \tag{7.7}$$

Where:

$$\begin{cases} \overrightarrow{w} = (-\theta, w_1, \ldots, w_m) \\ \overrightarrow{x} = (1, x_1, \ldots, x_m) \end{cases} \tag{7.8}$$

The perceptron divides a series of input data $x_1, x_2, \ldots, x_n$ into two different groups (A and B). For an example x_1 is in class A if the output of network for x_1 equals to 1 and x_1 belongs to group B if the output is 0. The Perceptron is only able to compute 14 Boolean logic functions out of 16. For more details about ANNs one may refer to (Haykin and Network 2004).

7.2.2 Applications of ANNs in Climatology

There are several publications indicating the applications of ANNs in climatology and meteorology. In most cases, the ability of ANN models in function approximation is used for weather forecast and climate prediction. Pakdaman et al. (2020) employed the ability of ANN for lightning prediction. They used the observation data for detecting lightning event based on binary classification algorithm. Pakdaman et al. (2020) used the MLP neural networks for monthly forecast of precipitation over Iran. The used the output of North American Multi-Model Ensemble data for monthly forecast of precipitation as inputs of ANN. Hussain et al. (2018) proposed a dynamic neural network architecture with immunology inspired optimization for weather data forecasting. They used the ability of recurrent neural networks and immune algorithm for forecasting of naturally occurring signals, including weather big data signals. Wang et al. (2020) combined the artificial bee colony algorithm and the backpropagation neural network to construct a precipitation prediction model. They collected the research data by 17 stations in the Wujiang River Basin from 1961 to 2018, and compiled into a time series of precipitation data. Ayzel et al. (2019) used deep all convolutional neural networks for radar-based precipitation nowcasting, which has a crucial role for early warning of hazardous events at small spatiotemporal scales. Hsu and Li (2010) proposed a data analysis method to cluster and explore spatio-temporal characteristics of the 22 years of precipitation data (1982–2003) for Taiwan. The wavelet transform self-organizing map framework combines the wavelet transform and a self-organizing map neural network. Nastos et al. (2014) used ANNs to forecast the maximum daily precipitation for the next coming year in Athens, Greece.

The use of ANNs is not limited just for prediction. For example, some authors used ANNs for downscaling and data assimilation. Downscaling is the procedure of

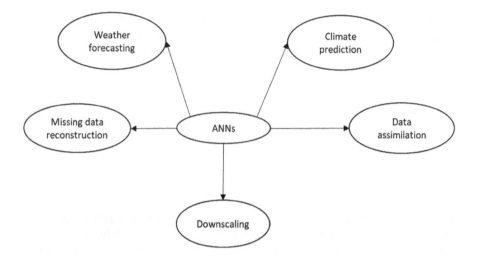

FIGURE 7.4   Some applications of ANNs in climatology and meteorology.

obtaining local-scale weather and climate information, particularly at the surface level, from regional-scale atmospheric variables that are provided by general circulation models. On the other hand, data assimilation is a procedure for providing reliable grid data for initial conditions from the observations. These reliable grid data for initial conditions are used for numerical weather prediction (for details see [Warner 2010] and [Coiffier 2011]). For example, Tomassetti et al. (2009) used a collection of one-year daily forecasts with the MM5 mesoscale model to investigate the possibility to downscale hourly precipitation fields from a horizontal grid spacing of 27 km to one at 3 km. They performed the downscaling using a multilayer Neural Network built with information of terrain, land use and predicted precipitation at the four adjacent grid points of the MM5 coarse grid. Wahle et al. (2015) proposed a novel approach of data assimilation based on ANN and applied to wave modeling in the German Bight. Their method takes advantage from the ability of NN's to emulate models and to invert them. They combined forward and inverse model ANN with the Levenberg–Marquardt learning algorithm to provide boundary values or wind fields in agreement with measured wave integrated parameters (See Figure 7.4).

However, ANNs usually are used for clustering and classification purposes in climatology, but there are also other applications of ANNs. Zhang and Li (2020) used deep learning for discover climate patterns and studied the climate change. Ishida et al. (2020) used a type of recurrent neural networks (long short-term memory) for a coastal sea level estimation at an hourly temporal scale.

7.3   DECISION TREE

As it is well-known, Decision Tree (DT) can be used for both classification and regression purposes. DT has a simple structure that can be used for discrimination and

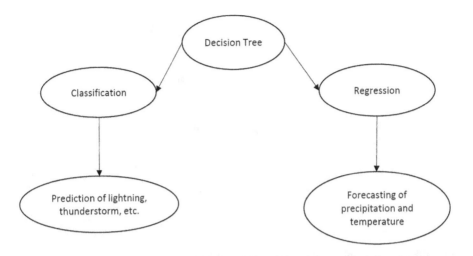

FIGURE 7.5   Some applications of DT in climatology and meteorology.

predictive modeling. Moreover, one may simply observe the graphical presentation of DT and interpret each node. For more details about DT see Myles et al. (2004).

Both classification and regression trees have important applications in climatology and meteorology (see Figure 7.5). Pakdaman et al. (2020) used DT for lightning prediction. They considered lightning event as a binary classification algorithm. They applied their model for a dataset in Iran. However, their data set for lightning event was class imbalance. Thus, they applied a bagging approach to overcome the imbalance dataset. Park et al. (2016) proposed an algorithm for detection of tropical cyclone genesis via quantitative satellite ocean surface wind pattern and intensity analyses using ensemble classification modeling by decision trees. Nourani and Molajou (2017) studied the hybrid application of two data mining techniques (decision tree and association rules) to discover affiliation between drought of Tabriz and Kermanshah synoptic stations (located in Iran).

7.4   SUPPORT VECTOR MACHINES

Similar to ANNs and DTs, Support Vector Machines (SVMs) are also a powerful tool for modeling and prediction in climatology and meteorology. In the theory of SVM, we look for an optimal separating hyperplane (as can be seen in Figure 7.6) for a given set of data. In order to attain the optimal hyperplane, we need to solve an optimization problem. From this point of view, SVM can be used for clustering. I what follows, we mention some important applications of SVM in climatology and meteorology.

Tian et al. (2018) analyzed the relation between soil moisture and drought and predicted agricultural drought in Xiangjiang River basin. They presented the agriculture droughts with the Precipitation-Evapotranspiration Index (SPEI) and used the Support Vector Regression (SVR) model incorporating climate indices to predict the agricultural droughts. Fan et al. (2018) proposed two machine learning algorithms, i.e. SVM and a novel simple tree-based ensemble method for accurate prediction of

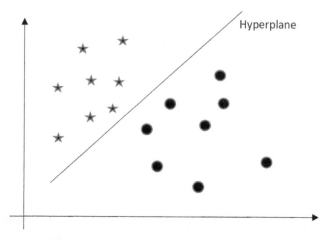

FIGURE 7.6 A simple example of separating hyperplane.

daily global solar radiation using limited meteorological data. Gizaw and Gan (2016) proposed a Regional Flood Frequency Analysis (RFFA) model based on SVR to estimate regional flood quantiles for two study areas, one with 26 catchments located in southeastern British Columbia (BC) and another with 23 catchments located in southern Ontario (ON), Canada. Belaid and Mellit (2016) studied an application of SVM for the prediction of daily and monthly global solar radiation on a horizontal surface in Ghardaïa (Algeria). The main advantage of their model is that the proposed SVM requires few simple parameters to get good accuracy.

In studies related to climatology and its applications we need information at fine spatial resolution. On the other hand, the outputs of general circulation models (GCMs), are on a coarse scale. Therefore, we need to downscale the outputs of GCM models. Tripathi et al. (2006) proposed an SVM approach for statistical downscaling of precipitation at a monthly time scale. Their SVM-based down-scaling model was applied to future climate predictions from the second generation Coupled Global Climate Model to obtain future projections of precipitation for the meteorological sub-divisions.

7.5 FUZZY SYSTEMS

In this section, first some preliminaries of fuzzy set theory will be provided and then, the applications of fuzzy set theory in climatology and meteorology will be introduced.

7.5.1 AN INTRODUCTION TO FUZZY SET THEORY

The concept of fuzzy logic was first introduced by Zadeh (1965). After Prof. Zadeh's paper (Zadeh 1965), extensive research works have been conducted on the development and application of fuzzy set theory in other science verticals. Many concepts of science and engineering were even redefined with the help of fuzzy logic. In the meantime, especially the various branches of mathematical science were developed with the help of fuzzy logic (for example, see Effati and Pakdaman (2010), Hadi Sadoghi Yazdi (2008), Pakdaman and Effati (2016a), Pakdaman and Effati (2016b) and Effati et al. [2011]).

Indeed, fuzzy logic is a many-valued logic, which the truth values of propositions can be any real number between 0 and 1. In probability, we have distribution functions while in fuzzy set theory, to show the degree of the membership of an element to a fuzzy set, we have a membership function. Suppose that $\tilde{S}$ is a fuzzy set. We indicate by $\mu_{\tilde{S}}(x)$ the degree of membership of x to the fuzzy set $\tilde{S}$. In this case, $\mu_{\tilde{S}}(x)$ is such that $0 \leq \mu_{\tilde{S}}(x) \leq 1$. There are several types of fuzzy sets and fuzzy numbers. Triangular and trapezoidal fuzzy numbers are the most widely used fuzzy numbers. For example, suppose that $\tilde{C}$., $\tilde{W}$ and $\tilde{H}$ indicate the fuzzy sets cold, warm and hot weather respectively. If we use trapezoidal fuzzy numbers for these three fuzzy sets, then we will have the membership functions as depicted in Figure 7.7.

The choice of the type of fuzzy number that is triangular or trapezoidal or other type depends on the type of application that is considered. Fuzzy numbs also can be presented by their $\alpha-$ cuts. For example, the $\alpha-$ cut representation of fuzzy set warm weather (as depicted in Figure 7.7) is as follows:

$$[\widehat{\tilde{W}}]^{\alpha} = [15 + 5\alpha, \quad 35 - 5\alpha], \quad 0 \leq \alpha \leq 1 \qquad (7.9)$$

As it can be determined from (9), the interval $[15, \quad 35]$ is the support (for $\alpha = 0$) of the fuzzy number $\tilde{W}$, the fuzzy set warm weather. Any temperature in $[20, 30]$ has membership value 1 to the fuzzy set $\tilde{W}$. Similarly, the $\alpha-$ cut representations of the other fuzzy sets can be determined. Generally, the $\alpha-$ cut representation of a fuzzy trapezoidal number $\tilde{T} = [a, b, c, d]$ (as depicted in Figure 7.8) can be obtained as follows:

$$[\widehat{\tilde{T}}]^{\alpha} = [a + (b - a)\alpha, d - (d - c)\alpha], \quad 0 \leq \alpha \leq 1 \qquad (7.10)$$

Also, the membership function of the trapezoidal fuzzy number $\tilde{T}$ is as follows:

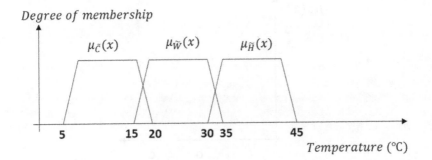

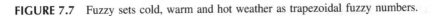

FIGURE 7.7 Fuzzy sets cold, warm and hot weather as trapezoidal fuzzy numbers.

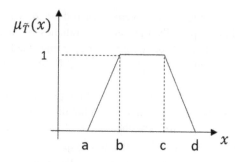

FIGURE 7.8 Trapezoidal fuzzy number $\tilde{T} = [a, b, c, d]$.

$$\mu_{\tilde{T}}(x) = \begin{cases} \frac{x-a}{b-a} & a \leq x \leq b \\ 1 & b \leq x \leq c \\ \frac{d-x}{d-c} & c \leq x \leq d \end{cases} \qquad (7.11)$$

Similarly, we can define the membership function and $\alpha-$ cut of the fuzzy triangular number $\tilde{R} = [a, b, c]$ as depicted in Figure 7.9.

The $\alpha-$ cut representation of the fuzzy triangular number $\tilde{R} = [a, b, c]$ is as follows:

$$[\tilde{R}]^{\alpha} = [a + (b-a)\alpha, \ c - (c-b)\alpha], \quad 0 \leq \alpha \leq 1 \qquad (7.12)$$

Finally, the membership function of $\tilde{R}$ is as follows:

$$\mu_{\tilde{R}}(x) = \begin{cases} \frac{x-a}{b-a} & a \leq x \leq b \\ \frac{c-x}{c-b} & b \leq x \leq c \end{cases} \qquad (7.13)$$

For more details about fuzzy set theory, see Pakdaman and Effati (2016b) and Hanss (2005).

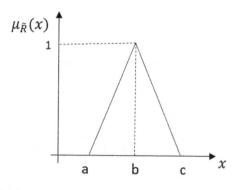

FIGURE 7.9 Triangular fuzzy number $\tilde{R} = [a, b, c]$.

7.5.2 APPLICATIONS OF FUZZY LOGIC IN CLIMATOLOGY AND METEOROLOGY

As it was mentioned in the introduction, in climatology and meteorology, we have intrinsic uncertainty in atmospheric phenomena. There are several tools for modeling uncertainty. Fuzzy logic is a powerful and natural tool for modeling uncertainty in climatology. In what follows, some important applications of fuzzy sets will be mentioned.

Pongracz et al. (2001) modeled monthly precipitation in Hungary using the Hess–Brezowsky atmospheric circulation pattern types and an ENSO index as forcing functions or inputs. In order to utilize the existing relationship between forcing functions and precipitation, they employed fuzzy rule base systems. Maskey et al. (2004) used fuzzy set theory for propagating the precipitation uncertainty through a deterministic rainfall-runoff-routing model for flood forecasting. Satyanarayana and Srinivas (2011) used a fuzzy clustering approach for regionalization of precipitation in data-sparse areas using large-scale atmospheric variables. They used large-scale atmospheric variables, location attributes and seasonality of rainfall to delineate regions. Cai et al. (2019) proposed an approach for control forecasts of four global weather centers were selected and assessed against the measured data using several verification metrics during the flood season (May–September) over the Shihe River catchment in the Huaihe River basin of China. To describe the uncertainty of precipitation forecasts for the safety of flood control, they proposed a new model using fuzzy probability and Bayesian theory on the basis of the generalized probability density function. Silver et al. (2020) proposed a fuzzy logic approach for improving weather radar precipitation maps.

7.6 CONCLUSIONS

In this chapter, the applications of soft computing in modeling and solving problems in the field of climatology and meteorology were explained. As can be seen in Figure 7.10, the important features of problems in this area are modeling, the complexity of atmospheric phenomena, uncertainty and the existence of big data. Soft computing is a great tool for dealing with these features.

The mentioned soft computing tools, such as neural networks, fuzzy systems and other soft computing tools are not only used in climatology and meteorology alone, but also their combination with each other has wide applications. For example, Bukhari et al. (2020) proposed a Neuro-fuzzy modeling approach for the prediction of summer precipitation with application to different meteorological stations. Indeed, they combined the ability of ANNs in approximation and the ability of fuzzy systems in modeling the uncertainty. Partal and Kişi (2007) studied a new conjunction method based on wavelet-neuro-fuzzy (discrete wavelet transform and neuro-fuzzy) approach for precipitation forecast. Chang et al. (2005) proposed a modified method, combining the inverse distance method and fuzzy theory, to precipitation interpolation. To determine the parameters of fuzzy membership functions, which represent the relationship between the location without rainfall records and its surrounding rainfall gauges, they used a genetic algorithm for the optimization step.

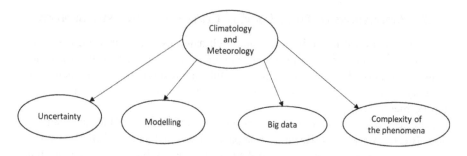

FIGURE 7.10 Some important aspects in climatology and meteorology.

Although there is a great deal of research in this scientific field, there is still room for further research and studies to apply soft computing methods in climatology and meteorology.

REFERENCES

Ayzel, G., Heistermann, M., Sorokin, A., Nikitin, O., & Lukyanova, O. (2019). All convolutional neural networks for radar-based precipitation nowcasting. *Procedia Computer Science*, 150, 186–192. https://doi.org/10.1016/j.procs.2019.02.036

Belaid, S., & Mellit, A. (2016). Prediction of daily and mean monthly global solar radiation using support vector machine in an arid climate. *Energy Conversion and Management*, 118, 105–118. https://doi.org/10.1016/j.enconman.2016.03.082

Bishop, C. M. (2006). *Pattern recognition and machine learning*. Springer.

Bukhari, A.H., Sulaiman, M., Islam, S., Shoaib, M., Kumam, P., & Zahoor Raja, M.A. (2020). Neuro-fuzzy modeling and prediction of summer precipitation with application to different meteorological stations. *Alexandria Engineering Journal*, 59(1), 101–116. https://doi.org/10.1016/j.aej.2019.12.011

Cai, C., Wang, J., & Li, Z. (2019). Assessment and modelling of uncertainty in precipitation forecasts from TIGGE using fuzzy probability and Bayesian theory. *Journal of Hydrology*, 577, 123995. https://doi.org/10.1016/j.jhydrol.2019.123995

Chang, C.L., Lo, S.L., & Yu, S.L. (2005). Applying fuzzy theory and genetic algorithm to interpolate precipitation. *Journal of Hydrology*, 314(1–4), 92–104. https://doi.org/10.1016/j.jhydrol.2005.03.034

Coiffier, J. 2011. *Fundamentals of numerical weather prediction*. Cambridge University Press.

Effati, S., Pakdaman, M., & Ranjbar, M. (2011). A new fuzzy neural network model for solving fuzzy linear programming problems and its applications. *Neural Computing and Applications*, 20(8). https://doi.org/10.1007/s00521-010-0491-4

Effati, Sohrab, & Pakdaman, M. (2010). Artificial neural network approach for solving fuzzy differential equations. *Information Sciences*, 180(8), 1434–1457.

Fan, J., Wang, X., Wu, L., Zhou, H., Zhang, F., Yu, X., Lu, X., & Xiang, Y. (2018). Comparison of Support Vector Machine and Extreme Gradient Boosting for predicting daily global solar radiation using temperature and precipitation in humid subtropical climates: A case study in China. *Energy Conversion and Management*, 164, 102–111. https://doi.org/10.1016/j.enconman.2018.02.087

Gizaw, M.S., & Gan, T.Y. (2016). Regional Flood Frequency Analysis using Support Vector Regression under historical and future climate. *Journal of Hydrology*, 538, 387–398. https://doi.org/10.1016/j.jhydrol.2016.04.041

Hadi Sadoghi Yazdi, M.P. and S.E. (2008). Fuzzy circuit analysis. *International Journal of Applied Engineering Research*, 3(8), 1061–1071.

Hammer, B. (2007). *Learning with recurrent neural networks* (Vol. 254). Springer.

Hanss, M. (2005). *Applied fuzzy arithmetic*. Springer.

Haykin, S., & Network, N. (2004). A comprehensive foundation. *Neural Networks*, 2(2004), 41.

Hsu, K.C., & Li, S.T. (2010). Clustering spatial-temporal precipitation data using wavelet transform and self-organizing map neural network. *Advances in Water Resources*, 33(2), 190–200. https://doi.org/10.1016/j.advwatres.2009.11.005

Hussain, A.J., Liatsis, P., Khalaf, M., Tawfik, H., & Al-Asker, H. (2018). A dynamic neural network architecture with immunology inspired optimization for weather data forecasting. *Big Data Research*, 14, 81–92. https://doi.org/10.1016/j.bdr.2018.04.002

Ishida, K., Tsujimoto, G., Ercan, A., Tu, T., Kiyama, M., & Amagasaki, M. (2020). Hourly-scale coastal sea level modeling in a changing climate using long short-term memory neural network. *Science of the Total Environment*, 720, 137613. https://doi.org/10.101 6/j.scitotenv.2020.137613

Latif, M. (2011). Uncertainty in climate change projections. *Journal of Geochemical Exploration*, 110(1), 1–7. https://doi.org/10.1016/j.gexplo.2010.09.011

Maskey, S., Guinot, V., & Price, R.K. (2004). Treatment of precipitation uncertainty in rainfall-runoff modelling: a fuzzy set approach. *Advances in Water Resources*, 27(9), 889–898. https://doi.org/10.1016/j.advwatres.2004.07.001

Myles, A.J., Feudale, R.N., Liu, Y., Woody, N.A., & Brown, S.D. (2004). An introduction to decision tree modeling. *Journal of Chemometrics*, 18(6), 275–285. https://doi.org/10.1 002/cem.873

Nastos, P.T., Paliatsos, A.G., Koukouletsos, K.V., Larissi, I.K., & Moustris, K.P. (2014). Artificial neural networks modeling for forecasting the maximum daily total precipitation at Athens, Greece. *Atmospheric Research*, 144, 141–150. https://doi.org/10.1 016/j.atmosres.2013.11.013

Nourani, V., & Molajou, A. (2017). Application of a hybrid association rules/decision tree model for drought monitoring. *Global and Planetary Change*, 159, 37–45. https:// doi.org/10.1016/j.gloplacha.2017.10.008

Nourani, V., Razzaghzadeh, Z., Baghanam, A.H., & Molajou, A. (2019). ANN-based statistical downscaling of climatic parameters using decision tree predictor screening method. *Theoretical and Applied Climatology*, 137(3–4), 1729–1746. https://doi.org/1 0.1007/s00704-018-2686-z

Pakdaman, M., & Effati, S. (2016a). Fuzzy Projection over a Crisp Set and Applications. *International Journal of Fuzzy Systems*, 18(2), 312–319. https://doi.org/10.1007/s4 0815-015-0125-1

Pakdaman, M., & Effati, S. (2016b). On fuzzy linear projection equation and applications. *Fuzzy Optimization and Decision Making*, 15(2). https://doi.org/10.1007/s10700-015-9222-8

Pakdaman, M., Falamarzi, Y., Sadoghi Yazdi, H., Ahmadian, A., Salahshour, S., & Ferrara, F. (2020). A kernel least mean square algorithm for fuzzy differential equations and its application in earth's energy balance model and climate. *Alexandria Engineering Journal*, 59(4), 2803–2810. https://doi.org/10.1016/j.aej.2020.06.016

Pakdaman, Morteza, Falamarzi, Y., Babaeian, I., & Javanshiri, Z. (2020). Post-processing of the North American multi-model ensemble for monthly forecast of precipitation based on neural network models. *Theoretical and Applied Climatology*, 141(1–2), 405–417. https://doi.org/10.1007/s00704-020-03211-6

Pakdaman, Morteza, Naghab, S.S., Khazanedari, L., Malbousi, S., & Falamarzi, Y. (2020). Lightning prediction using an ensemble learning approach for northeast of Iran. *Journal of Atmospheric and Solar-Terrestrial Physics*, 209, 105417. https://doi.org/1 0.1016/j.jastp.2020.105417

Park, M.S., Kim, M., Lee, M. I., Im, J., & Park, S. (2016). Detection of tropical cyclone genesis via quantitative satellite ocean surface wind pattern and intensity analyses using decision trees. *Remote Sensing of Environment*, 183, 205–214. https://doi.org/1 0.1016/j.rse.2016.06.006

Partal, T., & Kişi, O. (2007). Wavelet and neuro-fuzzy conjunction model for precipitation forecasting. *Journal of Hydrology*, 342(1–2), 199–212. https://doi.org/10.1016/ j.jhydrol.2007.05.026

Pongracz, R., Bartholy, J., & Bogardi, I. (2001). Fuzzy rule-based prediction of monthly precipitation. *Physics and Chemistry of the Earth, Part B: Hydrology, Oceans and Atmosphere*, 26(9), 663–667. https://doi.org/10.1016/S1464-1909(01)00066-1

Satyanarayana, P., & Srinivas, V.V. (2011). Regionalization of precipitation in data sparse areas using large scale atmospheric variables - A fuzzy clustering approach. *Journal of Hydrology*, 405(3–4), 462–473. https://doi.org/10.1016/j.jhydrol.2011.05.044

Silver, M., Svoray, T., Karnieli, A., & Fredj, E. (2020). Improving weather radar precipitation maps: A fuzzy logic approach. *Atmospheric Research*, 234, 104710. https:// doi.org/10.1016/j.atmosres.2019.104710

Tian, Y., Xu, Y.P., & Wang, G. (2018). Agricultural drought prediction using climate indices based on Support Vector Regression in Xiangjiang River basin. *Science of the Total Environment*, 622–623, 710–720. https://doi.org/10.1016/j.scitotenv.2017.12.025

Tomassetti, B., Verdecchia, M., & Giorgi, F. (2009). NN5: A neural network based approach for the downscaling of precipitation fields - Model description and preliminary results. *Journal of Hydrology*, 367(1–2), 14–26. https://doi.org/10.1016/j.jhydrol.2008.12.017

Tripathi, S., Srinivas, V.V., & Nanjundiah, R.S. (2006). Downscaling of precipitation for climate change scenarios: A support vector machine approach. *Journal of Hydrology*, 330(3–4), 621–640. https://doi.org/10.1016/j.jhydrol.2006.04.030

Veitch, D. (2005). *Wavelet Neural Networks and their application in the study of dynamical systems* (Issue August). University of York.

Wahle, K., Staneva, J., & Guenther, H. (2015). Data assimilation of ocean wind waves using Neural Networks: A case study for the German Bight. *Ocean Modelling*, 96, 117–125. https://doi.org/10.1016/j.ocemod.2015.07.007

Wang, Y., Liu, J., Li, R., Suo, X., & Lu, E. (2020). Precipitation forecast of the Wujiang River Basin based on artificial bee colony algorithm and backpropagation neural network. *Alexandria Engineering Journal*, 59(3), 1473–1483. https://doi.org/10.1016/ j.aej.2020.04.035

Warner, T.T. (2010). *Numerical weather and climate prediction*. Cambridge University Press.

Zadeh, L.A. (1965). Fuzzy sets. *Information and Control*, 8(3), 338–353.

Zhang, Z., & Li, J. (2020). Deep learning for climate patterns. In *Big data mining for climate change* (pp. 53–99). Elsevier. https://doi.org/10.1016/b978-0-12-818703-6.00008-8

8 Color Descriptor for Mobile Augmented Reality

Siok Yee Tan[1] and Haslina Arshad[2]
[1]Fakulti Teknologi dan Sains Maklumat, Universiti
Kebangsaan Malaysia, 43600 Bangi, Selangor, Malaysia
[2]Institute of IR 4.0, Universiti Kebangsaan Malaysia, 43600
Bangi, Selangor, Malaysia

8.1 INTRODUCTION

Mobile devices such as smartphones have been identified as one of the most potential and powerful tools for AR (Flavián et al. 2019). Smartphones nowadays can facilitate data access and processing with a large amount of computing power (Sung et al. 2016). Smartphones provide a different market in AR applications compared to the powerful personal computer. Most of the smartphone nowadays equipped with a built-in camera which is capable to run computer vision process such as AR application. To achieve optimum performance of mobile AR applications, the selection of tracking algorithms needs to be addressed carefully as smartphones have limited processing power and memory compared to personal computers. AR application requires tracking techniques to track the user's or device's position to register it with respect to the real world (Tan et al. 2019). The tracking algorithm must able to run efficiently in AR applications. Furthermore, the tracking algorithm must be robust in terms of scale changes, rotation changes, and lighting. Hence, the selection of a tracking algorithm is important to produce an AR application with optimum performance. The input image captured using a smartphone's camera and the reference image stored in the database will be converted into a grayscale image before the tracking process begin. The tracking process in the AR application can be divided into four main steps (Obeidy et al. 2013). The first step in the tracking process in the AR application is to detect the feature in the grayscale input image (camera image) and grayscale reference image (database image) using a detector algorithm. The second step is to describe the important features (keypoints) detected from the input image and the reference image. There are two categories of descriptors; binary descriptors and floating-point descriptors. SIFT and SURF are examples of floating-point descriptors while BRIEF, ORB, BRISK, and FREAK are examples of binary descriptors (Alahi et al. 2012; Bay et al. 2008; Calonder et al. 2012; Leutenegger et al. 2011; Lowe 2004; Rublee et al. 2011). The keypoints describes from the reference image using the feature descriptor will be stored in the database in advance. The keypoints describes from the input image will then matched with the keypoints stored in the database. If the matching accuracy is above a threshold, the pose estimation process will be carried out else it will start the detection process again. Pose estimation is to determine the position of a virtual object that will be superimposed on top of the input image. A 3D virtual object will be successfully augmented on top of the input image in the correct orientation in real-time once the tracking process is completed. AR researchers in recent years have been working hard to develop an efficient and robust AR application in both platforms; desktop and mobile. The terms efficiency and robustness are the general performance measures of tracking in AR application. Efficiency is generally defined as the ability to detect, extract, and match the corresponding keypoints between a reference image and input image in the shortest time. This term is often interchanged with words such as "fast". Robustness is defined as accurate matching the corresponding keypoints between a reference image and input image in the presence of large changes in rotation, scale, and lighting. This term usually interchanged with words such as "accuracy" (Tan et al. 2019).

Based on the tracking process, all the tracking algorithms such as the detector, descriptor, and matcher used in mobile augmented reality (MAR) applications will directly affect the performance of the application. Feature descriptors had been always the most popular component in research. The feature descriptor used in a MAR application will directly affect the efficiency and robustness of the application. Hence, this research is focused on the feature descriptor algorithm. A feature descriptor should able to perform tasks with high speed and robust to lighting, rotation, and scale changes. Fast Retina Keypoint (FREAK) has been proposed as the most appropriate descriptor for MAR application in the previous research due to FREAK able to act in a faster time compared to BRISK, BRIEF, and ORB. FREAK also achieved good accuracy in lighting, rotation, and scale-invariance (Tan et al. 2019). The robustness of MAR application towards various changes is still an important issue and high attention should be given. All the descriptors such as SIFT, SURF, BRIEF, ORB, BRISK, and even FREAK had ignored color space information and only able to extract features in the grayscale image (Alahi et al. 2012; Bay et al. 2008; Calonder et al. 2012; Leutenegger et al. 2011; Lowe 2004; Rublee et al. 2011). Color information such as RGB may provide important information or features in the description. Therefore, this study will propose an RGB color FREAK descriptor.

8.2 RGB FREAK DESCRIPTOR FRAMEWORK

The proposed framework for developing the RGB-FREAK 512-bits descriptor is shown in Figure 1. RGB FREAK is a combination of FREAK descriptors and RGB color space. The reference image and the input image are converted to RGB color space. The reference image and the input image must also be separated into three layers; red, green and blue. Thus, three images were created and the researcher named it IR, IG and IB in offline tracking and IIR, IIG and IIB in online tracking as shown in Figure 8.1.

The BRISK detector used to detect IR, IG, IB and generates red keypoints, green keypoints and blue keypoints. Thus, the three main types of keypoints; red, green, blue, tones, saturation, and values are generated and named as TR, TG and TB. All

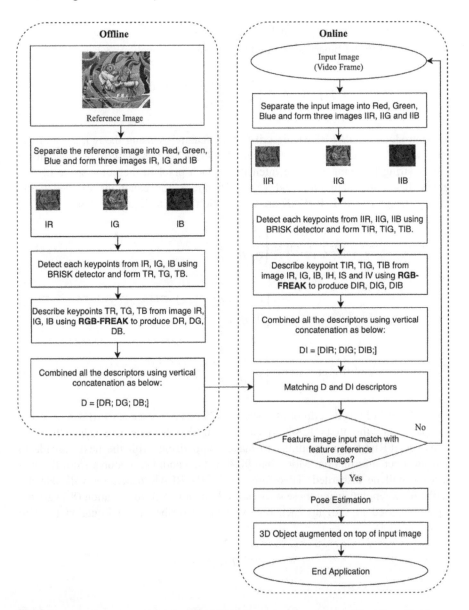

FIGURE 8.1   The proposed RGB-FREAK descriptor framework in mobile AR applications.

TR, TG and TB keypoints are stored in "RedtempDetector", "BluetempDetector" and "GreentemptDetector".

The next step is to describe each TR, TG and TB keypoints using the RGB-FREAK descriptor. FREAK generates a binary string by comparing the intensity of each pixel in a sampling pair. The binary string represents the area around the keypoint and find each sampling pair (p_x, p_y). When comparing the pairs of pixels, if the intensity at the point p_x is smaller than the intensity at the point p_y, then a binary value 1 is set in the binary string and 0 otherwise as Equation (8.1).

$$T(p; x, y): = \begin{cases} 1 & if \ I(p, x) < I(p, y) \\ 0 & if \ no \end{cases} \tag{8.1}$$

The introduced RGB-FREAK describes each feature by using the red, green, blue, hue, saturation and value color space. The RGB-FREAK descriptor generates a binary string by comparing the intensity of each pixel in the color space of red, green, blue, hue, saturation and value. Therefore, the equations for generating binary strings for RGB-FREAK are as Equation (8.2) to Equation (8.4):

$$T(p_{red}; x, y): = \begin{cases} 1 & if \ I(p_{red}, x) < I(p_{red}, y) \\ 0 & if \ no \end{cases} \tag{8.2}$$

$$T(p_{green}; x, y): = \begin{cases} 1 & if \ I(p_{green}, x) < I(p_{green}, y) \\ 0 & if \ no \end{cases} \tag{8.3}$$

$$T(p_{blue}; x, y): = \begin{cases} 1 & if \ I(p_{blue}, x) < I(p_{blue}, y) \\ 0 & if \ no \end{cases} \tag{8.4}$$

FREAK is a 512 bits descriptor (4 cascade - 128 bits per cascade). FREAK is first to compare only the first (128-bits) cascade. If the distance is smaller than the threshold, FREAK will continue to make comparisons with the next cascade to analyze finer information. More than 90% of the candidate features from the first cascade will be discarded. Therefore, the RGB-FREAK descriptor will also describe the keypoints using these 4 cascades. Equation (8.5) to Equation (8.7) are the equations used to sum up each binary string described from Equation (8.2) to Equation (8.4).

$$\sum_{1 \le i \le 512} 2^{i-1} T(p_{red}; x_i, y_i) \tag{8.5}$$

$$\sum_{1 \le i \le 512} 2^{i-1} T(p_{green}; x_i, y_i) \tag{8.6}$$

$$\sum_{1 \le i \le 512} 2^{i-1} T(p_{blue}; x_i, y_i) \tag{8.7}$$

After RGB-FREAK describes each TR, TG and TB keypoints, the descriptors for each color space were created and named as DR, DG and DB. All of these DR, DG and DB descriptors were combined using vertical concatenation technique and generated only one descriptor. Vertical concatenation technique is a technique to vertically combined all the keypoints. For instance, the 512-bits DR, DG and DB descriptors have 20 keypoints. These keypoints will be merged into a 60 keypoints descriptor but the descriptor size is still 512-bits because the keypoints are combined vertically.

Using this vertical concatenation technique can help to merge the existing descriptors and not increase the size of the descriptor. Steps for detecting and describing are repeated in the online tracking process to generate keypoints and descriptors. The TIR, TIG and TIB keypoints were generated after detecting the features from the input images of IIR, IIG and IIB. RGB-FREAK descriptor describes TIR, TIG and TIB to generate DIR, DIG and DIB. The DIR, DIG and DIB descriptors are combined using vertical concatenation techniques and generate DI descriptors. The DI descriptor of the input image is matched with the D descriptor of the reference image. The process tracking is repeated if the matching percentage between the DI descriptor and D descriptor is less than a threshold. Else the process of pose estimation and augmentation process will take place if the matching percentage is more than a threshold. An AR application process is considered successful when a 3D object is augmented on top of the input image.

8.3   ALOI DATASET

ALOI dataset is a color image collection of 1,000 small objects (Geusebroek et al. 2005). ALOI dataset systematically varied illumination color, illumination angle, viewing angle and captured wide-based line stereo images to collect sensory variation in object recording. They had recorded over 100 images of each object (1000 objects) and yielding a total of 110,250 images for this ALOI data collection. This research is focused on the illumination invariance of the feature descriptor. Thus, the dataset that will be used is only with varied illumination color and illumination angles.

Small objects with different illumination directions are varied in 24 configurations as shown in Figure 8.2. Each object was recorded with only one out five lights turned on to produce five different illumination angles (conditions l1–l5). The illumination bow is virtually turned by 15 degrees for camera 2 and 30 degrees for camera 3 by switching the camera and turning the stage towards that camera (cameras c2 and c3). Thus, the aspect of the small objects viewed by each camera is identical, but the light direction has shifted by 15 degrees and 30 degrees in azimuth and results in 15 different illumination angles. A combination of turning on the lights was used to illuminate the small object too. Turning on two lights (light 1 and light 2) at the sides of the object produced an oblique illumination from the right (condition l6). While turning on two lights (light 4 and light 5) at another side of the object produced an oblique illumination from left (condition l7). Turning on all lights yields a sort of hemispherical illumination (condition l8). After all the process of switching the camera and turning on a different light, a total of 24 different illumination conditions were generated (c1, c2, c3 and l1, l2, l3, l4, l5, l6, l7, l8).

Small objects with different illumination colors are varied in 12 configurations as shown in Figure 8.3. Each object was recorded with all five lights turned on. Illumination color temperature is changed from 2175K to 3075K. Each small object was illuminated under a reddish to white illumination color because the camera was white balanced at 3075K (condition i110 - i250)

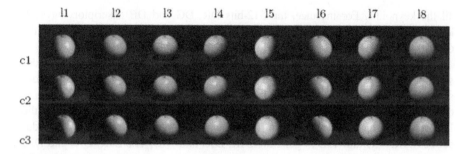

FIGURE 8.2 Object orange with different illumination direction is varied in 24 configurations.

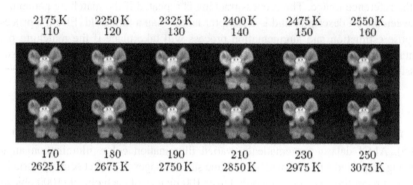

FIGURE 8.3 Object mouse with different illumination color is varied in 12 configurations.

8.4 TRACKING ACCURACY

The robustness of the proposed feature descriptors is evaluated using this ALOI dataset with the two different illumination changes; illumination direction and illumination color. The tracking accuracy of the feature descriptors is measured as Equation (8.8).

$$Accuracy\,(\%) = \frac{No.\ \ of\ \ Correct\ \ Matches\ (n)}{No.\ \ of\ \ Features\ \ Extracted\ (N)} x100\% \qquad (8.8)$$

The computation times were recorded in milliseconds for every 500 features extracted. Let t_s denote as the starting time, t_e denote the ending time, and t_f denote the final computation time. If $x\,(a,\,b)$ is the extracted function of the total number of features, then the computation time for $x\,(a,\,b)$ is defined by Equation (8.9).

$$x\ (a,\,b) \rightarrow t_f(t_e - t_s) \qquad (8.9)$$

The tracking accuracy for FREAK, RGB-FREAK, R-FREAK, G-FREAK and B-FREAK under light color changes and different lighting arrangements are shown in Figure 8.4 and Figure 8.5 respectively. The results are taking from the average of the accuracy values get from 1,000 images from ALOI dataset.

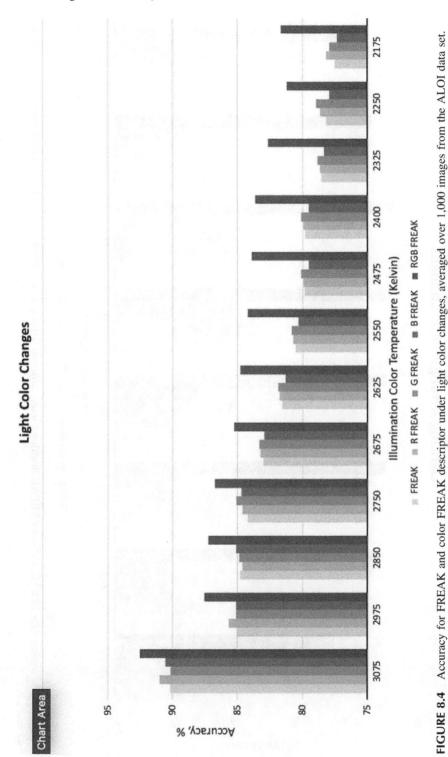

FIGURE 8.4 Accuracy for FREAK and color FREAK descriptor under light color changes, averaged over 1,000 images from the ALOI data set.

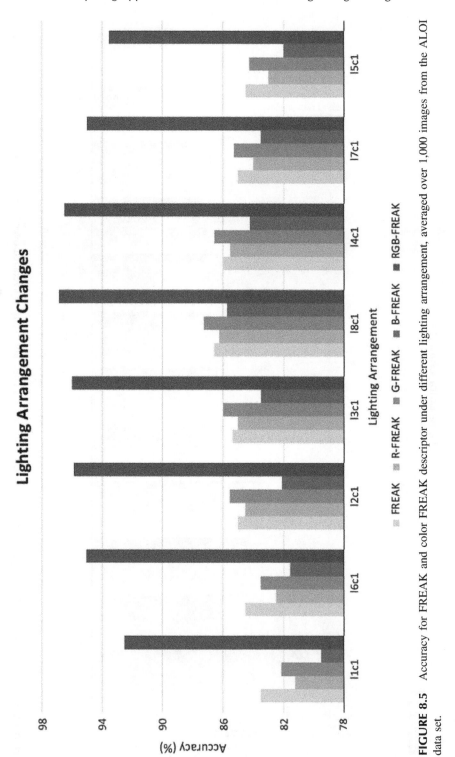

FIGURE 8.5 Accuracy for FREAK and color FREAK descriptor under different lighting arrangement, averaged over 1,000 images from the ALOI data set.

By observing the results with respect to light color changes, the combined RGB-FREAK descriptor has the highest invariance to this property. RGB-FREAK achieve 92.76% of tracking accuracy followed by G-FREAK (83.47%), FREAK (82.29%), R-FREAK (81.66%) and B-FREAK (80.69%). There is a clear distinction in performance between RGB-FREAK and FREAK due to the use of RGB color extension.

From the results shown in Figure 5, it can be seen that the RGB-FREAK still remains invariant and robust to lighting arrangement changes compared to others (FREAK, R-FREAK, G-FREAK and B-FREAK). RGB-FREAK achieved the highest accuracy in the lighting arrangement change with 95.18%, followed by FREAK and G-FREAK which achieve the same accuracy with 85.07%, R-FREAK with 84.01% and B-FREAK with 82.78%.

RGB-FREAK descriptor under the extended diagonal model is normalized and the gradient magnitude changes have no effect on the final descriptor and make the RGB-FREAK descriptor invariant to light changes. From the results in both Figure 8.4 and Figure 8.5, the theoretical invariance properties of RGB color extension descriptors are validated.

8.5 CONCLUSION

This study focuses on improving the mobile tracking process by introducing an RGB-FREAK descriptor that meets the basic needs of mobile AR applications. In recent times, AR has become a very popular field of research as AR technology has impacted people's daily lives. A literature review was carried out in detail and many key components such as the tracking process in AR were also discussed in this study to provide a better understanding of the challenges of AR in mobile devices. The biggest challenge faced in mobile AR applications is real-time functionality and robustness to changes such as scale, rotation, lighting color, lighting direction, and lighting value. Therefore, to address this challenge, a FREAK-based descriptor is proposed and developed in this study. The results and contributions of this study prove that this research is very important in the field of AR because tracking has been recognized as an important element in the field of AR. This study not only contributes to the field of AR but can lead to a new direction in the field of image recognition or computer vision as an image recognition element; descriptors have been implemented and tested in this study.

ACKNOWLEDGMENT

This study was supported by the Fundamental Research Grants, Ref. NO.: FRGS/1/2018/ICT01/UKM/02/5, awarded by the Malaysia Ministry of Higher Education.

REFERENCES

Alahi, A., Ortiz, R., & Vandergheynst, P. (2012). FREAK: fast retina keypoint, In *2012 IEEE Conference on Computer Vision and Pattern Recognition* (pp. 510–517). https://doi.org/10.1109/cvpr.2012.6247715

Bay, H., Ess, A., Tuytelaars, T., & Van Gool, L. (2008). Speeded-up robust features (SURF). *Computer Vision and Image Understanding,* 110(3), 346–359.

Calonder, M., Lepetit, V., Özuysal, M., Trzcinski, T., Strecha, C., & Fua, P. (2012). BRIEF: Computing a local binary descriptor very fast. *IEEE Transactions on Pattern Analysis and Machine Intelligence,* 34(7), 1281–1298.

Flavián, C., Ibáñez-Sánchez, S., & Orús, C. (2019). The impact of virtual, augmented and mixed reality technologies on the customer experience. *Journal of Business Research,* 100, 547–560.

Geusebroek, J.M., Burghouts, G.J., & Smeulders, A.W.M. (2005). The Amsterdam library of object images. *International Journal of Computer Vision,* 61, 103–112.

Leutenegger, S., Chli, M., & Siegwart, R.Y. (2011). BRISK: Binary Robust invariant scalable keypoints, In *2011 International Conference On Computer Vision* (pp. 2548–2555). IEEE.

Lowe, G. (2004). SIFT - The scale invariant feature transform. *International Journal,* 2, 91–110.

Obeidy, W.K., Arshad, H., Chowdhury, S.A., Parhizkar, B., & Huang, J. (2013). Increasing the tracking efficiency of mobile augmented reality. In *International Visual Informatics Conference* (pp. 447–457).

Rublee, E., Rabaud, V., Konolige, K., & Bradski, G. (2011). ORB: an efficient alternative to SIFT or SURF, In *2011 International Conference on Computer Vision* (pp. 2564–2571). https://doi.org/10.1109/ICCV.2011.6126544

Sung, Y.-T., Chang, K.-E., & Liu, T.-C. (2016). The effects of integrating mobile devices with teaching and learning on students' learning performance: A meta-analysis and research synthesis. *Computers & Education,* 94, 252–275.

Tan, S. Y., Arshad, H., & Abdullah, A. (2019). Distinctive accuracy measurement of binary descriptors in mobile augmented reality. *PLoS ONE* 14(1). https://doi.org/10.1371/journal.pone.0207191

9 Cryptosystem for Meshed 3D through Cellular Automata

R. Sulaiman[1], M.A. Al-Jabbar[1], A. Ahmadian[1], and A.M.A. Abdalla[2]

[1]The National University of Malaysia
[2]Al-Zaytoonah University of Jordan

9.1 INTRODUCTION: BACKGROUND AND DRIVING FORCES

In general, data may refer to text, images, audio, video or graphics. All 3D images and 3D objects are two main types of graphics. A 3D image may be processed by anyone using different techniques to produce 3D effects such as Stereoscopy, Integral Imaging, and Holography.

Stereoscopy is a method of recording details of 3D objects for imaging by mimicking the work of the eyes. Two eyes perceive two images from two different angles with a small visual difference due to the difference in eyes' locations, and then the brain merges the two images into a 3D image useful in evaluating the depths of objects in the picture. Integral imaging is an auto-stereoscopic or a multi-subject 3D view. It views the 3D image on behalf of the viewer without special glasses by placing an array of micro-lenses in front of the image, where each lens varies depending on its viewing angle. (Arimoto and Javidi 2001).

Holography is a technique that produces 3D images, called holograms, formed by the interference of light beams. This includes the use of a light source (such as a laser), diffraction, and interference, light intensity, and appropriate illumination. The produced hologram changes according to the position and orientation of the viewing system. The hologram may not be considered an image since it has a structure of varying intensity, density, and profile (Yamaguchi and Zhang 1997). A 3D object is considered a form of graphic data that may be classified based on how it is read and stored into four main types as follows.

i. The first type is the 3D object defined by voxels where a 3D object of dimensions (W×H×D) can be represented with a 3D matrix. Each cell is '1' if the analogous position in the solid object is occupied and '0' if it is empty.

ii. The second type of 3D objects is defined by the general features of 3D object file formats, such as 3D object geometry, appearance, scene, and animations. Popular formats of this type include STL, OFF, OBJ, FBX, and

COLLADA (McHenry and Bajcsy 2008). The geometry of the object is determined by the polygons of each surface. The polygons can have a massive number of faces and vertices organized and connected in the form of a Mesh (Smith 2006).

iii. The third type of 3D objects is defined by the point cloud, which is a set of data points in space typically produced by 3D scanners that measure a large number of points on the outer surfaces of surrounding objects. The point cloud is used for many purposes, including 3D CAD object creation for built parts, metrology and quality inspection, visualization, animation, rendering, and mass customization applications (Rusu and Cousins 2011).

iv. The final type is a 3D printed object where 3D printing is one of the various processes in which a material is mixed or solidified under computer control to create a 3D object. Printed objects can be of almost any shape or geometry and are typically produced using digital data of a 3D object created with a computer-aided design (CAD) package, a 3D scanner or a plain digital camera with photogrammetry software (Hoy 2013).

Note that the second and fourth types of 3D objects above use meshes to create objects, unlike the other two types. Overall, 3D objects are widely used in 3D graphics and in various fields such as medical applications, film, video games, natural sciences, architecture, engineering, earth science, and many **Industrial Revolution** (IR4.0) techniques and devices.

9.2 THREE-DIMENSIONAL OBJECTS DEFINED BY MESH

As previously mentioned, 3D objects can be represented in different ways such as with voxels or using general features of 3D object file formats like boundary representation, point clouds, and 3D printer objects. The most common geometric representation for boundary 3D geometric objects is the irregular polygonal meshes that consist of a set V of vertices (nodes, points), a set E of edges that connect the vertices, and a set F of faces. Faces and vertices may have attributes such as colors, texture coordinates, and normal. This is called a static 3D mesh. Meshed 3D objects represent a physical body and can be created by hand, algorithmically (procedural modeling) or scanned. Their surfaces may be further defined with texture mapping.

A texture map is a bitmap image or a procedural design mapped to the surface of a shape or polygon and can be stored in common image file formats. It was pioneered by Edwin Catmull in 1974. A textured object needs to include a texture map (also known as texture coordinates, UV map or UV coordinates) to lay a 2D image on the 3D surface effectively. The locations of vertices and faces of the 3D object are defined with 3D-coordinates, where a UV map projects the locations of those vertices and faces onto the 2D plane. UV-axes are used to express the vertical and horizontal axes of the texture space, and to reduce opacity along the x-axis and y-axis, which correspond to the geometry coordinates of the 3D object. Therefore, working with UV-coordinates allows automatic or manual adjustment of the mapping coordinates without changing the 3D object. The UV map must be taken into consideration when performing encryption because it must be transmitted with the encrypted object and its textured image, and this may undermine its security (Segal et al. 1992; Malzbender et al. 2001).

Objects in 3D may be combined and animated to create movement using several common techniques, such as rigging, key framing, kinematics, and motion capture. In addition, Twinning and Morphin are two processes that automatically find the difference between key frames. Rigging is a digital skeleton tied to 3D meshes. It is made up of joints and bones, each acting as a "handle" that animators can use to bend the character to the desired pose (Magnenat-Thalmann et al. 1988). Kinematics is the technique of using the kinetic equations of a robot to calculate the position of the end-effector from the values specified for the joint parameters, where the end-effector is the device at the end of the interacting robot arm. An environment for this system can be designed (Aristidou et al. 2018). Motion capture is the process of recording the movement of objects or people, and then using this information to animate digital character objects in 2D or 3D computer animation (Yamane and Hodgins 2009). Key framing is a system where the object has an initial state or condition and will change over time to a final shape that is different in position, form, color or any other property.

9.3   COMPRESSION OF 3D ANIMATED MESH

Essentially, a 3D object defined by a mesh originates from very small points (vertices) that are connected to form a mesh (static mesh) of polygons. Three or more vertices specify the outer form and shape of the polygon where the construction of polygons plays an essential role in the completeness of the object and its suitability for animation. Animation specifies how the object moves and deforms over time as an animated object consists of a sequence of static 3D meshes (Mamou et al. 2005) with the same connectivity throughout the mesh sequence or Dynamic Mesh (Corsini et al. 2013).

A dynamic mesh gives life to static 3D objects. It garnered attention from marketing, art, science, television, and special effects in the computer game industry and films. In animation, objects can change over time and various methods can be used to model the animation. Typically, animation can either be generated using a motion capturing system or simulated by sophisticated software tools such as Maya, Blender or 3ds Max. The popular representation of these animated objects is a mesh of triangular polygons.

A dynamic 3D object is a sequence of meshes (Amjoun and Straßer 2007), where each mesh represents a frame (also called a mesh frame). During the animation, vertex positions (geometry) change from frame to frame. Connectivity or the number of vertices can also change over time. Very often, the number of vertices and the connectivity of the mesh are defined first, and then the vertices are moved or deformed to generate the desired animation. Various 3D animation formats such as MAX, MDL, MS3D, BLEND or FBX will be discussed.

As animation techniques and animated mesh compression become more developed and accessible, their applications become more widespread (Mamou et al. 2008; Maglo et al. 2015). Applications in computer games, movies, education, medicines, etc. often demand animated 3D models and scenes with a high degree of realism. As the animation becomes more realistic, the corresponding frame meshes become larger and more complex, so it becomes necessary to compress the animation dataset. Key frames are among the most prominent animation representations used in the animation industry. With this technique, a set of key frames is selected to describe some important key poses in the animation sequence where other frames can be generated using interpolation techniques. However, the number of key frames can be very large, requiring effective compression. Overall, it is necessary to find efficient compression methods to provide a compact way to represent dynamic 3D models and reduce data size for storage and transmission.

Current static compression techniques of mesh sequences are mostly inefficient because the difference between neighboring frames in meshes is often very small. This leads to large redundancy between the neighboring frames (temporal redundancy) and between the neighboring vertices in the same frame (spatial redundancy). To develop compact representations that significantly reduce the storage space of an animated model, the coherence of both space and time must be exploited. Current coders are dedicated to compressing triangular webs of fixed connectivity so that connectivity is encoded, stored or transmitted, and then geometry coding is applied. The focus on animated meshes with fixed connectivity can be justified by the fact that animation creators often maintain easy contact throughout the sequence, allowing easy and efficient manipulation of the sequence.

9.4 IMAGE MINING IN 2D

Data mining is an advanced technology that plays an important role in data extraction and expansion. It is a method for achieving and retrieving data accurately and efficiently as required by the user (Lee and Siau 2001). Data mining techniques can be classified and differentiated based on the algorithms used. Data mining applications are of three tiers, from the inside out, classified according to data access and computing (Tier I), data privacy and domain knowledge (Tier II), and Big Data mining algorithms (Tier III). In general, mining techniques can be classified according to data into several categories such as image mining, text mining, and content-based mining.

Image mining, which is a branch of data mining, is the process of retrieving data based on the information and patterns contained in images such as keywords, alphanumeric data, and patterns. Images differ from text, especially in terms of their nature, storage mechanisms, and republication. Image mining starts with image data sources and goes through the phases of pre-processing, transformation and extraction, mining, interpretation and evaluation, and knowledge discovery (Yasodha and Yuvaraj 2013). Image mining techniques used by image miners include image acquisition, image enhancement and restoration, object recognition, image indexing and retrieval, image segmentation and feature extraction, representation and description, and association rule mining (Shekhar 2017). Data mining is useful when hidden pattern mining is required, but unfortunately, it still does not give enough thought to the mining of 3D objects, especially animated ones where it can be used to find patterns that can hide parts of the sequence of animated data. This technique may be better than the compression of 3D animated objects because mining does not require analyzing complex descriptions of these objects.

9.5 CELLULAR AUTOMATA AND CRYPTOGRAPHY

A Cellular Automaton (CA) is a discrete system that was introduced in the 1940s by Stani-Slum Ulm and John von Neumann, and it has applications in mathematics, computer science, physics, complexity science, microstructure modeling, and theoretical biology. The CA is composed of a systematic grid of cells with a limited number of dimensions. Each cell of the grid has one of two states: either ON (1) or OFF (0). For each cell, the group of cells adjacent to it is called its neighborhood. An initial state, when time t = 0, is generally dependent on some well-known rules that provide a state for each cell. The next generation is created when adding 1 to t based on certain rules that determine the new state of each cell based on its current state and the states of its neighbors. Typically, the rules in each generation are applied to all cells in a grid simultaneously and similarly.

CA has been used effectively for key cryptography (Nandi et al. 1994). To be suitable for this, however, cellular automata must be reversible and have some boundary conditions. Using rules, the next generations can be explicitly enumerated, but it is much more difficult to produce the preceding generations. The CA boundary conditions help identify which cell is the correct neighbor of the best cell. Common alternative boundary conditions include periodic (cyclic) and static (closed) boundaries. CA should be kept balanced where equilibrium means that in each generation, the generated CA requires approximately the same number of ones and the zeros.

9.6 CHALLENGES IN USING DATA

Common forms of data include text, images, videos, sounds, and more recently, 3D images and objects with or without animation. Telecommunications and data transmission networks have also evolved significantly, leading to an increased need for data security and encryption. Therefore, developing data security strategies and plans must focus on four emerging problems as explained below.

One problem in data security is the emerging need for efficient encryption of new forms of data, such as 3D images and objects. The protection of these data is important because they are more descriptive than traditional fixed images. Furthermore, encryption of this type of images and objects should be simple, efficient, robust, and reliable. Another problem in data security is the need for flexibility in choosing the required level of encryption. Based on data sensitivity, some data require a very high degree of encryption and need a huge key space, and consequently, more storage space and execution time while other data may not need all this robustness and extra resources. Therefore, the encryption algorithm should have enough flexibility to provide the degree of encryption that efficiently provides the required level of security.

Another problem that must be considered is the simplicity of the encryption algorithm. For researchers and programmers, it is preferable that the proposed encryption system is easy to understand and apply while maintaining its effectiveness. In addition, there is a need for a standard dataset of 3D objects to be used in the evaluation and testing of encryption algorithms.

Finally, data security algorithms must address the need to increase their overall efficiency by summarising and compressing 3D animated objects in an efficient, simple, and fast way without the heavy analysis and extraction of their features. Unfortunately, the majority of the existing research focused on encrypting text and images where audio and video received less work and work on 3D objects was the least. Moreover, recent algorithms for encrypting 3D objects did not take into consideration all aspects of encrypting these objects. For example, most algorithms overlooked encrypting UV maps of the 3D objects. They only encrypted points of faces, faces and vertices or faces and vertices with the texture image. Existing literature does not encrypt full 3D objects, i.e. faces, vertices, and UV map, and does not provide specialized methods for handling animation.

Existing encryption algorithms only allow a fixed degree of encryption or a fixed key space in spite of the different requirement of end-users. In addition, previous research in cryptography generally appears ambiguous and challenging to new researchers due to the use of advanced mathematical equations and complex rules of cryptography. Moreover, existing algorithms for the compression of animated 3D objects tend to extract their features, which is computationally expensive.

Combining simplicity, flexibility, and reliability is not easily obtainable in a cryptosystem, especially for larger and more complex data items. Therefore, proposing a new cryptosystem for encrypting 3D objects with these properties will be very beneficial to the fields of sophisticated data encryption and transmission.

9.7 STATE-OF-THE-ART ALGORITHMS AND DESCRIPTORS

Ideally, the systems should be compared with the previous research on 3D object encryption. Most of the previous algorithms on 3D object encryption did not provide their datasets. In addition, they did not fully encrypt 3D textured objects and did not encrypt 3D animated objects. Therefore, to be able to use the same datasets and the same metrics to compare our algorithms with the state-of-the-art algorithms, the new results are compared with the state-of-the-art image encryption algorithms exploiting the similarity in the representation of 2D images and 3D objects with matrices. Nevertheless, there are many differences between 2D images and 3D objects as seen in Table 9.1. These differences do not preclude encrypting them by the proposed cryptosystems in the same way. Note that a 2D image consists of a finite flat x-y plane whereas a 3D object adds a third dimension (z) to represent the depth and introduce the concept of object volume. In addition, this 3D model presents additional visualizations and transformations.

These existing algorithms developed different techniques depending on different methods. Chai et al. (2018) developed a *memristive* chaotic system that utilizes elementary CA and compressive sensing. Initially, they extensively scramble the wavelet coefficients of the plain image using elementary CA in a zigzag path and employ a hashing method to obtain some encryption parameters. Then, they compress and encrypt the scrambled image by compressive sensing that utilizes a

TABLE 9.1

Comparisons between RGB Images and 3D Objects

	RGB Image	3D Object
Structure	One matrix of size N×M×3	Multiple N×M matrices where N is either 2 or 3
Shape	Each N×M component forms a square or a rectangle	Each N×M component forms a very long and thin bar
Pre-processing	No need (already a matrix)	Needs to be converted from .off /.obj format into matrices
Processing	As three matrices (R, G, B) of size N×M	As two matrices for objects without texture (faces, vertices) and as seven matrices for textured objects (faces, vertices, VN, VT, R, G, B) where texture is an RGB image.
Encryption Time	Relatively lower	Relatively higher
Encryption Method	Same steps	Same steps

circular measurement matrix produced by a magnetic-controlled *memristive* chaotic system. This method conserves the energy consumption of data transmission, enlarges the key space, and increases the resistance of the encryption algorithm to brute-force attacks.

An encryption system based on the intertwining logistic map and cellular automata was introduced. In this system, the primary key is formed by an intertwining logistic map and the secondary key is generated by the attractors of cellular automata. Then, the first and second keys are combined to form the encryption key. Noshadian et al. (2018) developed a system that uses a logistic map as a chaos function to confuse the image and a modified Knuth shuffling algorithm for diffusion. Then, they attempt to speed up the optimization process using Teaching-Learning-Based Optimization and Gravitational-Search evolutionary algorithms.

An encryption system using permutation and substitution processes has been developed. The permutation process performs pixel shuffling using a 2D Logistic-adjusted-Sine map. Then, substitution is performed by a second-order life-like CA with balanced rules that maintain the equilibrium of the distribution of 0's and 1's in the CA during iteration. The second-order CA maintains the reversibility by preserving the CA result after each iteration. In addition, the initial conditions of the 2D Logistic-adjusted-Sine map are controlled with the key and the weighted histogram of the plain image to increase the system's resistance to different attacks. The traditional confusion method was replaced with a self-adaptive method of selective permutation.

9.8 FLEXIBLE FcCA Cryptosystem

The suggested cryptosystem, named **Flexible cryptosystem based on Cellular Automata** (FcCA), employs flexible techniques based on CA to perform the encryption of images and 3D objects. One flexibility feature of FcCA is allowing the modification of encryption sub-key sizes. This offers easier control over the encryption and decryption strength and enables the handling of massive objects and images of varying types and dimensions. The advantages of this flexibility include simplifying the programming and reducing memory requirements.

In order to make the cellular automata (CA) reversible, FcCA provides simplified creation of a robust flexible encryption system that performs lossless encryption of 3D objects and images of different formats. For diffusion, FcCA proposed using pure random CA. For confusion, FcCA expanded and modified an existing technique by replacing the static start point with suggested multi-dynamic intersected start points. Moreover, FcCA contributed various factors including the random configuration with open boundary conditions, the g-th order memory independent-cell technique, and collating the encryption key from two sub-key segments. Since the sub-keys rely on flexible parameters, this adds flexibility to the length and complexity of the sub-keys. The scrambling level of FcCA was tested and validated with several criteria. Experimental results demonstrated the efficacy of FcCA as a cryptosystem and its suitability for encrypting images and 3D objects.

The configuration of FcCA entails an adaptable size of CA that does not rely on the size of the plain information lattices. This extends the properties of CA with a new component called expanded CA (expCA). If the original data matrix A has a size of W × H, then expCA will have a size of $(W+N_1) × (H+N_2)$, where $N_1, N_2 \in$ [0, 1000] are nonnegative integers. To strengthen the cryptosystem without significantly increasing execution time, the upper limit for N_1 and N_2 has been set to 1000.

The diffusion phase in FcCA employs CA with random configuration. After that, more generations are produced by filling the CA with 0's and 1's randomly, in the absence of any neighborhood rules. The confusion phase is a modified adaptation of the method where FcCA uses **multiple dynamic intersected start points** (iDL) instead of their one static start point. Hence, rather than pairing each pixel in the original data matrix with a pixel in the CA in the same position, FcCA couples matrix locations with locations specified after shifting the original data matrix based on the predefined iDL values. The expCA matrix has more rows and columns than the matrix of original data. A pixel in the original matrix can be placed in any location in the region of the cells in the expCA matrix.

Consider the example shown in Figure 9.1 where A is an original 4 × 4 matrix and E is a 6 × 6 expCA matrix. Then, the starting point of the original matrix, in this case, will be the point (3, 2) in matrix E and iDL will have the coordinates of this starting point. After that, the encryption of matrix A will be based on the 1's and 0's of the matrix E-based starting point (3, 2) instead of (0, 0). Hence, laying location and the iDL point can be altered simply inside the expCA matrix.

Furthermore, if the original data comprises multiple matrices, every matrix can be scrambled with the same expCA. Nonetheless, the iDL point should be altered for every matrix without exceeding the expCA boundaries. For the example in Figure 9.2, iDL was (6,5) in Plain Matrix 1, and it was altered into (3,7) for Plain Matrix 2. Subsequently, the confusion component of FcCA mainly aims to shuffle the locations of points in the original image or 3D object.

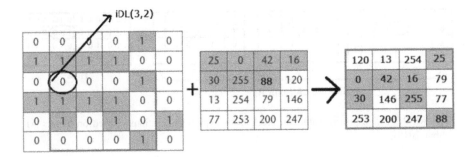

FIGURE 9.1 Example of FcCA with the matrices for expCA, original data and encrypted data (Based on Thesis Al-Jabbar 2018).

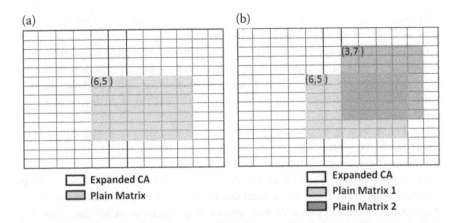

FIGURE 9.2 iDL for original data matrix a) with one plain matrix b) with two plain matrices (Based on Thesis Al-Jabbar 2018).

The FcCA framework employs open-boundaries. It can start with a CA having the same size as the original data matrix where each cell in the CA has its value excluded at every generation starting at the initial randomization. Subsequently, FcCA does not require defining any boundary conditions for the cells' values at the subsequent generations since they are completely independent of the cells' values of the preceding generations.

A 2D CA is reversible if its reverse evolution can be calculated. On the other hand, reversibility for CA of two or more dimensions cannot be firmly established by default. Hence, the decidability of CA is often established by a g-th order memory independent-cell method. This method assumes binary states for the cells in each CA generation and these cells are kept in sequence in corresponding locations in the Hybrid Cellular Automata (HCA). The HCA is a new 2D CA with the same size as the expCA in the cryptosystem and it will generate the first sub-key for the FcCA cryptosystem. Figure 9.3 shows an example of combining the values of HCA from different expCA generations.

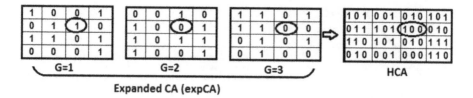

Expanded CA (expCA)

FIGURE 9.3 Composing values in HCA from expCA generations (Based on Thesis Al-Jabbar 2018).

There are three main benefits of the reversibility technique suggested above. First, it meaningfully reduces the number of stored states. For example, when the CA matrix has a size of 8 × 8, the number of required states is 26 instead of 2^{64}. Second, this technique eliminates ancestor configurations with no predecessors in traditional cellular automata. Third, it eliminates the requirement of storing the states of neighboring cells from the previous steps.

The flexibility of our FcCA cryptosystem is high, especially when encrypting meshed 3D objects. This type of object has a considerable difference between the numbers of rows and columns in the Face and Vertex matrices. FcCA flexibility is mainly the result of the two new techniques for the expansion of the HCA matrix and the insertion into it.

The FcCA system involves two stages: cipher and decipher. The cipher stage consists of three phases, which are pre-processing (input/extract matrices), pre-encryption and encryption/output.

An original image is given to FcCA as input, and it is transformed into its component matrices. Then, the system creates the expCA and HCA matrices and assigns values of iDL points, Ps and number of generations. After that, expCA is filled randomly with ones and zeros, and HCA is created. Finally, the secret key is used to apply the diffusion and confusion phases on the data for a specified number of generations and the scrambled data are produced as output. The cipher stage, described in Figure 9.4, consists of three phases.

The proposed FcCA cryptosystem has three distinguished benefits compared with the existing systems. Firstly, the FcCA system showed preponderance due to its ability to control the number of times the cryptosystem can repeat the shuffling and permutation procedures, while most of the other systems implemented these procedures for a constant number of iteration. This indicates that FcCA can control its encryption level contrary to the other systems with constant encryption levels. Moreover, the algorithm is not completely random, so it reproduces the same encrypted object when the same original object is used.

Secondly, most conventional cryptosystems have fixed sizes for their key spaces in contrast to FcCA, which has extendable and resizable keys. This makes it appropriate for a larger variety of data types that can be represented with 2D matrices, and it allows changing the security level as desired to suit specific applications. Therefore, FcCA provides a very flexible cryptosystem that combines key flexibility with encryption level flexibility.

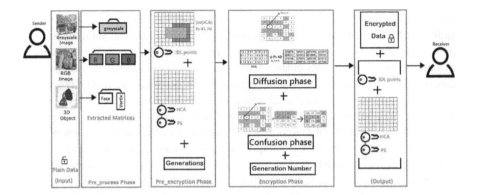

FIGURE 9.4 Sketch of FcCA phases with different types of input (Based on Thesis Al-Jabbar 2018).

Thirdly, FcCA applies innovative simplified rules for reverse 2D CA and for encryption. Many existing algorithms relied on conventional complex encryption rules or maps, or they utilized heavy 3D cellular automata. Other existing algorithms employed Arnold's Cat Map in encryption to benefit from its simplicity, but this has the disadvantage of producing an inadequate security level because of its periodic nature and its work with square images.

9.9 IMPROVED FLEXIBLE CRYPTOSYSTEM (iFcCA)

The improved FcCA (iFcCA) cryptosystem uses the same diffusion idea from the FcCA encryption system where FcCA is a simplified flexible encrypting system based on cellular automata (CA). The simplified techniques were introduced to make CA reversible with the creation of a robust flexible encryption system that performs lossless encryption of 3D objects and 2D images of various types. FcCA proposed pure random CA as a diffusion procedure, and it uses an improved existing confusion procedure where multi-dynamic intersected start points were used instead of the single static start point. Furthermore, FcCA proposed using a mixture of features such as the random configuration with open boundary conditions, the g-th order memory independent-cell technique, and the categorization of two portions of the encryption key as sub-keys. The length and complexity of FcCA sub-keys can be controlled in a simple manner because they depend on flexible parameters. FcCA is distinguished by its simplicity, flexibility, and reliability, but it has two drawbacks. First, the original data are shuffled without changing their values, which produces the same histogram for the original data and its encrypted data. Furthermore, it causes the unified averaged changed intensity (UACI) standard for this encryption procedure to fall out of the standard range. The second drawback of FcCA is that it requires many generations to make the key space large enough for the desired encryption level. Consequently, the proposed iFcCA system presents solutions to eliminate these drawbacks of FcCA while encrypting 3D textured objects completely with their UV maps. This will also cover the missing part of encrypting textured objects in the system as they did not encrypt the UV maps. In addition, iFcCA will surpass FcCA through its ability to encrypt 3D textured objects completely with their texture maps. The enhancements to FcCA include making intersect start points change with every generation and encrypting the values of the original data while scrambling them using cellular automata. Hence, the original 3D object will be extracted into vertices, faces, and texture, in addition to its texture map before it is encrypted using iFcCA.

The improvements by the proposed iFcCA system overcome the weaknesses of FcCA by presenting two new techniques: random dynamic intersected start points (rDL) and selective masking for plain data histogram (sHist). In contrast, the technique employed by FcCA is multiple dynamic intersected start points (iDL) where matrix locations are paired with the locations found after shifting the original matrix, depending on predefined iDL values. This method keeps the same iDL point throughout all CA generations for each input matrix in FcCA. To overcome this problem, iFcCA alters the values of iDL points in every generation. This is achieved by using a matrix of rDL points for the input matrix rather than using one point for each matrix. For example, if a cellular automaton has four generations, then the vertices matrix will have at least an rDL matrix of four points such as rDL = ((90,27), (2,58), (16,4), (65,30)). Moreover, rDL matrices will have bogus rDL points where a **Hybrid Cellular Automaton** (HCA) will be created with bogus bits. This new technique of using random dynamic intersected start points significantly enlarges and strengthens the key space.

Another novel technique presented by iFcCA is selective masking for plain data histogram (sHist). In FcCA, the original matrix elements are permuted based on the 1's in the cellular automata. Since these elements are constant, they will produce identical histograms for the original and encrypted matrices. This significant weakness may undermine the security of the data because it provides hints to the original data within the encrypted data. Increasing the sensitivity of the encrypted data is essential to the robustness of the algorithm against various attacks. Consequently, iFcCA presents a technique, named sHist, to alter the original matrix values while they are permuted by CA in every generation.

The masking changes the matrix values based on the configuration of the CA at every generation as the CA shuffles their locations. At every CA generation, each matrix value is incremented with one of two random numbers used at that generation. Nonetheless, the values paired with 1's will have the same increment and the rest will use the other increment amount. These restrictions ensure keeping the random values and the new values within the range specified by the minimum and maximum values of the original matrix. Any new value that exceeds the maximum by any excess value will be replaced with the minimum plus that excess value. This method creates new mask values for each matrix in every generation. Furthermore, these generated random values are included in the security key, which is a new enhancement to key strength. Figure 9.5 provides an example of applying CA with masking and rDL points to perform confusion. This confusion process is a part of iFcCA, which is illustrated in Figure 9.6.

As shown in Figure 9.6, iFcCA transforms an input image or 3D textured object into its corresponding matrix or matrices. Then, it creates the expCA and HCA

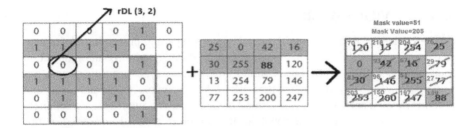

FIGURE 9.5 Confusion example showing CA with rDL, plain data, and scrambled data with masking, respectively (Based on Thesis Al-Jabbar 2018).

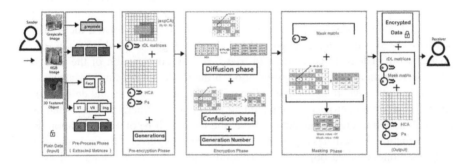

FIGURE 9.6 A sketch of iFcCA phases with different types of input (Based on Thesis Al-Jabbar 2018).

matrices and determines the values of rDL points for the first generation, and assigns values to Ps, the number of generations, and masking numbers. After that, it assigns random 1's and 0's to expCA and creates HCA. Finally, the secret key and the input data undergo the diffusion, confusion, and masking phases for a required number of generations to generate the scrambled output with the new mask and rDL.

9.10   ROBOTIC MOVEMENT ENCRYPTION (APPLIED CASE)

The demand for robot technology has increased significantly in the last few years with uses in many areas including military applications. Hence, the security of the data of a robot movement has emerged as an important research area. The preceding works targeted the encryption of communication among robots or the encryption of the distinct kinds of stiff three-dimensional objects. That will be performed through simulating the motion steps in a computer via the use of key frames and then shuffling key frames points using the iFcCA cryptosystem. Outcomes of practical experiments show that this proposed scheme is capable of encrypting and decrypting robotic movements efficiently. Moreover, its propagation level surpassed 99.8% and it was shown to resist statistical and brute-force attacks employing a very robust key.

9.11 PREVIOUS WORK

Cyber-resilience invokes a long-term strategy of preparing, preventing, defending, recovering, and evaluating what happens before, during, and after an organization encounters a digital threat. Furthermore, an effective cyber-security system has numerous layers of protection where networks, programs, important data, and endpoint devices such as computers, smart devices, routers, and robots are definitely not an exception. From simple robots to those used in medical or military fields, whether used individually or cooperatively, it is evident that safety, security, and privacy of robotic systems are critical.

3D robot modeling could be used to characterize the formation procedure of the shape of a robot. Robot models can be created by a 3D modeling tool on the computer or by scanning real robots into a computer. Essentially, a robot model is generated from very small dots, called vertices, connected to form a mesh. These vertices specify the external form and the shape polygons. A polygon is a region shaped from at least three vertices (a triangle). The construction of the polygons plays an essential role in the representation of the model and its appropriateness for use in animation where animation indicates how the robot moves and deforms over time. There are numerous common animation techniques where they are often used in combination to create movement. Here, the focus will be on the animation done by kinematics. Nonetheless, present techniques in this direction take into account only the non-animated objects such as solid objects, the point cloud objects, the meshes, the textures of 3D objects, and the textured objects.

For securing robotic systems, an effort was presented for the authentication of the communication between connected robots (Yfantis and Fayed 2014), while the encryption of aerial robotics communication was discussed. Then, message encryption in robot operating systems was proposed by (Rodríguez-Lera et al. 2018).

Additionally, there was some effort done to secure the key frame itself in movies, rather than the relationships between key frames that yield the movement of the 3D model. Some researcher treated video key frames separately during the encryption method. Himeur and Boukabou (2018) encrypted watermark information and included it in the key frames extracted from video stream.

9.12 PROPOSED APPLIED CASE (EncKin)

In this subsection, the applied case (EncKin) is described. It aims for encrypting the steps of robot movement by using the iFcCA cryptosystem where this movement is produced by kinematics. This case is applied in five phases: 1) Prepare movement data by using a robot kinematics simulator. 2) Generate the iFcCA cryptosystem. 3) Encrypt key frames. 4) Detect threats. 5) Decrypt key frames. These phases are explained in detail below.

Phase 1 (Preparation phase–Performed by the simulator): a) Create the mesh that constructs the robot's body. b) Determine the points of joints and the segments in the robot's body by the programmer. c) Determine Kinematics; how the joints and the segments will move in the space (key frames for animation) where the values of these key frames can be generated either manually or automatically; d) Store the values of the new positions or key frames for all joints in all time-steps in a 2D matrix, called the key frames matrix, where each matrix cell holds one key frame.

Phase 2 (Generating phase): The generations for the CA will be created by the iFcCA cryptosystem where the initial generation will have a random configuration.

Phase 3 (Encryption phase): Generated cellular automata generations are used as a map for the diffusion process. The values of cells in the key frames matrix are scrambled depending on the indices of 1's in the CA at every generation. Then, the encrypted key frames matrix is applied to the robot's arm. During the confusing phases, safeguarding two exceptions about joints key frames must be considered: joint hierarchy and forward kinematics. These two exceptions are responsible for keeping joints moving coherently even when they move in random steps.

Phase 4 (Threat detection phase): a) The robot keeps its plain key frame matrix in a hidden secure place and presents a scrambled one. b) To put the robot in ON mode, an operator offers a key to unscramble the key frames. c) If the scrambled key frames are identical to the hidden ones, the robot turns ON; otherwise, the robot will activate a threat alarm. See Figure 9.7 for an illustration.

Phase 5 (Decryption phase): This phase takes the scrambled key frames matrix and the related secret keys as input. Then, it yields the recovered real points of the key frames and the real steps of the robot movement. This phase is similar to the encryption phase, but with some procedural steps inverted.

FcCA is distinguished by its simplicity, flexibility, and reliability, but it has two drawbacks. First, the plain data are shuffled without changing their values, which yields the same histogram for plain data and its encrypted data. This causes the randomness of this encryption technique to fall out of the standard range of the unified averaged changed intensity (UACI) standard. The second drawback of FcCA is that it needs many generations to make the key space very large. Thus, the

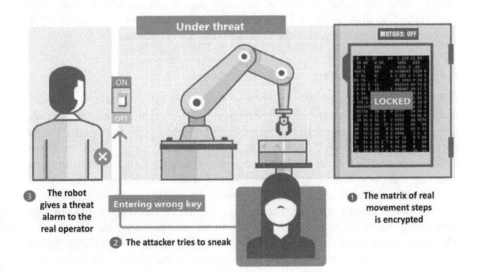

FIGURE 9.7   Phase 4: Threats Detection (Based on Thesis Al-Jabbar 2018).

proposed iFcCA system overcomes these drawbacks of FcCA and fully encrypts 3D textured objects with their UV maps—the missing part of encrypting textured objects in the system. iFcCA overcomes the drawbacks of FcCA by presenting two new techniques: random dynamic intersected start points (rDL) and selective masking for plain data histogram (sHist).

The rDL points are changed in every generation contrary to FcCA where iDL points are fixed over all generations, so instead of having a point for each data matrix, the data matrix will have a matrix of rDL points. This reduces the need for many generations and overcomes one of the drawbacks of FcCA. Using rDL, iFcCA can have a keyspace of up to $2^{26,818,167}$ by using only one generation while FcCA needs nearly 17 generations to achieve the same keyspace. Furthermore, iFcCA maintains the same high degree of encryption as FcCA.

The second new technique in iFcCA is sHist, which is the selective masking for the plain data histogram. sHist changes the values of plain data bits during the shuffling of the plain matrix in each CA generation. This causes the randomness of this encryption technique to fall in of the standard range of the unified averaged changed intensity (UACI) standard contrary to the FcCA cryptosystem and it overcomes the second drawback of FcCA. The UACI values of FcCA are near 0.2%, which are theoretically unacceptable, while iFcCA UACI values are between 0.331594 and 0.337677, which are theoretically acceptable.

Keyspace in encryption schemes has to be very large to impede brute-force attacks. For that reason, the secret key used by the FcCA cryptosystem is comprised of two flexible sub-keys: HCA and a numeric set containing the Ps series and iDL coordinates. Unlike most existing encryption schemes with conventional CA, this key structure provides more flexibility to change the sizes of those sub-keys freely and easily, based on the required level of protection. The dimensions of CA and the length of the generated keys partially depend on the size of the original image or object. Nonetheless, the lengths of sub-keys depend on numerous parameters; specifically, the dimensions of HCA, the (G + Ps)-bit length of each cell in HCA, the number of elements within the Ps series, and the coordinates of iDL points.

9.13 CONCLUSION

Due to the importance of 3D objects' encryption and their increased use in animation, this chapter introduced and elaborated a new system for summarising and compressing sequences of rigid objects and then encrypting the results by the previously introduced iFcCA encryption algorithm. It is composed of three new techniques: identification of rigid object by one meaningful point, summarisation by selecting rigid key objects, and compression of selected rigid key objects. It was tested under thirty different cases to choose the most suitable descriptors for summarisation. Results showed that merging the use of mean absolute error with subtracting the difference for the vertices of objects produced the best results. Moreover, experiments and analyses showed that it could compete with human users as it can reduce encrypted data while preserving the quality and the integrity of the sequence of motion. Consequently, it can reduce the time and space complexity of the whole encryption system. This chapter highlighted the encryption of non-traditional data as a new field of cryptography that handles different types of 3D object animation techniques with applications in the data mining of animated 3D objects. In addition, it provided a standard dataset of 3D objects to be used as a benchmark or a test suite by future researchers.

REFERENCES

Amjoun, R., & Straßer, W. (2007). Efficient compression of 3d dynamic mesh sequences. *Journal of WSCG*, 15(1–3): 99–106.

Arimoto, H., & Javidi, B. (2001). Integral three-dimensional imaging with digital reconstruction. *Optics letters*, 26(3): 157–159.

Aristidou, A., Lasenby, J., ChrD.ysanthou, Y., & Shamir, A. (2018). Inverse kinematics techniques in computer graphics: A survey. *Computer Graphics Forum*, 37(6): 35–58.

Chai, X., Fu, X., Gan, Z., Lu, Y., & Chen, Y. (2019). A color image cryptosystem based on dynamic DNA encryption and chaos. *Signal Processing*, 155: 44–62.

Chai, X., Zheng, X., Gan, Z., Han, D., & Chen, Y. (2018). An image encryption algorithm based on chaotic system and compressive sensing. *Signal Processing*, 148: 124–144.

Corsini, M., Larabi, M.-C., Lavoué, G., Petřík, O., Váša, L., & Wang, K. (2013). Perceptual metrics for static and dynamic triangle meshes. *Computer Graphics Forum*, 32(1): 101–125.

Han, J., Kamber, M., & Pei, J. (2011). Data mining concepts and techniques third edition. *The Morgan Kaufmann Series in Data Management Systems*, 5(4): 83–124.

Himeur, Y., & Boukabou, A. (2018). A robust and secure key-frames based video watermarking system using chaotic encryption. *Multimedia Tools and Applications*, 77(7): 8603–8627.

Hoy, M.B. (2013). 3D printing: making things at the library. *Medical reference services quarterly*, 32(1): 93–99.

Koenderink, J. J., van Doorn, A. J., & Kappers, A. M. (1994). On so-called paradoxical monocular stereoscopy. *Perception*, 23(5): 583–594.

Lee, S. J., & Siau, K. (2001). A review of data mining techniques. *Industrial Management & Data Systems*, 101: 41–46.

Maglo, A., Lavoué, G., Dupont, F., & Hudelot, C. (2015). 3d mesh compression: Survey, comparisons, and emerging trends. *ACM Computing Surveys (CSUR)*, 47(3): 44.

Magnenat-Thalmann, N., Laperrire, R., & Thalmann, D. (1988). Joint-dependent local deformations for hand animation and object grasping. In *Proceedings on Graphics interface'88*.

Malzbender, T., Gelb, D., & Wolters, H. (2001). Polynomial texture maps. *Proceedings of the 28th annual conference on Computer graphics and interactive techniques*. 519–528.

Mamou, K., Stefanoski, N., Kirchhoffer, H., Muller, K., Zaharia, T., Preteux, F., Marpe, D., & Ostermann, J. 2008. The new MPEG-4/FAMC standard for animated 3D mesh compression. *2008 3DTV Conference: The True Vision-Capture, Transmission and Display of 3D Video*. 97–100.

Mamou, K., Zaharia, T., & Preteux, F. (2005). A preliminary evaluation of 3D mesh animation coding techniques. *Mathematical Methods in Pattern and Image Analysis*, 5916: 591605.

McHenry, K., & Bajcsy, P. (2008). An overview of 3d data content, file formats and viewers. *National Center for Supercomputing Applications*, 1205: 22.

Nandi, S., Kar, B., & Chaudhuri, P. P. (1994). Theory and applications of cellular automata in cryptography. *IEEE Transactions on Computers*, 43(12): 1346–1357.

Noshadian, S., Ebrahimzade, A., & Kazemitabar, S.J. (2018). Optimizing chaos based image encryption. *Multimedia Tools and Applications*, 77(19): 25569–25590.

Ping, P., Fan, J., Mao, Y., Xu, F., & Gao, J. (2018a). A chaos based image encryption scheme using digit-level permutation and block diffusion. *IEEE Access*, 6: 67581–67593.

Ping, P., Wu, J., Mao, Y., Xu, F., & Fan, J. (2018b). Design of image cipher using life-like cellular.

Rodríguez-Lera, F.J., Matellán-Olivera, V., Balsa-Comerón, J., Guerrero-Higueras, Á.M., & Fernández-Llamas, C. (2018). Message encryption in robot operating system: Collateral effects of hardening mobile robots. *Frontiers in ICT*, 5: 2.

Rusu, R.B., & Cousins, S. (2011). 3d is here: Point cloud library (pcl). *2011 IEEE international conference on robotics and automation*. 1–4.

Schnars, U., Falldorf, C., Watson, J., & Jüptner, W. (2015). Digital holography. *Digital Holography and Wavefront Sensing*. Springer, 39–68.

Segal, M., Korobkin, C., Van Widenfelt, R., Foran, J., & Haeberli, P. (1992). Fast shadows and lighting effects using texture mapping. *ACM Siggraph Computer Graphics*, **26**(2): 249–252.

Shekhar, S. (2017). Java Topology Suite (JTS). In S. Shekhar et al. (eds.), *Encyclopedia of GIS*, Springer International Publishing. AG 2017.

Smith, C. (2006). On vertex-vertex systems and their use in geometric and biological modelling. Thesis Doctor THE UNIVERSITY OF CALGARY, CALGARY, ALBERTA.

Smith III, A.R. (1971). Cellular automata complexity trade-offs. *Information and Control*, 18(5): 466–482.

Smith, J.R., & Chang, S.-F. (1996). Tools and techniques for color image retrieval. *Storage and Retrieval for Still Image and Video Databases IV*. 2670: 426–437.

Wu, J., Liao, X., & Yang, B. (2018). Image encryption using 2D Hénon-Sine map and DNA approach. *Signal Processing*, 153: 11–23.

Wu, X., Zhu, X., Wu, G.-Q., & Ding, W. (2013). Data mining with big data. *IEEE Transactions on Knowledge and Data Engineering*, 26(1): 97–107.

Yamaguchi, I., & Zhang, T. (1997). Phase-shifting digital holography. *Optics Letters*, 22(16): 1268–1270.

Yamane, K., & Hodgins, J. (2009). Simultaneous tracking and balancing of humanoid robots for imitating human motion capture data. *2009 IEEE/RSJ International Conference on Intelligent Robots and Systems*. 2510–2517.

Yasodha, K., & Yuvaraj, K. (2013). A study on image mining techniques. *International Journal of Applied*, 1(1): 1–6.

Ye, G., Pan, C., Huang, X., & Mei, Q. (2018). An efficient pixel-level chaotic image encryption algorithm. *Nonlinear Dynamics*, 94(1): 745–756.

Yfantis, E. A. & Fayed, A. (2014). Authentication and secure robot communication. *International Journal of Advanced Robotic Systems*, 11(2): 10.

10 Evolutionary Computing and Swarm Intelligence for Hyper Parameters Optimization Problem in Convolutional Neural Networks

Senthil kumar Mohan[1], A John[2], and Ananth kumar Tamilarasan[3]
[1]School of Information Technology and Engineering, VIT University, Vellore, India
[2]School of Computing Science and Engineering, Galgotias University, Greater Noida, India
[3]Dept of Computer Science and Engineering, IFET College of Engineering, Tamil Nadu, India

10.1 INTRODUCTION

The convolutional neural network (CNN) along with the unsupervised method, is introduced. It relies based on the variable which is used on the neighborhood search approach for improving the classification performance during hyperparameter tuning of the CNN architectures. The network displays the predictive results in significant improvement in robustness, power and validating the CNN (Araújo et al. 2017). The Evolutionary Stochastic Gradient Descent (ESGD) is used in deep neural networks (DNN). The ESGD is used as the single framework by combining Stochastic Gradient Descent with gradient algorithm. The effectiveness of ESGD is checked in various applications like speech, image recognition with different deep architectures, and so on (Cui et al. 2018). Successive Halving and Classification (SHAC) works with comparable k stages evaluations and perfumes cascading the training of binary classifiers into undesirable regions in the search space. The adoption of tree-based classifiers along with SHAC, which results in significant improvements in the results during the optimization of architectures and hyperparameters functions (Dahl.). The PSF-HS technique is used to adjust the

157

hypermeters with harmony. The memory of harmony is generated, and updates have taken place on the basis of CNN loss. The CNN with LeNet-5 is proposed with MNIST dataset, the simulation with CNN generated by using CifarNet and a Cifar-10 dataset. Based on the two simulation results, the CNN architectures performance improved by hyperparameters tuning (Lee et al. 2018).

The robust and simple hyperparameter tuning technique is introduced, namely ASHA, the technique exploits parallelism as well as early-stopping in an aggressive manner. The ASHA outperforming the hyperparameter tuning effectively, balance the number of workers in shared settings and converges the configuration which results in 50% improvements in quality used by Vizier. The hyperparameter tuning which is used internally in Google known as Vizier, which takes 500 people's tasks and produced the results for LSTM architecture which is double time the training into the single model (Li et al. 2018). A multi-level convolutional neural network (ML-CNN) is anticipated for the classification of a lung nodule. It is used for the optimization of the hyperparameter configuration in the proposed technique of the non-stationary kernel-based Gaussian surrogate model. The proposed techniques keep on performing the searches which provide a place holder for hyperparameter to make optimal settings in the strategy. The experiments conducted to perform manual tuning, as well as hyperparameter optimization techniques like Gaussian processes, Random search in the kernel, the latest technique, is introduced by HORD (Zhang et al. 2007). The CNN architecture with an evolutionary algorithm framework is used for performance optimization automatically by hyper-parameters. The framework extends toward the joint optimization of CNN to control the special activities in the individual networks (Kennedy and Eberhart 1995).

The detection and termination of bad runs in the networks become essential and extrapolates the performance by using the probabilistic model. The broad range of experiments with neural networks (NN) architectures conducted which performs object recognition benchmarks displays the results of hyperparameter optimization technique with twofold of DNNs. The performance results in significant improvement compared to human experts (Domhan et al. 2015). The novel hyperparameter optimization techniques introduced for finding the optimal hyperparameters based on the sequence of action. It is performed in a predicted network leveraged on the uninterrupted in-depth learning process. The object tracking activities becomes more complex in nature which incomparable traditional problem, the existing deep learning techniques can't be processed directly. The challenge needs to be overcome by applying the heuristic approach to improve the behavior of convergence (Dong et al. 2018).

The expected improvement needs to be achieved by applying the new greedy sequential technique with random search is proposed. The random search is performing various activities in the NN for several datasets. The sequential algorithm becomes realistic for deep belief networks (DBN) learning issues (Bergstra et al. 2011; Bergstra and Bengio 2012). The GPEI is introduced and becomes an effective technique for optimizing the various hyperparameters. The DNGO which is used along with NN results in an alternative way of Gaussian process. The proposed technique is associated with MSMLEO (multiscale and multilevel evolutionary optimization) to enhance the performance of hyperparameters (Cui and Bai 2019).

The hyperparameters optimization technique performs over and over again in the hyberband, Bayesian optimization on various problems. For example, the problems can be classified like SVM, FNN, BNN, deep reinforcement learning and CNN. The technique becomes robust and adaptable, as well as easy to implement (Falkner et al. 2018). Hyperparameter optimization (HPO) is proposed, the optimization method based on the blackbox technique is used on model fee as well as Bayesian optimization. The demand for high computational for various machine learning applications becomes more costly with blackbox optimization. Due the cost-effectiveness, the multi-fidelity is proposed which is cheaper compare to black box methods and assessments made to achieve the quality hypermeters settings in the CNN (Feurer and Hutter 2019). The HOIST, a fast hyperparameter optimization technique used to intermediate as well as complete the data evaluation to improve the performance of DNN in the hyperparameter optimization (Goldberg 1989). The novel method introduced to perform learning and transfer the values small dataset into the of hyperparameters which comparable performance of dataset. The existing transfer learning techniques are opposed to the proposed method because of no usage of features hand-designed. Instead of the place holder of the model performs error distribution of the datasets train and learns the function of hyperparameters (Koutsoukas et al. 2017; Ilievski and Feng 2016).

Autotune is proposed to perform automation of parallel derivative which combines the various sampling, search methods used for effective in tuning the ML (machine learning) models. The autotune gives significant result improvement by using the hyperparameters default settings (Koch et al. 2018). The Bayesian technique is introduced which adapts the monotonicity constraints. The results are comparable with monotonicity performs significant improvements in various machine learning applications with hyperparameter tuning applications (Wang and Welch 2018). The novel method HORD is introduced, finding the placeholder for the most potential value of hyperparameter tuning evaluations. HORD works in low dimensions well and exceptionally produces better in high dimensions (Ilievski and Shoemaker; Shoemaker 2012). The NN used as the alternative method for GP in the distributions of the functions. The adaptive function regression with NN used in the form of parametric entirely the scaling took place linearly rather than cubically. The hyperparameter optimization performs on large scale, rapidly searching the models which are competitive in the object recognition of CNN (Snoek et al. 2012). The EGO (Efficient Global Optimization) method is proposed which performs optimization and configuration of CNN architectures automatically. The configuration of CNN architecture fully depends on convolutional layers to perform the optimization of tasks (Stein et al. 2019).

The lower-dimensional depiction of the original information identifies quickly and shows potential in the hyperparameter space. The values that can be used to perform initializing, optimizing the method for higher-dimensional data. The hyperparameter standard course of action taken place to get optimized with the original input of data. Various methods of optimization of hyperparameters have been used, including the tree of partial evaluators, random search, genetic algorithms, and sequence model-based configuration algorithms (Hinz et al.). The proposed CMA-ES (Co-variance Matrix Adaptation Evolution Strategy) and the CMA-ES for derivative-free optimization and few useful invariance features are also the solutions for parallel assessments (Loshchilov and Hutter 2016).

The PSO method introduced in deep neural networks which is the combination of the steepest gradient descent technique with hyperparameter selection makes automated for finding the optimal network configuration in DNN. In the PSO search method, this method was encoded with network settings with a real number of m-dimensional vectors (Ye 2017). The Nelder-Mead methods and the easier coordinate search for hyperparameters. DNNs for character recognition and gender/age classification were compared with the different hyperparameter optimization techniques (Ozaki et al. 2017).

10.1.1 BAYESIAN OPTIMIZATION

Bayesian hyperparameter tuning technique is inspired by classifier statistical learning theory for optimization. We understand this by using strategically placed directional derivative signs in the search space of the hyperparameter in order to look for a more complex model than the one obtained with tiny data. We show the efficacy of our approach in the tuning tasks of the hyperparameters of many machine learning algorithms (Joy et al. 1999). Deep metric learning is used to learn meta-functionalities through datasets to efficiently measure the similarity between its associated meta-functions by the distance between Euclides. The Siamese network is made of profound features and meta-featuring extractors. A deep extractor functionality is represented in a dataset semantically in each case. The several in-depth features are combined to encode a single image through a meta-feature extractor dataset—optimization-focused Bayesian hyperparameter tuning technique, inspired by the mathematical learning theory of classifiers.

A Bayesian-based optimization method is introduced in the system, which is known as FABOLAS. It models the loss and training time automatically according to the size of the data sets and trades high gains in data against device costs over the global optimum (Klein et al. 2017). Grid and Random Search are said to be unreliable and too exclusive due to different architectural hyperparameters. Sequential optimization from Bayesia is therefore, a promising option to solve a model-based extreme unknown cost function. The lowest error report on the CIFAR-10 benchmark was obtained by Snoek's last Bayesian Optimization study on nine convolutionary network parameters (Murugan 2017).

10.1.2 APPLICATIONS

By including molecular biomarkers in a routine diagnostic panel, cancer detection is currently undergoing a paradigm change. This groundbreaking finding guides researchers to investigate the role of microRNA in cancer, as almost all human tumors are also associated with its deregulation. These variations again recur in tumor-specific microRNA signatures that are useful for the diagnosis of tissue of origin and subtype tumors. In this chapter, a new paradigm for automatically optimizing LSTM using differential evolution (DE) proposes to apply a convolutionary neural network evolutionary optimized classifier to this complex task (Lopez-rincon et al. 2018). This is the first systematic emotion classification study in hyperparameter optimization. In this chapter, the proposed method is tested and compared with other state-of-the-art hyperparameter optimization processes using (simulated annealing, particle swarm optimization, random search, and the tree of Parzen estimators) a new dataset or informations obtained from wearable sensors. The computation DE algorithm is less complicated but provides more diversity in finding optimal solutions (Nakisa et al. 2018). Handwritten digital recognition is an issue which has been significantly improved by neural networks in recent years. Previous research has shown that 96% accuracy for 1,000 epochs and 16 hidden neurons can be achieved within 1 minute by a three-layer feed-forward neural network with a backpropagation system. Although neural network efficiency relies heavily on the choice of various hyperparameters, a new challenge will soon be good optimization of hyperparameters. Further research and modifications on Genetic Algorithm hyperparameter optimization indicate that a 1-hour search will find a 96.5% accuracy of the neural network that operates for less than 5 seconds (Su).

10.2 DEEP LEARNING OVERVIEW

10.2.1 DEEP LEARNING

Deep learning is the sub-set of human-neuronic feature-based learning. The human neuron patterns are used to take decision like the human brain. It is capable of solving unsupervised learning problems with unlabeled data and unstructured data. Using deep learning techniques (Wang and Welch 2018), several different problems can be solved easily, such as diagnosing system, false data prediction, future data prediction.

10.2.2 CONVOLUTIONAL NEURAL NETWORKS

A CNN is an algorithm for deep learning that acquires an image input, attaches importance to it, and then differentiates among many aspects/objects of the image. Compared to other classification algorithms the pre-processing required in ConvNet is much lower (Ye 2017).

ConvNets can acquire these scanners/features with the right training, while scanners are produced in rudimentary processes. A ConvNet's architecture is similar to the human brain neurons' contact pattern. The whole framework of Visual Cortex influenced this. Individual neurons only respond to stimuli in an environment known as the receptive field in the visual field. A group of these fields overlap to protect the whole region. With suitable screens, a ConvNet can successfully capture spatial and time dependencies in an image. The architecture is best suited for the image data set because the number of parameters involved is reduced and weight reusability is decreased. The network can also understand the sophistication of the image better (Zhang et al. 2007).

10.2.3 HYPER PARAMETERS PROBLEM OPTIMIZATION

Optimizing or tuning hyperparameters poses a problem in machine learning, which can be solved by choosing a collection of sufficient hyperparameters for learning algorithms. A hyperparameter is a parameter that tracks the learning process using its value. Comparison values of other parameters (usually node weights) are learned. The same model is used for generalizing diverse data patterns with different limits, weights, or speeds of learning. These steps are called hyperparameters, and they have to be optimized in such a way that the machine learning problem can be solved optimally by the model (Goldberg 1989). Hyperparameter optimization seeks a tuple of hyperparameters that produce an optimized model that minimizes the independent data supplied with a predefined loss function. The Machine Learning models consist of two distinct parameter types:

> Hyperparameters = are all the parameters that the user will randomly set before beginning training (e.g. the number of Random Forest estimators).
> Model parameters = In place of learning through the model training

Using input data, the model parameters decide how to get the desired output and are learned at training time. Hyperparameters, instead, determine in the first place how our model is ordered. A kind of optimization problem is tuning machine learning models (Kennedy and Eberhart 1995). A range of hyperparameters are used to determine the best combination of their values to help find the minimum loss/ maximum accuracy of a function. When comparing how various machine learning models work on a dataset, this can be especially relevant. In fact, for example, comparing an SVM model with the best hyperparameters against a Random Forest model that has not been optimized would be unreasonable. The different hyperparameter such as 1. Grid Search, 2. Random Search, 3. Artificial Neural Networks Tuning, 4. Manual Search, 5. Automated Hyperparameter Tuning.

10.3 METAHEURISTIC IN HYPER PARAMETERS OPTIMIZATIONS

10.3.1 EVOLUTIONARY COMMUTING

EC is an approach towards computational intelligence inspired by natural evolution. With an EC algorithm, the development of a population consisting of people representing solutions to the problem begins. Generating the first population at random or feeding it into the algorithm was feasible. Individuals are evaluated with a fitness function, and the function's output shows how well this individual solves the problem or is close to solving it (Yang et al. 2009). Then, individuals are applied to those workers impacted by natural evolution, including crossover, mutation, selection, and reproduction. A new population is created based on the fitness values of newly established individuals, as the population size needs to be preserved as it is in nature, certain individuals are excluded. This process continues until the dismissal condition is met. The most used criterion for stopping the algorithm is to exceed the number of generations specified. Natural evolution is used as a role model for a technique of evolutionary calculation to find optimal or near-optimal solutions for a particular problem. In genetic algorithms, the solution candidates are encoded in a string, a significant class of evolutions, often a binary string of only '0's and '1's. Evolution takes place by changing a candidate's genetic code.

For optimization problems, evolutionary approaches are usually applicable. Many of these concerns are problems of combinatorial optimization, which are difficult to compute (NP-hard). This means that programs are supposed to take a calculation time, which will increase exponentially with the problem's size. One of these issues is tour operators' problem when a number of cities are provided along with the distance matrix that gives each couple of cities the distance or cost of travel. The problem is that the traveling salesman leaves a certain city and must sit in all the other cities for the shortest roundtrip possible before returning to the first city. There are n towns, except the city of birth. There are n!-There are n! Different round trips, since each city has a direct connexion. A large proportion of the trips must be tested before one can be sure that the perfect round trip has been identified (Mirjalili and Lewis 2016).

The number of computing steps thus increases with the number of cities to be reached exponentially. This means that it is impractical to have the required computing time to find the optimum solution except for the moderate number of cities on fast computers today and computers foreseen in the short term. As a result, instead of an ideal solution, one must be satisfied with a satisfactory solution [38].

10.3.2 PARTICLE SWARM INTELLIGENCE

Particle Swarm Optimization (PSO), which optimizes a problem, is a computational approach that seeks to improve a candidate solution concerning a particular quality measurement. Kennedy & Eberhart introduced it in 1995 (Kennedy et al., 1995), and is used to optimize non-linear functions. However, it is also related to evolutionary estimation and has both genetic and evolutionary programming relations. The PSO has two main advantages such as 'nearest-neighbour velocity' 'matching' and 'craziness'. Some of the main advantages of PSO are as given below.

- Non-sensitive to design variables
- Easy to implement
- Concurrent parallelized
- Free derivatives
- Algorithm parameters
- Optimized global search

The some of the main application areas of PSO are as follows.

- Training the neural networks
- Topology optimization
- Identifying Parkinson's disease
- Structural optimization
- Extraction of fuzzy networks using rules
- Image recognition
- Optimizing distribution networks
- Structural optimization
- Procedure of biochemistry & Structure identification in biomechanics.

PSO consists of three steps, repeated until the condition meet or until the fitness values meet.

1. Assess the fitness of any particle
2. Update the individual and international best fitness and places
3. Update each particle's speed and position.

The two first measures are very trivial. Fitness assessment is carried out by presenting the candidate solution for the objective purpose. Person and world-leading fitness and positions are updated by comparing the newly assessed fitness with previous person and global fitness and substituting for best fitness and positions as needed (Strumberger et al. 2019). The velocity and location update is responsible for optimising the PSO algorithm. The speed of any particle in the swarm is updated by the following equation::

$$Vtmaxcount = WtV \ it + c1r1 (pit - xtt) + c2r2(p2t - xtt)$$

Where i is the object index, w is the inertia coefficient, $c1$; $c2$ are acceleration coefficients

Finally, the PSO is evaluated using parameters such as precision, error rate, sensitivity, specificity, entropy, etc.

10.3.3 EVOLUTIONARY COMPUTING AND CONVOLUTIONAL NEURAL NETWORK

In recent years, convolutionary neural networks (CNNs) have gained considerable recognition and significant influence, partly owed to their outstanding performance in incredibly composite supervised learning jobs. These structured neural networks have proven remarkably effective in addressing di-verse signals and time series, images, audio, and video processing. A fundamental solution to these problems is designing a significant system for pre-processing the signals and extraction systems to generate adequate data structures suitable for classification tasks. However, due to their ability to automatically extract useful features, CNNs made pre-processing unnecessary in many domains where it was an integral and necessary part of the classification task. In some instances, the coevolutionary layers of CNNs may perform automated pre-processing with an efficiency comparable to that achieved by human experts after rigorous and careful design processes. Without manual function engineering or further data transformation, comparable or even better results, can be obtained for handwritten character classification, which is the subject of study in this work.

CNN architecture design, however, remains a rigorous and repetitive process requiring industry expert involvement. In this job, we try to resolve this uncomplicated method in such a way as not to use pre-processing or other forms of a priori data processing, nor to build and parameterize CNN architecture. The critical contribution of this chapter is to suggest a new approach focused on the use of evolutionary algorithms to automatically discover the most suitable components of the CNN, both for the architecture and the hyperparameters concerned, and to implement for the first time a revolutionary coding scheme covering the evolution of the most important parameters of all aspects of CN classification. This methodology is part of the area known as 'neuroevolution,' and while it has been used effectively for nearly three decades, its application is revolutionary to some specific CNN design aspects. To validate this proposal and evaluate its efficiency, we chose a well-known and widespread problem: handwriting recognition. Recognition of handwritten characters today presents no real challenge, much less since the discovery and growth of CNNs, which have been extensively applied to this area, achieving human-like recognition performance in recent years. However, this problem is a good environment for testing the effectiveness of classification methods, as shown by the interest this problem has created in the scientific community in recent years. A CNN-based neural system architecture is complex, requiring a large number of parameters to de-terminate the efficacy of the network in solving a problem. In this chapter, we try to facilitate this task by developing a method that automatically generates a complete design of explicitly generated convolutionary neural networks to solve a specific problem, such as classifying handwritten text. This means that certain aspects of the architecture can be changed, such as a number of layers, connectivity, etc., as well as parameters for network activity, such as activation functions, learning rates, etc.

10.3.4 SWARM INTELLIGENCE AND CONVOLUTIONAL NEURAL NETWORK

CNN has recently emerged as a good option for achieving greater precision in the field of identification. There are numerous deep learning fields, including artificial intelligence, neural networks, pattern recognition, optimization, signal processing, and visual model. Deep learning is also an essential outcome in implementing, for example, the Colorful Image Colorization in several fields, an algorithm that takes black and white images and returns its color version (Yang and Hossein Gandomi 2012). To identify and colour objects/regions, the algorithm uses deep learning. The CNN definition involves numerous architectures, such as LeCun et al.'s first LeNet architecture proposed in 1998, and LeNet is implemented in OCR documents and character recognition.

ConvNet architecture, which uses seven layers, is also a CNN architecture; each layer has a necessary feature to describe it in different methods. ConvNet architecture is used to project in our designed scheme because it showed useful digital and character recognition tasks.

Overall, CNN can use different techniques including "Adam Optimizer", "Adadelta Optimizer", "Adagrad Optimizer" and "Stochastic Gradient Descent (SGD)" to train the proposed model. The latter is widely used in CNN based training since many samples are easier to implement and perform better. However, much manual tuning is needed to optimise their arguments (Wang et al. 2015). Here, the ConvNet's output layer weights is tried using the Particle Swarm Optimization (PSO) algorithm to improve image recognition accuracy on MNIST data sets.

10.4 PROBLEMS AND CHALLENGES

Hyperparameters are the magic numbers of the model; values are set before using any model data. ie. the number of trees in a random forest or hidden layers within a deep neural net. The method by which "right" hyperparameters can be searched is commonly called hyperparameter optimization. It can only have a small amount of your hyperparameter values to impact your model's efficiency significantly (Bacanin and Tuba 2015). Optimizing hyperparameters is a powerful technique to access the model's full potential, but only when properly implemented. Here, seven common issues are covered when optimizing hyperparameters.

10.4.1 TRUSTING DEFAULTS

In optimizing the hyperparameter, not optimizing the hyperparameter is the key error. If you don't explicitly is hyperparameters, you depend implicitly on the model maker's default hyperparameters, and these values might be totally different for the issue. In an example, a blog of TensorFlow ConvNet to predict the SHVN dataset Google Street View house numbers, 315 percent improvement is achieved over the default baseline hyperparameters hand configured for a comparable task using the related MNIST dataset.

10.4.2 FAKE METRICS

Microsoft researchers used the total search number as an indicator of their algorithmic search engine performance. They noticed that searches had actually improved after optimization of their search engine for this metric, but search results were worse after optimization on manual analysis. The fundamental assumption is that, as the number of searches increases, the algorithm works better because it is difficult for people to search to find what they are looking for. Stories like this demonstrate a major problem in hyperparameter optimization; it is to amplify the assessment criterion that you have chosen. If you have incorrect metric assumptions, the optimisation of hyperparameters will amplify the underlying assumptions. You can balance various competing measuring metrics such as sales and efficiency with models.

10.4.3 OVERFITTING

Overfitting is the issue in which, during training and optimization, The model performs exceptionally well and out of sample very poorly. Using strategies such as cross-validation, backtesting or regularisation can prevent overfitting. The evaluation of the hyperparameter optimization model is the average of k model evaluations from each k-fold of your data using a technique such as k-fold cross validation. Techniques like this can help ensure that the data is generalised by the calculation that you optimise, even uncertain, for correlations.

10.4.4 HIGH HYPERPARAMETERS

Construction of a machine learning pipeline will require tunable parameters such as transformations or trained feature representations, from raw data to extraction features to model development. Remember to optimize the feature parameters even to get optimum efficiency. An xgboost classifier is developed for SVHN digits in this example from the SigOpt blog and demonstrate compelling results for tuning the function parameters alongside the model hyperparameters. It is recommended that optimizing the model's hyperparameters includes varying design parameters and model parameters.

10.4.5 HAND-TUNING

An optimization approach is a technique that proposes the following set of hyperparameters for hyperparameters optimisation. Several optimization approaches are available and they all have different configuration metrics, time requirements and performance results.

When the value of the hyperparameter, like an optimisation tool, is changed manually, it becomes an inefficient optimisation process. With high dimensional, non-convex optimization in their brains, people are at the end of the day inherently slow. In this SigOpt blog example, we show that optimising algorithms for a deep neural net can be done by hand in a matter of hours requiring knowledge of an algorithmic weight bounding box or of neural network structure hyperparameters.

10.4.6 RANDOM SEARCH

Random search is easier to understand and execute as a grid search and also more effective technically. Space for the hyperparameter is achieved by evaluating n random points uniformly and selecting which results are better. The negative consequence of random searches is excessive variance. After all, the technique is absolutely random, with no information to select which points to pursue. You rely on luck to achieve good results. Ingenious techniques such as simulated annealing, Bayesian optimization (used by SigOpt), genetic algorithms, convex optimizers and swarm intelligence methods can provide enhanced performance over grid and random searching to the model.

10.5 CONCLUDING REMARKS

The conventional neural network is an inspired structure and it is based on the basic concepts of neural network. It is useful for different applications such as object detection, future prediction of data, analysis of data, missing data predictions and etc. The layers of the CNN used for different purpose such as filtering, analysis and detection/prediction. The combination of CNN with hyperparameter produce effective optimization in each layer of the CNN. The evolutionary algorithm is inspired based on the natural knowledge and activities. The different evolutionary algorithms such as genetic algorithm, ant colony and particle swarm optimization etc. These natural optimizations are combined with various meta optimization techniques and produced new hyperparameter procedure various applications. In this chapter summarized various optimization techniques combined with hyperparameter procedure. The finally presented various challenges and issues related to hyper parameter optimizations.

REFERENCES

Araújo, T., Aresta, G., Almada-Lobo, B., Mendonça, A.M., & Campilho, A. (2017). "Improving convolutional neural network design via variable neighborhood search." In Karray, F., Campilho, A., & Cheriet, F. (eds.) *Image Analysis and Recognition.* Lecture Notes in Computer Science, vol. 10317.

Bacanin, N., & Tuba, M. (2015). "Fireworks algorithm applied to constrained portfolio optimization problem". In Proceedings of the 2015 IEEE Congress on Evolutionary Computation (CEC), Sendai, Japan, 25–28 May.

Bergstra, J., et al. (December 2011). "Algorithms for hyper-parameter optimization." In NIPS'11: Proceedings of the 24th International Conference on Neural Information Processing Systems (pp. 2546–2554).

Bergstra, J., & Bengio, Y. (2012). "Random search for hyper-parameter optimization." *Journal of Machine Learning Research, 13*, 281–305.

Cui, H., & Bai, J. (2019). "PT US CR." *Pattern Recognition Letters*, 125, 828–834.

Cui, X., Zhang, W., Tüske, Z., & Picheny, M. (2018). "Evolutionary stochastic gradient descent for optimization of deep neural networks." arXiv:1810.06773.

Dahl, G.E. (2018). "Parallel architecture and hyperparameter search via successive halving and classification." arXiv:1805.10255.

Domhan, T., Springenberg, J.T., & Hutter, F. (July 2015). "Speeding up automatic hyperparameter optimization of deep neural networks by extrapolation of learning curves." In IJCAI'15: Proceedings of the 24th International Conference on Artificial Intelligence (pp. 3460–3468).

Dong, X., Shen, J., Wang, W., Shao, L., & Porikli, F. (2018). "Hyperparameter Optimization for Tracking with Continuous Deep Q-Learning." In IEEE/CVF Conference on Computer Vision and Pattern Recognition.

Falkner, S., Klein, A., & Hutter, F. (2018). "BOHB: Robust and efficient hyperparameter optimization at scale." arXiv:1807.01774.

Feurer M., & Hutter F. (2019). "Hyperparameter Optimization." In Hutter F., Kotthoff L., Vanschoren J. (eds). *Automated Machine Learning. The Springer Series on Challenges in Machine Learning.* Springer, Cham. https://doi.org/10.1007/978-3-030-05318-5_1.

Goldberg, D.E. (1989). *Genetic Algorithms in Search, Optimization and Machine Learning*, 1st ed. Addison-Wesley Longman Publishing Company: Boston, MA, USA.

Hinz, T., Magg, S., & Wermter, S., "Speeding up the Hyperparameter Optimization of Deep Convolutional Neural Networks." arXiv:1807.07362.

Ilievski, I. & Feng, J. (31 Jul 2016). "Hyperparameter transfer learning through surrogate." arXiv: 1608. 00218v1 [cs. LG].

Ilievski, I. & Shoemaker, C. A. (2012). "Efficient Hyperparameter Optimization of Deep Learning Algorithms Using Deterministic RBF Surrogates." arXiv:1607.08316.

Joy, T. T., Rana, S., Gupta, S., & Venkatesh, S. (1999). "Derivatives," Vapnik.

Kennedy, J., & Eberhart, R. 1995). "Particle swarm optimization." In Proceedings of the ICNN'95—International Conference on Neural Networks, Perth, WA, Australia, 27 November–1 December, Volume 4, pp. 1942–1948.

Kim, J., Kim, S., & Choi, S. (2017). "Learning to warm-start bayesian hyperparameter optimization." arXiv:1710.06219.

Klein, A. (2018). "Towards automated deep learning: efficient joint neural architecture and hyperparameter search," arXiv:1807.06906.

Klein, A., Falkner, S., & Bartels, S. (2017). "Fast bayesian optimization of machine learning hyperparameters on large datasets," vol. 54, arXiv: 1605. 07079v2 [cs. LG] 7 Mar 2017.

Koch, P., Gardner, S., Wujek, B., & Griffin, J. (2018). "Autotune: A derivative-free optimization framework for hyperparameter tuning." arXiv:1804.07824.

Koutsoukas, A., Monaghan, K. J., Li, X., & Huan, J. (2017). "Deep learning: investigating deep neural networks hyper parameters and comparison of performance to shallow methods for modeling bioactivity data." *Journal of Cheminformatics*, 9, 1–13.

Lee, W., Park, S., & Sim, K., (2018). "Optik optimal hyperparameter tuning of convolutional neural networks based on the parameter-setting-free harmony search algorithm." *Optik - International Journal for Light and Electron Optics*, 172 (May), 359–367.

Li, L. *et al.* (2018). "Massively parallel hyperparameter tuning." arXiv:1810.05934.

Lopez-rincon, A., Tonda, A., & Elati, M. (2018). Evolutionary optimization of convolutional neural networks for cancer miRNA biomarkers classification. *Applied Soft Computing - Journal*, 65, 91–100.

Loshchilov, I., & Hutter, F. (2016). "CMA-ES for hyperparameter optimization of deep neural networks." arXiv:1604.07269.

Mirjalili, S., & Lewis, A. (2016). "The whale optimization algorithm." *Advances in Engineering Software - Journal*, 95, 51–67.

Murugan, P. (2017). "Hyperparameters optimization in deep convolutional neural network/ Bayesian approach with Gaussian process priors," pp. 1–10. arXiv:1712.07233.

Nakisa, B., Rastgoo, M.N., & Rakotonirainy, A. (2018). "Long short term memory hyperparameter optimization for a neural network based emotion recognition framework." *IEEE Access*, 6, 49325–49338.

Ozaki, Y., Yano, M., & Onishi, M. (2017). "Effective hyperparameter optimization using Nelder-Mead method in deep learning." *IPSJ Transactions on Computer Vision and Applications*, 9, 20.

Shoemaker, C.A. (2012). "Efficient Hyperparameter Optimization of Deep Learning Algorithms Using Deterministic RBF Surrogates," arXiv:1607.08316.

Snoek, J., Rippel, O., & Adams, R.P. (2012). "Scalable Bayesian optimization using deep neural networks," arXiv:1502.05700.

Stein, B.V., Wang, H., & Bäck, T. (2019). "Automatic configuration of deep neural networks with parallel efficient global optimization," In 2019 International Joint Conference on Neural Networks (IJCNN) (pp. 1–7), Budapest, Hungary.

Strumberger, I., Bacanin, N., Tuba, M., & Tuba, E. (2019). "Resource scheduling in cloud computing based on a hybridized whale optimization algorithm." *Applied Sciences*, 9, 4893.

Su, Y., "Neural network hyperparameter optimization with genetic algorithm on handwritten digit problem, and the observation on neuron network by distinctiveness."

Wang, G.G., Deb, S., & dos S. Coelho, L. (2015). "Elephant herding optimization". In Proceedings of the 2015 3rd International Symposium on Computational and Business Intelligence (ISCBI) (pp. 1–5), Bali, Indonesia, 7–9 December.

Wang, W., & Welch, W. J. (2018). "Bayesian optimization using monotonicity information and its application in machine learning hyperparameter tuning," 1–13. arXiv:1802.03532.

Yang, X.S., & Hossein Gandomi, A. (2012). Bat algorithm: A novel approach for global engineering optimization." *Engineering with Computers*, 29, 464–483

Yang, X.S., Watanabe, O., & Zeugmann, T. (2009). "Firefly algorithms for multimodal optimization." In: *Stochastic Algorithms: Foundations and Applications*. Springer: Berlin, Germany, Volume 5792.

Ye, F. (2017). "Particle swarm optimization-based automatic parameter selection for deep neural networks and its applications in large-scale and high-dimensional data." *PLoS ONE* 12(12), e0188746. https://doi.org/10.1371/journal.pone.0188746

Zhang, M., Li, H., Lyu, J., Ho, S., & Su, S. (2007). "Multi-level CNN for lung nodule classification with Gaussian Process assisted hyperparameter optimization," Huiqi Li.

11 New Approach for Efficiently Computing Factors of the RSA Modulus

Muhammad Rezal Kamel Ariffin[1],
Amir Hamzah Abd Ghafar Ghafar[1],
Wan Nur Aqlili Wan Mohd Ruzai[2], and
Nurul Nur Hanisah Adenan[2]

[1]Institute for Mathematical Research and Department of Mathematics, Universiti Putra Malaysia, 43400 UPM Serdang, Selangor, Malaysia
[2]Institute for Mathematical Research, Universiti Putra Malaysia, 43400 UPM Serdang, Selangor, Malaysia

11.1 INTRODUCTION: BACKGROUND AND DRIVING FORCES

The RSA cryptosystem is one of the most widely used asymmetric cryptosystems in the world. Constructed in 1978, due to the commutative property of the RSA cryptosystem, it has been efficiently used to ensure confidentiality, integrity, authenticity and to disallow repudiation of the data being transmitted. The lower bound complexity of the power modulo operation surrounding the execution of the RSA algorithm is $O(n^3)$ where n is the length of the input, ensures fast computational time for the algorithm. This leads to its fast adoption rate worldwide. Moreover, the complexity of the execution time can be further reduced to $O(n^2 \log n)$. In order for the RSA cryptosystem to be accepted as a practical cryptosystem, the underlying mathematical problem that provides confidence for potential users has to be scrutinized in detail. This chapter discusses the underlying mathematical problem surrounding the RSA modulus $N = pq$ and $N = p^2q$ where p and q are large distinct primes. A large prime refers to a specific length of the parameter p and q which is more than the lower bound of the most efficient factoring algorithm available. The challenge is, upon obtaining the value of N, one has to produce its factors. This challenge is well known as the integer factorization problem. This seemingly trivial challenge has eluded a global audience of cryptanalysts. In general, one would need exponential time in order to factor the RSA modulus. On the flip side, to be able to efficiently compute the factors of N, it would deem the RSA cryptosystem insecure. This chapter discusses the recent

TABLE 11.1

Complexity and Running Time of Current Strategies to Solve Integer Factorization Problem

Algorithm	Complexity	Running Time
Trial Divisions	$O(n^2\sqrt{N})$	Exponential
Pollard $p - 1$ Factorization Algorithm	$O(\log m)$	Logarithmic
Factorization via Difference of Square	$O(\sqrt{N})$	Exponential
Quadratic Sieve Factoring	$O(\sqrt{n \cdot n})$	Subexponential
Pollard ρ Method	$O(p^{1/2} (\log n)^2)$	Subexponential
Elliptic Curve Method	$O(e^{\sqrt{2+o(1)\log p \log \log p}})$	Subexponential
Continued Fraction Method	$O(e^{\sqrt{\log p \log \log p}})$	Subexponential
Number Field Sieve	$O\left(e^{(c+o(1))\sqrt[3]{\log n}\sqrt[3]{(\log \log n)^2}}\right)$	Subexponential

advancements in cases where the RSA modulus N can be efficiently factored in polynomial time. We introduce to the readers the results where a 32-bit processor can be utilized to obtain the factors of N. Apart from providing the analytical results, we provide the algorithms for an easy implementation by interested readers.

Since the ultimate goal of our attack is to factor the modulus N, we describe here briefly some of the algorithms that are purposely designed to factorize N. However, these algorithms are efficient under certain conditions. As such, the Integer Factorization Problem still remains secure until today. We provide information on the complexity and running time of the algorithms through Table 11.1.

In the next subsections, we introduce some of the cryptanalytic tools that are needed throughout our discussions in order to ensure they are workable to factor the modulus N.

11.1.1 Continued Fractions

One of the important methodologies that are being utilized to launch algebraic cryptanalysis upon RSA and its variants is via the continued fractions (CF). (Wiener 1990) produced the first result that managed to factor N by using this method. We begin by reviewing the fundamental knowledge of CF and its related concepts.

Definition 11.1: The continued fractions expansion of a real number X can be defined and written in the following form

$$X = [x_0, x_1, x_2, \cdots] = x_0 + \cfrac{1}{x_1 + \cfrac{1}{x_2 + \cfrac{1}{x_3 + \cdots}}}$$

where x_0 is an integer and x_i are the positive integers with $i > 0$.

As seen from Definition 11.1., the numbers $x_1, x_2, x_3, \cdots$ are called the partial quotients. When $i \geq 0$, the fractions $\frac{a_i}{b_i} = [x_0, x_1, x_2, \cdots, x_i]$ are called the convergents of an expansion X. When $X = \frac{a}{b}$ where a and b are co-prime, the continued fractions algorithm such as the Euclidean algorithm computes the convergents in polynomial time with complexity $\mathcal{O}((\log b)^2)$ (Nitaj 2008).

Consequently, the following theorem by Legendre is a significant result on continued fractions that can be found in most of kinds of literature related to cryptanalysis of RSA via Diophantine approximations.

Theorem 11.2: (Legendre's Theorem) *Suppose $\mathscr{X}$ is a rational number and y and z are co-prime integers. If*

$$\left| \mathscr{X} - \frac{y}{z} \right| < \frac{1}{2z^2},$$

then $\frac{y}{z}$ is a convergent of the continued fractions expansion of $\mathscr{X}$.

11.1.2 LLL Algorithm

This algorithm was introduced by Lenstra et al. in 1982 with the objective of producing the shortest basis vector. Since then, this algorithm has been exploited by

---

ALGORITHM 11.3   LLL ALGORITHM

Input: A basis $\{v_1, v_2, \ldots, v_n\}$ for lattice $\mathcal{L}$.
   Output: Return LLL reduced basis $\{b_1, b_2, \ldots, b_n\}$

1. Set $k = 2$
2. Set $v_1^* = v_1$
3. **while** $k \leq n$ **do**
4.   **for** $j = 1$ to $k + 1$ **do**
5.   Set $v_k = v_k - [\mu_{k,j}]v_j^*$ where $\mu_{k,j} = \frac{v_k \cdot v_j^*}{\|v_k\|^2}$
6.   **end for**
7.   **if** $\|v_k^*\|^2 \geq \left(\frac{3}{4} - \mu_{k,k-1}^2 \right) \|v_{k-1}^*\|^2$ **then**
8.   Set $k = k + 1$
9.   **else**
10.   Swap v_{k-1} and v_k
11.   Set $k = \max(k - 1, 2)$
12. **end if**
13. **end while**

numerous researchers in their attempts to attack the RSA cryptosystem. The following algorithm and theorem describe the result of the algorithm.

Theorem 11.4: (LLL Algorithm) *Let $\mathcal{L}$ be a lattice with n -dimension. The LLL outputs a reduced basis $\{b_1, b_2, ..., b_n\} \in \mathcal{L}$ such that*

$$\prod_{i=1}^{n} \|b_i\| \leq 2^{\frac{n(n-1)}{4}} \, det(\mathcal{L})$$

for all $1 \leq i \leq n$.

11.1.3 COPPERSMITH'S METHOD

Next, we introduce another method that is very essential in the cryptanalysis of RSA. In 1996, Coppersmith proposed a method with a primary aim to find the integer roots of univariate or bivariate polynomials modulo of a given integer. The polynomial can be written in the form

$$F(x) = x^n + a_{n-1}x^{n-1} + ... + a_1x + a_0 \pmod{N}.$$

Coppersmith showed that there exists a small solution x_0 such that $F(x_0) \equiv 0$ (mod N) provided $x_0 < N^{1/n}$. This solution can be found by applying the LLL algorithm. Coppersmith presented his method in the following theorem.

Theorem 11.5: *Let N be an integer and $F \in \mathbb{Z}[x]$ be a monic polynomial of degree n over the integers. Let $X = N^{\frac{1}{n}-\varepsilon}$ for $\frac{1}{n} > \varepsilon > 0$. From the given N and F, then all the integers $x_0 < X$ satisfying $F(x_0) \equiv 0$ (mod N) can be found in polynomial time.*

11.1.4 CONTINUOUS MIDPOINT SUBDIVISION ANALYSIS

Now, we introduce the concept of continuous midpoint subdivision analysis (CMSA). It is a technique that manipulates the interval containing Euler's totient function via continued fractions of certain related numbers. Recall that, the Euler's totient function is denoted by $\phi(N) = (p - 1)(q - 1)$. The interval containing $\phi(N)$ is described in the following lemma.

Lemma 11.6: *Let $N = pq$ represents the modulus of RSA with $q < p < 2q$. Suppose a public exponent e satisfies an equation $ed - k\phi(N) = 1$ for the positive integers d, k and $\phi(N) = (p - 1)(q - 1)$. Then, $N + 1 - \frac{3}{\sqrt{2}}\sqrt{N} < \phi(N) < N + 1 - 2\sqrt{N}$.*

Proof. Refer to (Bunder and Tonien 2017).

11.1.5 JOCHEMSZ MAY'S STRATEGY

Jochemsz and May (2006) invented a strategy to solve for small roots of polynomials either in integer or modular form. Besides, this strategy is also used to find the unsafe bound for RSA decryption exponent d where $ed \equiv 1 \bmod \phi(N)$ and e is the public RSA exponent. By reformulating the idea by (Coron 2004), they described their strategy in a more structured manner. They utilized the lattice-based Coppersmith's method to solve for the small roots. The following algorithms show the steps that are needed to find the intended roots and bound. However, we only provide the algorithm to solve for integer polynomial since it will be used later in our attack.

ALGORITHM 11.7   FINDING SMALL INTEGER ROOTS

Input: A set of integer multivariate polynomial f.
   Output: The primes p and q.

1. Define the set

$$S = \bigcup_{0 \le j \le t} \{x_1^{i_1}, \ldots, x_n^{i_n+j} | x_1^{i_1}, \ldots, x_n^{i_n} \text{ monomial of } f^{m-1}\}$$

$$M = \{\text{monomials of } x_1^{i_1}, \ldots, x_n^{i_n} f | x_1^{i_1}, \ldots, x_n^{i_n} \in S\}$$

2. Find the expansion of f^{m-1} where $m \in \mathbb{Z}$ and characterize the monomials into set S and M.
3. Define $W = \|f(x_1 X_1, \ldots, x_n X_n)\|_\infty$, with $\|f(x_1 X_1, \ldots, x_n X_n)\|_\infty := |\max a_{i_1, \ldots, i_n}|$.
4. Define $R = W \prod_{j=1}^n X_n^{d_j(m-1)}$.
5. Define $f' = a_0^{-1} f \bmod R$, where a_0 is the constant term of f. We have to ensure $a_0 \ne 0$ and $\gcd\{a_0, R\} = 1$.
6. Define

$$g_{i_1, \ldots i_n} = x_1^{i_1} \ldots x_n^{i_n} f'(x_1 \ldots x_n) \prod_{j=1}^n X_j^{l_j - i_j} \quad \text{for } x_1^{i_1} \ldots x_n^{i_n} \in S$$

$$h_{i_1, \ldots i_n} = x_1^{i_1} \ldots x_n^{i_n} R, \qquad\qquad \text{for } x_1^{i_1} \ldots x_n^{i_n} \in M \backslash S$$

where l_j is the largest exponent of x_j. Polynomial g and h have the roots $x_1^{(0)} \ldots x_n^{(0)} \bmod R$.

7. Build a lattice $\mathcal{L}$ I a lower triangular form by using the coefficient vectors from both polynomials g and h as its lattice basis.
8. Perform LLL to the lattice $\mathcal{L}$ which will output $n - 1$ reduced basis vectors correspond to $n - 1$ polynomials $h_i(x_1, \ldots, x_n)$ with $h_i(x_1^{(0)}, \ldots, x_n^{(0)}) = 0$.
9. Extract the roots from the polynomial of f and h_i by using resultant computations.
10. Use the revealed roots to factor N.

**ALGORITHM 11.8 FINDING THE BOUND FOR THE DECRYP-
TION EXPONENT D.**

Input: A set of integer multivariate polynomial f.
  Output: Bound for d.

1. Refer Steps 1–7 in Algorithm 11.7.
2. Find the determinant of the lattice that satisfies Howgrave-Graham's
   bound which is $\det(\mathcal{L}) < R^{\omega+2-n}$. This condition can be reduced to

$$\prod_{j=1}^{n} X_j^{s_j} < W^{s_W}, \quad \text{for } s_j = \sum_{x_1^{i_1}\dots x_n^{i_n}\in M\setminus S} i_j, \quad \text{and } s_W = |S|. \qquad (11.1)$$

   Find all the values of s_j as it represents the cardinality of x_j in the
   diagonal of the lattice.
3. Set $t = \tau m$. Then substitute the value of t into s_j. The purpose is to
   determine the values of s_j when m approaches a higher value.
4. Substitute all the values of H_j, s_j, W and s_W into equation (11.1). To
   solve the inequalities, only the values of the indices will be considered.
5. Differentiate with respect to τ for the equation that we gained after
   Step 4. The find the optimal value for τ.
6. Substitute the optimal value of τ into the equation from Step 4, then
   solve for the value of δ in terms of other monomials.

The following three sections will present our analytical factoring results upon
modulus N in polynomial time. For the first two cases, we consider the case when
$N = pq$. For the third case, we produce results for $N = p^2 q$.

11.2 ATTACKING RSA KEY EQUATION USING ARBITRARY PARAMETER

In this section, we take a different approach from the past attacks. By defining a new
parameter, u to be the sum of the upper and lower bounds of $\phi(N)$, we incorporate it
into the generalized key equation. It should be noted that u can be modified to other
values that is suitably larger than N and related to the bounds of $\phi(N)$.

Here, we present two new attacks that apply this approach. The first attack focuses on a single RSA key equation upon an RSA modulus. Given RSA public keys
(N, e), $u = \phi_a + \phi_b$ and suitably large $X, Y, Z \in \mathbb{Z}$, we modified RSA key equation to

$$eX - uY = Z - \phi_b \qquad (11.2)$$

where ϕ_a and ϕ_b are respectively the best known upper and lower bounds of $\phi(N)$. By combining the continued fraction method in (Wiener 1990) and Coppersmith's method (Coppersmith 1997), we showed that N can be factored in polynomial time when

$$1 \le Y < X < \frac{u}{2\left(\phi(N)-\phi_b\right)}, \quad \phi(N) + \frac{p-q}{p+q} N^{\frac{1}{4}} < N - 2N^{\frac{1}{2}},$$

$$|Z - \phi(N)| < \frac{p-q}{p+q}N^{1/4}.$$

Note that this equation is not derived from the RSA key equation. It is also not a generalized RSA key equation. We also estimated there are at least $N^{\frac{1}{2}-\epsilon}$ numbers of $e < N$ that satisfies equation (11.2).

In the second attack, we show that the first attack can be modified to accommodate k instances of weak public keys e_i with its corresponding RSA moduli $N_i = p_i q_i$. If there exist an integer $X < N^\delta$ and k integers $Y_i < N^\delta$ and $|Z_i - \phi(N_i)| < \frac{p_i - q_i}{p_i + q_i}N^{1/4}$ such that

$$e_i X - Y_i u_i = Z_i - \phi_b \qquad (11.3)$$

for $i = 1, ..., k$, and $|Z\_i - \phi_{b_i}| < \lambda N^{\delta+\frac{1}{4}}\}$ where $\lambda < \frac{3}{2}(2^{\frac{k+5}{4}} - 3)$ then N_i can be factored simultaneously in polynomial time.

From these two attacks, we showed that there is a pressing danger for users of RSA that intends to generate their own RSA keys since many pairs of (N, e) can be transformed into weak keys of RSA using a suitable arbitrary u without suitable precautions.

11.2.1   FIRST ATTACK

We begin by introducing the new parameter u.

Definition 11.9: Let ϕ_a be the smallest integer value of the known upper bound of $\phi(N)$. Let ϕ_b be the largest integer value of the known lower bound of $\phi(N)$. Then we define $u = \phi_a + \phi_b$.

Observe that in (Nitaj 2013),

$$2\sqrt{N} < p + q < \frac{3}{\sqrt{2}}\sqrt{N}. \qquad (11.4)$$

From (11.4), we can obtain the best approximation of ϕ_a to be $\lfloor N - 2\sqrt{N} + 1 \rfloor$ while the best approximation of ϕ_b is $\lceil N - \frac{3}{\sqrt{2}}\sqrt{N} + 1 \rceil$. The parameter u is an arbitrary value that satisfies two conditions; (i) u is suitably larger than N, and (ii) u is related to the bounds of $\phi(N)$.

The following lemmas enable the conditions for our attack.

Lemma 11.10: Suppose $N = pq$ is an RSA modulus with $q < p < 2q$. Given an approximation S of $p + q$ such that $S > 2N^{1/2}$, $\sqrt{S^2 - 4N} > p - q$ and

$$|p + q - S| < \frac{p-q}{p+q}N^{1/4}.$$

Then $P' = \frac{1}{2}(S + \sqrt{S^2 - 4N})$ is an approximation of p where $|p - P'| < N^{1/4}$.

Proof. Refer to (Ariffin 2020).

Lemma 11.11: Suppose $N = pq$ is an RSA modulus with $q < p < 2q$. Suppose e satisfies the equation $eX - uY = Z - \phi_b$ where X, Y are positive integers with $\gcd(X, Y) = 1$. If $1 \le Y < X < |\frac{u}{2(\phi(N) - \phi_b)}|$ and $|Z - \phi(N)| < \frac{p-q}{p+q}N^{1/4}$ then $\frac{Y}{X}$ is a convergent of $\frac{e}{u} - \frac{N^{1/4}}{2u}$.

Proof. Refer to (Ariffin 2020).

Based on the previous lemmas, we show that N can be factored in polynomial time in the following theorem.

Theorem 11.12: Suppose $N = pq$ is an RSA modulus with $q < p < 2q$. Given that e satisfies the equation $eX - uY = Z - \phi_b$ where X, Y are suitable positive integers with $\gcd(X, Y) = 1$. If

$$1 \le Y < X < \frac{u}{2\left(\phi(N) - \phi_b\right)}, \quad \phi(N) + \frac{p-q}{p+q}N^{\frac{1}{4}} < N - 2N^{\frac{1}{2}},$$

$$|Z - \phi(N)| < \frac{p-q}{p+q}N^{1/4}.$$

then N can be factored in polynomial time.

Proof. Refer to (Ariffin 2020).

Now we present a theorem to estimate the number of RSA public key pairs that are susceptible to our attack.

Theorem 11.13: Suppose $N = pq$ be the product of two balanced prime integers such that $p + q > \sqrt{N}$. The number of the parameter $e < N$ from Theorem 11.12 where

$$e = \frac{Z - \phi_b + uY}{X}$$

and $\gcd(X, Y) = 1$ with

$$1 \le Y < X < \frac{p-q}{p+q}N^{\frac{1}{4}}, \quad |Z - \phi(N)| < \frac{p-q}{p+q}N^{1/4}$$

is at least $N^{\frac{1}{2}-\epsilon}$ where $\epsilon > 0$ is arbitrarily small for suitably large N.

Proof. Refer to (Ariffin 2020).

To understand properly the proof given in Theorem 11.12., we advise readers to refer to Lemma 3 and 4 in (Ariffin 2020).

11.2.2 SECOND ATTACK

In this section, we apply the previous attack on k RSA public key e_i with its corresponding RSA moduli $N_i = p_i q_i$ and u_i where u_i follows Definition 11.9, i.e. $u_i = \phi_{a_i} + \phi_{b_i}$. In this attack, we show that we are able to factor k RSA moduli simultaneously if there exists X and Y that satisfy conditions required in the following theorem.

Theorem 11.14: For $k \ge 2$, let $N_i = p_i q_i$, $1 \le i \le k$, be k RSA moduli. Let $N = \min_i N_i$. Let e_i where $i = 1, ..., k$, be k public exponents. Let $\delta = \frac{k}{2(k+1)}$. If there exist an integer $X < N^\delta$ and k integers $Y_i < N^\delta$ with $\gcd(X, Y_i) = 1$ and $|Z_i - \phi(N_i)| < \frac{p_i - q_i}{p_i + q_i}N^{1/4}$ such that $e_i X - Y_i u_i = Z_i - \phi_{b_i}$ for $i = 1, ..., k$, and $|Z_i - \phi_{b_i}| < \lambda N^{\delta+\frac{1}{4}}$ where

$$\lambda < \frac{3}{2}(2^{\frac{k+5}{4}} - 3)$$

then one can factor the k RSA moduli $N_1, ..., N_k$ in polynomial time.

Proof. Refer to (Ariffin 2020).

From the two presented attacks, we can see that our results did not utilize the RSA Diophantine equation either in its original or generalized form. Our equation of the form $eX - uY = Z - \phi(b)$ does not originate from the RSA Diophantine equation. As a result, our strategy enables us to factor $N = pq$ for $d \approx N$. This is a major finding.

11.3 ON THE CONTINUOUS MIDPOINT SUBDIVISION ANALYSIS UPON RSA CRYPTOSYSTEM

In this section, a brief review of the cryptanalytic work via the continuous midpoint subdivision analysis (CMSA) on the RSA cryptosystem is scrutinized. Recall from Lemma 11.6., we propose CMSA that can be explained as follows.

First, suppose that $\phi(N) \in (\theta_1, \theta_2)$ where $\phi(N) = (p - 1)(q - 1)$, $\theta_1 = N + 1 - \frac{3}{\sqrt{2}}\sqrt{N}$ and $\theta_2 = N + 1 - 2\sqrt{N}$, then we find a midpoint of interval (θ_1, θ_2) and denote it as $\mu_{(0,0)}$ as shown in Figure 11.1. This process is marked as $i = 0$.

As observed from Figure 11.1, regardless of where $\phi(N)$ is situated at, this relation always holds

$$|\phi(N) - \mu_{(0,0)}| < \frac{\theta_2 - \theta_1}{2}.$$

Later, we divide equally between the intervals $(\theta_1, \mu_{(0,0)})$ and $(\mu_{(0,0)}, \theta_2)$, which return another set of midpoints denoted $\mu_{(1,0)}$ and $\mu_{(1,1)}$ as illustrated in Figure 11.2.

For simplicity, this process is denoted with $i = 1$. Then, regardless of where $\phi(N)$ is situated at, we always have

$$|\phi(N) - \mu_{(1,j)}| < \frac{\theta_2 - \theta_1}{4}, \quad 0 \le j \le 1.$$

The same method is repeated and this process is denoted with $i = 2$ and is illustrated as in Figure 11.3.

In this process, the following relation always holds regardless of where $\phi(N)$ is situated at;

$$|\phi(N) - \mu_{(2,j)}| < \frac{\theta_2 - \theta_1}{8}, \quad 0 \le j \le 3.$$

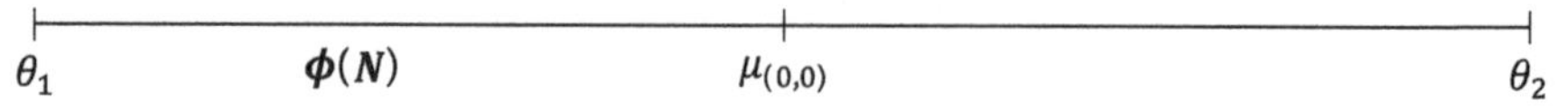

FIGURE 11.1 The continuous midpoint subdivision analysis when $i = 0$.

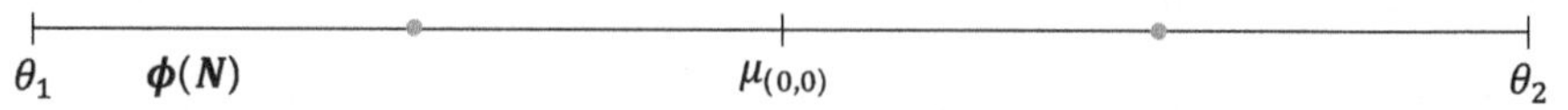

FIGURE 11.2 The continuous midpoint subdivision analysis when $i = 1$.

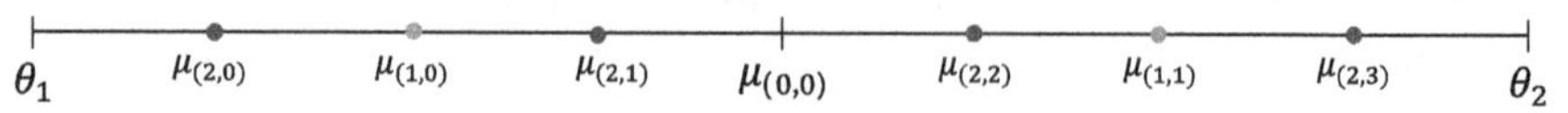

FIGURE 11.3 The continuous midpoint subdivision analysis when $i = 2$.

The same method is applied continuously and thus; we obtain the following general result.

Definition 11.18: Let $\phi(N) \in (\theta_1, \theta_2)$ where $(N) = (p-1)(q-1)$ $\theta_1 = N + 1 - \frac{3}{\sqrt{2}}\sqrt{N}$, and $\theta_2 = N + 1 - 2\sqrt{N}$. Let i and j be fixed positive integers of the midpoint term $\mu_{(i,j)}$ given by

$$\mu_{(i,j)} = N + 1 - \sqrt{N}\left(\frac{1 + 2j}{2^i} + \frac{3(2^{i+1}) - 3 - 6j}{2^{i+2}}\sqrt{2}\right),$$

then

$$\left|\phi(N) - \mu_{(i,j)}\right| < \frac{\theta_2 - \theta_1}{2^{i+1}}$$

for the specific $\mu_{(i,j)}$.

Remark 11.19: *Parameter $i \in \mathbb{Z}$ can be viewed as the number of subdivision processes between the midpoints in the interval of $\phi(N)$ where $\phi(N) \in \left(N + 1 - \frac{3}{\sqrt{2}}\sqrt{N}, N + 1 - 2\sqrt{N}\right)$ while parameter $j \in \mathbb{Z}$ denotes each midpoint term in i -th subdivision process.*

11.3.1 OUR PROPOSED ATTACK

This section discusses an improved result in terms of the upper cryptanalytic bound of private exponent d as opposed to previous results by Bunder & Tonien (2017) and Tonien (2018).

Theorem 11.20: *Let i be a fixed positive integer. Consider a public key pair (N, e) of an RSA cryptosystem such that $N = pq$ with $q < p < 2q$. If $e < (p-1)(q-1)$ satisfies an equation $ed - k(p-1)(q-1) = 1$ for some positive integer k and d with*

$$d < \sqrt{\frac{B \cdot 2^i}{e \cdot (A + 2^{i+2})}},$$

where $A = \left(\frac{3}{\sqrt{2}} - 2\right)\sqrt{N}$ and $B = N^2 - \frac{6}{\sqrt{2}}N^{1.5} + \frac{9}{2}N$, then $\frac{k}{d}$ can be found among the convergents of the public rational number $\frac{e}{\mu_{(i,j)}}$ given that $\mu_{(i,j)} = N + 1 - \sqrt{N}\left(\frac{1 + 2j}{2^i} + \frac{3(2^{i+1}) - 3 - 6j}{2^{i+2}}\sqrt{2}\right)$ for some $j \in [0, 2^i - 1]$.

Proof. Let $\phi(N) = (p-1)(q-1)$ is the Euler totient function such that $\phi(N) \in (\theta_1, \theta_2)$ where $\theta_1 = N + 1 - \frac{3}{\sqrt{2}}\sqrt{N}$ and $\theta_2 = N + 1 - 2\sqrt{N}$. Let $\mu_{(i,j)} = N + 1 - \sqrt{N}\left(\frac{1+2j}{2^i} + \frac{3(2^{i+1}) - 3 - 6j}{2^{i+2}}\sqrt{2}\right)$ is the general term of midpoint of interval (θ_1, θ_2). Then, for every $\mu_{(i,j)}$ we have

$$|\phi(N) - \lfloor\mu_{(i,j)}\rfloor| < \frac{\theta_2 - \theta_1}{2^{i+1}} < \frac{\theta_2 - \theta_1}{2^{i+1}} + 1. \tag{11.5}$$

From the equation $ed - k\phi(N) = 1$, we divide with $d\phi(N)$ to obtain

$$\frac{e}{\phi(N)} - \frac{k}{d} = \frac{1}{d\phi(N)}.$$

Let $\mu_{(i,j)}$ be the approximation of $\phi(N)$ and observe

$$\left|\frac{e}{\lfloor\mu_{(i,j)}\rfloor} - \frac{k}{d}\right| = \left|\frac{e}{\lfloor\mu_{(i,j)}\rfloor} - \frac{e}{\phi(N)} + \frac{e}{\phi(N)} - \frac{k}{d}\right| \le \left|\frac{e}{\lfloor\mu_{(i,j)}\rfloor} - \frac{e}{\phi(N)}\right| + \left|\frac{e}{\phi(N)} - \frac{k}{d}\right|$$

$$\le \frac{e\left|\phi(N) - \lfloor\mu_{(i,j)}\rfloor\right|}{\lfloor\mu_{(i,j)}\rfloor \lfloor\phi(N)\rfloor} + \frac{1}{d\phi(N)}. \tag{11.6}$$

Since $d = \frac{1 + k\phi(N)}{e}$ and from (11.5), then (11.6) yields

$$\left|\frac{e}{\lfloor\mu_{(i,j)}\rfloor} - \frac{k}{d}\right| < \frac{e\left(\frac{\theta_2 - \theta_1}{2^{i+1}} + 1\right)}{\lfloor\mu_{(i,j)}\rfloor \cdot \phi(N)} + \frac{1}{\frac{1 + k\phi(N)}{e} \cdot \phi(N)}$$

$$< \frac{e(\theta_2 - \theta_1 + 2^{i+1})}{2^{i+1} \cdot \lfloor\mu_{(i,j)}\rfloor \cdot \phi(N)} + \frac{e}{\phi(N) \cdot [1 + k\phi(N)]}. \tag{11.7}$$

Now, observe that from Lemma 11.6., $\theta_1 < \phi(N) < \theta_2 \Rightarrow \frac{1}{\theta_2} < \frac{1}{\phi(N)} < \frac{1}{\theta_1}$ and lead (11.7) to

$$\left|\frac{e}{\lfloor\mu_{(i,j)}\rfloor} - \frac{k}{d}\right| < \frac{e(\theta_2 - \theta_1 + 2^{i+1})}{2^{i+1}(\theta_1)(\theta_1)} + \frac{e}{(\theta_1)(\theta_1)} = \frac{e(\theta_2 - \theta_1 + 2^{i+2})}{2^{i+1}(\theta_1)^2}$$

$$< \frac{e(\theta_2 - \theta_1 + 2^{i+2})}{2^{i+1}(\theta_1 - 1)^2}$$

$$< \frac{e\left(\left(\frac{3}{\sqrt{2}} - 2\right)\sqrt{N} + 2^{i+2}\right)}{2^{i+1}\left(N - \frac{3}{\sqrt{2}}\sqrt{N}\right)^2}. \tag{11.8}$$

For simplicity, let $A = \left(\frac{3}{\sqrt{2}} - 2\right)\sqrt{N}$ and $B = N^2 - \frac{6}{\sqrt{2}}N^{1.5} + \frac{9}{2}N$. Then, (11.8) becomes

$$\left|\frac{e}{\lfloor \mu_{(i,j)} \rfloor} - \frac{k}{d}\right| < \frac{e(A + 2^{i+2})}{B \cdot 2^{i+1}}. \tag{11.9}$$

To ensure (11.9) meets the condition of Legendre's Theorem,

$$\frac{e(A + 2^{i+2})}{B \cdot 2^{i+1}} < \frac{1}{2d^2}. \tag{11.10}$$

Hence, $\frac{k}{d}$ can be found amongst the convergents of $\frac{e}{\mu_{(i,j)}}$ via the continued fractions algorithm. ∎

Consequently, the knowledge of k and d implies that one is able to solve the prime factorization of modulus N. This can be done by solving for the roots of quadratic polynomial $X^2 - (N - \phi(N) + 1)X + N = 0$ where $\phi(N) = \frac{ed - 1}{k}$; which output the primes $p = X_1$ and $q = X_2$.

Remark 11.21: Based on the attack proposed in Theorem 11.20., our method is applicable whenever $e > N^{0.5}$.

In contrast with the previous results obtained as in the work of (Bunder and Tonien 2017) and (Tonien 2018), we successfully raise the security bound of d exponentially. That is, d is increased from $d < \sqrt{8}\,N^{0.25}$ (Bunder and Tonien 2017) and $d < \sqrt{8t}\,N^{0.25}$ (Tonien 2018) to $d < \sqrt{2^i}\,N^{0.25}$. Note that, t and i are both fixed positive integers.

According to the current technological advancement, $i = 112$ (Barker 2016) is an achievable target. In our case, if $i = 112$ is considered, then we are able to increase the security bound of d up to $d < N^{0.305}$ for 1024-bit of modulus N and $d < N^{0.277}$ for 2048-bit of modulus N. Hence, this shows some significant improvement as compared to the previously proposed attacks on RSA.

11.4 ATTACK ON $N = p^2q$ WHEN THE PRIMES SHARE LEAST SIGNIFICANT BITS

In this attack, we describe a case when the primes of the modulus $N = p^2q$ share an amount of Least Significant Bits(LSBs). Based on key equation $ed - k\phi(N) = 1$, where $\phi(N) = p(p - 1)(q - 1)$, we find the substitution for $\phi(N)$ by utilizing the given information on p and q. We present our attack in the following lemma and theorem. Note that our lemma is a reformulation from (Nitaj et al. 2014).

Lemma 11.22: *Let $N = p^2 q$ be the modulus and suppose that $p - q = 2^b u$ for a known value of b. Let $p = 2^b p_1 + u_0$ and $q = 2^b q_1 + u_0$ where u_0 is a solution to $p^3 \equiv N \pmod{2^b}$. If $s_0 \equiv u_0^{-1}(N - u_0^3)\pmod{2^{3b}}$ then $p^2 + pq - p = 2^{3b}s + s_0 - v$ where*

$$v = (2^b p_1 + 2^{2b} p_1 q_1 - 2^b p_1 u_0 - 2u_0^2 + u_0).$$

Through this lemma, we manage to find a substitution for some part of the $\phi(N)$. We then use Lemma 11.22. to prove our theorem.

Theorem 11.23: *Let $N = p^2 q$ be the modulus such that $p - q = 2^b u$ where $2^b \approx N^\alpha$. Let e be a public exponents satisfying $e \approx N^\gamma$ and $ed - k\phi(N) = 1$. Suppose that $d < N^\delta$. Then N can be factored in time polynomial if*

$$\delta < \frac{11}{9} - \frac{2}{9}\sqrt{4 + 18\gamma}.$$

Proof. Based on the key equation $ed - k\phi(N) = 1$, replacing $\phi(N) = p(p - 1)(q - 1)$ then we would have

$$ed - k(N - (p^2 + pq - p)) = 1. \tag{11.11}$$

From Lemma 11.22, it had been proved that $p^2 + pq - p = 2^{3b}s + s_0 - v$. Thus, substituting this value into (11.11), we get

$$ed - k(N - (2^{3b}s + s_0 - v)) = 1. \tag{11.12}$$

Rearranging (11.12),

$$ed - k(N - s_0) + k(2^{3b}s - v) - 1 = 0. \tag{11.13}$$

We then transform (11.13) into

$$a_1 x_1 + a_2 x_2 + x_2 x_3 + a_3 = 0.$$

We fix the known and unknown parameters as follows.

$$a_1 = e; \quad a_2 = -(N - s_0); \quad a_3 = -1; \quad x_1 = d; \quad x_2 = k; \quad x_3 = 2^{3b}s - v;$$

Now, we consider the polynomial

$$f(x_1, x_2, x_3) = a_1 x_1 + a_2 x_2 + x_2 x_3 + a_3.$$

Then $(d, k, 2^{3b}s - v)$ is a root of polynomial $f(x_1, x_2, x_3)$ and can be found by using Coppersmith's technique (Coppersmith 1997). We use the extended strategy of (Jochemsz and May 2006) in order to find the small roots of $f(x_1, x_2, x_3)$ and the following bounds will be needed.

- $\max(e_1, e_2) = N^\gamma$;
- $\max(d) < X_1 = N^\delta$;
- $k = \frac{e_1 d_1 - 1}{\phi(N)} < X_2 = N^{\gamma+\delta-1}$;
- $p - q = 2^b u$ with $2^b \approx N^\alpha$ and $\alpha < \frac{2}{9}$.
- $p^2 + pq - p = 2^{3b}s + s_0 - v$ with $2^{3b}s - v < X_3 = N^{2/3}$

Next we define the sets S and M based on the following properties. Let $m, t \in \mathbb{Z}^+$

$$S = \bigcup_{0 \le j \le t} \left\{ x_1^{i_1} x_2^{i_2} x_3^{i_3+j} | x_1^{i_1} x_2^{i_2} x_3^{i_3} \text{ monomials of } f^{m-1} \right\}$$

and

$$M = \left\{ \text{monomials of } x_1^{i_1} x_2^{i_2} x_3^{i_3} f | x_1^{i_1} x_2^{i_2} x_3^{i_3} \in S \right\}$$

Next, we find the expansion of polynomial $f^{m-1}(x_1^{i_1} x_2^{i_2} x_3^{i_3})$ by using Binomial expansion and we get

$$f^{m-1}\left(x_1^{i_1} x_2^{i_2} x_3^{i_3}\right) = \sum_{i_1=0}^{m-1} \sum_{i_2=0}^{m-1-i_1} \sum_{i_3=0}^{i_2} x_1^{i_1} x_2^{i_2} x_3^{i_3}$$

Particularly, the monomials in set S can be characterized as

$$i_1 = 0, \ldots, m-1, \quad i_2 = 0, \ldots, m-1-i_1, \quad i_3 = 0, \ldots, i_2+t$$

For set M, the characterization of the monomials are

$$i_1 = 0, \ldots, m, \quad i_2 = 0, \ldots, m-i_1, \quad i_3 = 0, \ldots, i_2+t$$

Define $W = \| f(x_1 X_1, x_2 X_2, x_3 X_3) \|_\infty$. Then W satisfies

$$W \geq |a_1|X_1 = ed \approx N^{\gamma+\delta}. \qquad (11.14)$$

Next, define

$$R = WX_1^{m-1}X_2^{m-1}X_3^{m-1+t}.$$

Suppose that a_4 is relatively prime with R. We define $f'(x_1^{i_1}x_2^{i_2}x_3^{i_3}) = a_4^{-1}f'$ $(x_1^{i_1}x_2^{i_2}x_3^{i_3})$ mod R so that $f'(0, 0, 0) = 1$. Next define the polynomials

$G = (x_1^{i_1}x_2^{i_2}x_3^{i_3})f'X_1^{m-1-i_1}X_2^{m-1-i_2}X_3^{m-1-i_3+t}$ with $x_1^{i_1}x_2^{i_2}x_3^{i_3} \in S$

$H = (x_1^{i_1}x_2^{i_2}x_3^{i_3})R$ with $x_1^{i_1}x_2^{i_2}x_3^{i_3} \in M\backslash S$

The coefficients of polynomials G and H are used to construct a basis of a lattice $\mathcal{L}$ with dimension

$$\omega = \sum_{x_1^{i_1}x_2^{i_2}x_3^{i_3} \in M} 1 = \frac{1}{6}(m+1)(m+2)(m+3t+3).$$

In order to construct an upper triangular matrix, we perform the following ordering of the monomials: if $\Sigma\, i_j < \Sigma\, i'_j$ then $x_1^{i_1}x_2^{i_2}x_3^{i_3} < x_1^{i'_1}x_2^{i'_2}x_3^{i'_3}$ and the monomials are lexicographically ordered if $\Sigma\, i_j = \Sigma\, i'_j$. The diagonal entries of the matrix are of the form

$$\begin{cases} (X_1X_2)^{m-1}X_3^{m-1+t} & \text{for the polynomials } G \\ WX_1^{m-1+i_1}X_2^{m-1+i_2}X_3^{m-1+i_3+t} & \text{for the polynomials } H \end{cases}$$

Define

$$s_j = \sum_{x_1^{i_1}x_2^{i_2}x_3^{i_3} \in M\backslash S} i_j, \quad \text{for } j = 1, \ldots, 3 \qquad (11.15)$$

The determinant of $\mathcal{L}$ becomes

$$\det(\mathcal{L}) = W^{|M\backslash S|}X_3^{(m-1+t)\omega+s_3} \prod_{j=1}^{2} X_j^{(m-1)\omega+s_j}.$$

All the polynomials G and H and their combinations share the root $(d, k, 2^{3b}s - v)$ modulo R. We get a new basis with short vectors by applying the LLL algorithm to the lattice $\mathcal{L}$. Let $f_i(x_1 X_1, x_2 X_2, x_3 X_3)$ for $i = 1, 2$ be two short vectors of the reduced basis. Each f_i is a combination of G and H, and then shares the root $(d, k, 2^{3b}s - v)$. Then, applying the theorem of lattice reduction from (Lenstra et al. 1982), we have for $i = 1, 2$

$$\| f_i(x_1 X_1, x_2 X_2, x_3 X_3) \| < 2^{\frac{\omega(\omega-1)}{4(\omega-2)}} \det(\mathcal{L})^{\frac{1}{\omega-2}}.$$

For $i = 1, 2$, we force the polynomials f_i to satisfy the bound from (Howgrave-Graham 1997) which is $\| f_i(x_1 X_1, x_2 X_2, x_3 X_3) \| < \frac{R}{\sqrt{\omega}}$. The condition suffices when

$$2^{\frac{\omega(\omega-1)}{4(\omega-2)}} \det(\mathcal{L})^{\frac{1}{\omega-2}} < \frac{R}{\sqrt{\omega}}.$$

which can be transformed into $\det(\mathcal{L}) < R^\omega$, that is

$$W^{|M \setminus S|} X_3^{(m-1+t)\omega+s_3} \prod_{j=1}^{2} X_j^{(m-1)\omega+s_j} < (W X_1^{m-1} X_2^{m-1} X_3^{m-1+t})^\omega.$$

Using $\omega = |M|$ and $|M| - |M \setminus S| = |S|$, we get

$$\prod_{j=1}^{3} X_j^{s_j} < W^{|S|}. \tag{11.16}$$

Using (11.15), we would have

$$s_1 = \sum_{x_1^{i_1} x_2^{i_2} x_3^{i_3} \in M \setminus S} i_1 = \frac{1}{6} m(m+1)(m+3t+2),$$

$$s_2 = \sum_{x_1^{i_1} x_2^{i_2} x_3^{i_3} \in M \setminus S} i_2 = \frac{1}{6} m(m+1)(2m+3t+4),$$

$$s_3 = \sum_{x_1^{i_1} x_2^{i_2} x_3^{i_3} \in M \setminus S} i_3 = \frac{1}{6}(m+1)(m^2+3mt+2m+3t^2+3t).$$

Similarly, we get

$$|S| = \sum_{x_1^{i_1} x_2^{i_2} x_3^{i_3} \in M \setminus S} 1 = \frac{1}{6} m(m+1)(m+3t+2).$$

Setting $t = \tau m$, then

$$s_1 = \frac{1}{6}(3\tau + 1)m^3 + o(m^3),$$

$$s_2 = \frac{1}{6}(3\tau + 2)m^3 + o(m^3),$$

$$s_3 = \frac{1}{6}(3\tau^2 + 3\tau + 1)m^3 + o(m^3),$$

$$|S| = \frac{1}{6}(3\tau + 1)m^3 + o(m^3).$$

We then simplify all the equations above by m^3. After substituting all the values of $|S|$, s_j and X_j for $j = 1, 2, 3$ into (11.16) and simplifying the inequality, we would have

$$\frac{1}{3}\tau^2 + \frac{1}{6}(3\delta - 1)\tau + \frac{1}{36}(6\gamma + 12\delta - 8) < 0.$$

Differentiate the equation above with respect to τ, we get the optimal value $\tau = \frac{1-3\delta}{4}$, this reduces to

$$-27\delta^2 + 66\delta + 24\gamma - 35 < 0$$

which is valid if

$$\delta < \frac{11}{9} - \frac{2}{9}\sqrt{4 + 18\gamma}.$$

Under this condition of δ, we find our reduced polynomial f, f_1, f_2 with the roots $(d, k, 2^{3b}s - v)$. Assuming all the polynomials are algebraically independent, the roots can be extracted by using the resultant technique. Utilizing the third root $2^{3m}s - v$, we compute $p^2 + pq - p = 2^{3m}s + s_0 - v$. From here, we can compute $\phi(N)$. Taking $\gcd(\phi(N), N)$ would retrieve p which means the modulus N has been factorized. This terminates the proof. ∎

11.5   CONCLUSION

In this chapter, we provide a brief introduction to the RSA cryptosystem and the strategies to factor the RSA modulus. Next, we describe three new recent advancements where the RSA modulus N can be efficiently factored in polynomial time. We proved that either the standard modulus or the multi-power modulus i.e. $N = p^2q$ is susceptible to the attacks if certain properties are satisfied. Thus, one really needs to be extra cautious in designing the RSA cryptosystem or its variants to avoid vulnerability in any attack.

REFERENCES

Ariffin, M.R. (2020). Attacking RSA using an arbitrary parameter. In *International Conference on Cryptology in Africa* (pp. 382–399). Springer. https://doi.org/10.1007/978-3-030-51938-4_19

Barker, E. (2016). NIST Special Publication 800-57 Part 1 Revision 4; Recommendation for Key Management Part 1: General. http://dx.doi.org/10.6028/NIST.SP.800-57pt1r4

Bunder, M., & Tonien, J. (2017). A new attack on the RSA cryptosystem based on continued fractions. *Malaysian Journal of Mathematical Sciences, 11*(S3), 45–57.

Coppersmith, D. (1997). Small solutions to polynomial equations, and low exponent RSA vulnerabilities. *Journal of Cryptology, 10*(4), 233–260. https://10.1007/s001459900030

Coron, J.S. (2004). Finding small roots of bivariate integer polynomial equations revisited. In *International Conference on The Theory and Applications of Cryptographic Techniques*. Springer, Berlin, Heidelberg. https://10.1007/978-3-540-24676-3_29

Hardy, G., & Wright, E. (1965). *An Introduction to the Theory of Numbers*. Oxford University Press, London.

Howgrave-Graham, N. (1997). Finding small roots of univariate modular equations revisited. In Proceeding of *IMA Conference on Cryptography and Coding* (pp. 131–142). https://10.1007/BFb0024458

Jochemsz, E., & May, A. (2006). A strategy for finding roots of multivariate polynomials with new applications in attacking RSA variants. *International Conference on the Theory and Application of Cryptology and Information Security* (pp. 267–282). https://10.1007/11935230_18

Lenstra, A.K., Lenstra, H.W., & Lovasz, H.W. (1982). Factoring polynomial with rational coefficients. *Mathematische Annalen, 261*(4), 515–534. https://10.1007/BF01457454

Nitaj, A. (2008). Another generalization of Wiener's attack on RSA. In *International Conference on Cryptology in Africa* (pp. 174–190). Springer, Heidelberg. https://10.1007/978-3-540-68164-9_12

Nitaj, A. (2013). Diophantine and lattice cryptanalysis of the RSA cryptosystem. In *Artificial Intelligence, Evolutionary Computing and Metaheuristics* (pp. 139–168). Springer. https://10.1007/978-3-642-29694-9_7

Nitaj, A., Ariffin, M.R.K., Nassr, D.I., & Bahig, H.M. (2014). New attack on the RSA cryptosystem. In Proceeding *International Conference on Cryptology in Africa* (pp. 178–198). https://10.1007/978-3-319-06734-6_12

Rivest, R., Shamir, A., & Adleman, L. (1978). A method for obtaining digital signatures and public-key cryptosystem. *Communication of the ACM, 21*(2), 17–28. https://doi.org/10.1145/359340.359342

Ruzai, W.N.A., Ariffin, M.R.K., Asbullah, M.A., Mahad, Z., & Nawawi, A. (2020). On the improvement attack upon some variants of RSA cryptosystem via the continued fractions method. *IEEE Access, 8*(1), 80997–81006.

Tonien, J. (2018). *Continued fractions and their applications, Doctor of Philosophy thesis, School of Mathematics and Applied Statistics*. University of Wollongong. https://ro.uow.edu.au/theses1/216

Wiener, M.J. (1990). Cryptanalysis of short RSA secret exponents. *IEEE Transactions on Information Theory, 36*(3), 553–558. https://doi:10.1109/18.54902

12 Vision-Based Efficient Collision Avoidance Model Using Distance Measurement

A.F.M Saifuddin Saif[1],
Zainal Rasyid Mahayuddin[2], and Haslina Arshad[3]
[1]Faculty of Science and Technology, American International University – Bangladesh, Dhaka, Bangladesh
[2]Faculty of Information Science and Technology, Universiti Kebangsaan Malaysia, 43600 UKM, Bangi, Selangor, Malaysia
[3]Institute of IIR 4.0, Universiti Kebangsaan Malaysia, 43600 UKM, Bangi, Selangor, Malaysia

12.1 INTRODUCTION

A cautionary vehicle detection model integrated with a collision-avoidance system refers to a safety system designed to reduce the severity of a collision in the context of fourth industrial revolution (IR 4.0). Almost 10 million automobile accidents per year, approximately 27,000 accidents occur every day of which fatal accidents leading to deaths is nearly 1.3 million per year which averages to over 3,300 deaths per day (Dagan et al. 2004). Road crashes cost low and middle-income countries USD $65 billion annually, exceeding the total amount received in developmental assistance. Unless action is taken, road traffic injuries are predicted to become the fifth leading cause of death by 2030 demanding for efficient collision avoidance model proposed in this research.

Vehicle collision avoidance in order to design intelligent transportation systems has been a very significant area of research for its practical impact on the lives of people towards fourth industrial revolution (IR 4.0). Vehicle collision avoidance means to prevent running vehicles from colliding with other running or stationary vehicles, pedestrians or any other objects in the real-time scenario which also can be considered as the key to inventing technologies like self-driven vehicles. Various technologies and methods have been applied so far in vehicle collision avoidance researches. Some of them use various sensors to get the necessary data from the camera to validate various methods, models or frameworks to justify the feasibility and efficiency. This research proposed an efficient collision avoidance model by establishing a relation between distance and the size of the vehicle in live video to generate an approximate notion about the distance between the vehicles.

The proposed collision avoidance model uses live video from both offline and online cameras and runs a tracking algorithm on it to detect vehicles. Along with vehicles, tracking of roads and lanes was also performed which makes it possible to run surveillance on the vehicles about changing lanes and other traffic laws. Section 12.2 depicts previous research to state the demand for efficient collision avoidance model, section 12.3 depicts contribution by this research, section 12.4 illustrates the proposed collision avoidance model and demonstrates experimental results with analysis and discussion, section 12.5 presents observation and discussion and section 12.6 depicts concluding remarks.

12.2 RESEARCH BACKGROUND

Vehicle collision avoidance has always been an area of fertile research interest for a long time where a single camera is composed with a collision warning system that uses images and then with the help of data gathered from images, a forward collision warning is generated. Various types of works have been done previously on vehicle collision avoidance mentioned in Figure 12.1. Meyer et al. (Meyer et al. 2020) applied proximal policy optimization on the dual-objective problem of controlling an underactuated autonomous surface vehicle to follow a previously known path while avoiding collisions with non-moving obstacles along the way. They demonstrated the possibility of programming intelligence into safety-critical applications, that is Automatic Identification System (AIS). However, research by Meyer et al. (Meyer et al. 2020) does not work for non-moving obstacles of circular shapes. Besides, their proposed work immensely depends on a massive number of trained parameters. In addition, they did not apply their research in real-time environment as they only performed the analog experiments in 2D. In this context, Havenstrøm et al. (Havenstrøm et al. 2020) also applied proximal Optimization for a collision which was used to train the neural networks. They inherited trade-off parameter concepts from Meyer, et al. (Meyer et al. 2020) and added penalties to roll, roll rate and the use of control actuation to form the complete reward function. Besides, in their research, a deep reinforcement learning agent was trained and used to tackle the hybrid objective of 3D path-following and 3D collision avoidance. Their obtained experimental results indicate that reinforce learning could play a vital role to achieve truly capability of human-level decision-making in order to avoid collision in real time. However, they did not consider sensor noise in their research to receive satisfactory results. Peng et al. (Peng et al. 2020) proposed a data mining model based on a systematic "driver-vehicle-road traffic" arrangement for evaluating driving safety in near-crashes. In their research, the involvement of crash risk in a certain emergency situation is linked with the real-time conditional attributes i.e. driver behavior, vehicle motion through an improved rough set model, which can be trained and validated using driving data. The improved rough set model in their research indicated the input-output relationships characterized by extracted rules, which are interpretable and easy to understand, while other models are black boxes in nature and their input-output relationships cannot be interpreted

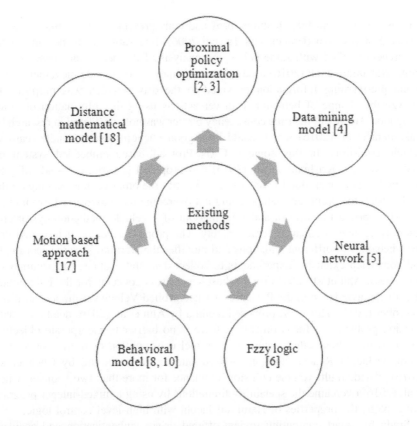

FIGURE 12.1 Existing methods for vehicle collision avoidance.

or verified explicitly. However, the database they used in their research, the influence of multi factors on the driving risk was not fully addressed. Only longitudinal driving safety situation assessment was processed and evaluated during experimentation Lee and Yeo (2015) proposed to rear-end collision warning system by considering different perception-reaction times using a multi-layer perceptron neural network. However, the proposed method by Lee and Yeo (2015) lacks sufficient evidence of robust performance due to not considering safety distance among vehicles.

Lee and Wang (1994) used fuzzy logic control for automated guided vehicle navigation in order to avoid collision by using an algorithm to detect probable collision from any sides or angles. Research by Lee and Wang (1994) demonstrated experimentation to validate the method was only performed with a theoretical framework causes the method to be efficient. Fuzzy logic control-oriented method needed to be integrated to some practical experimental models like any model-based framework to achieve more proper and real data from the real world scenario and then evaluate the accuracy using various performance evaluation parameters.

A recent study on Pedestrian Collision Avoidance Strategy generates good works on collision avoidance systems for pedestrians with vehicles which summarizes various cameras and their features, pros and cons present great documentation in this area of research (Gandhi and Trivedi 2006). Integrating with the same field, researchers worked with some behavioral analysis of the pedestrians based on regions. Nakamura et al. (2016) used behavioral analysis for vehicle movement using signal pre-warning information provided to the driver which was proposed to analyze the change of behavior in driver actions using the information of voice navigation. However, the time consistency barrier was not considered in research by Nakamura et al. (2016) which could be a good phenomenon to handle rear-end vehicle collisions. In this context, CAN Protocol-based embedded system by Kedareswar and Krishnamoorthy (2015) was proposed to avoid rear-end collision of vehicles. However, due to the inability to notify the other vehicle running on the road expect, the proposed method could not overcome the drawback. Trivedi et al. (2007) proposed Looking-In and Looking-Out of a vehicle methodology for collision avoidance to enhance vehicle safety. The proposed method determined drivers' behavior in different situations and modifies the warning system accordingly and conducted extensive experiments to collect data and evaluate the accuracy of the system. Ahn et al. (2016) used robust supervisors concepts for the intersection of collision avoidance in the Presence of Uncontrolled Vehicles using a centralized controller (2016). However, proposed method by Ahn et al. (2016) dealt only with decision problems to focus on safety, there is no barrier to incorporate objective functions to address other issues such as fuel consumption or traffic congestion. Hamilton-Jacobi Reachability and Mixed Integer Programming by Chen et al. (2016) provide multi-vehicle collision avoidance for more than two vehicles. Chen et al. (2016) overcame the scalability limitations by using a mixed-integer program that exploits the properties of Hamilton-Jacobi with high-level control logic.

Study by smart computing review offered driver authentication and accident avoidance for vehicles which can be considered as advanced collision avoidance system for automobiles (Abdalla and Abaker 2016; Ujjainiya and Chakravarthi 2015; Mahayuddin and Saif 2020; Mahayuddin and Saif 2020). Later on, ultrasonic sensors used by Ujjainiya and Chakravarthi (2015) are engaged to identify the motion of the objects and measured the distance between obstacles and instantaneously notified the driver accordingly to avoid collision. However, research by Ujjainiya and Chakravarthi (2015) has some limitations; i.e. ill-disposed weather conditions like foggy, harsh and extreme rainy environment were still the barriers to achieve better results. In addition, Ujjainiya and Chakravarthi (2015) produced errors to differentiate between shadows and monotone.

Later, research on safety distance mathematical model using pro-active head restraint in rear-end collision avoidance frame were proposed and applied by Yin and Wang (2015) in complex and variable traffic environments. Their model is simple and easy to operate to process data and improve the performance of automotive anti-collision methods for automotive security. However, their research did not take the vehicle lane changing into consideration and hence the model still needs further investigation. Then, one of the crucial factors for cautionary vehicle detections further progressed by Samiee et al. (2016) who proposed Lane Change Algorithm. After that, to overcome the lack of considering sufficient risk factors to avoid collision, periodical of sensors and techniques for vehicle detection and tracking were proposed by Mukhtar et al. (2015) for better measurement. In this context, Winkler et al. (2016) considered drivers reaction on multistage threat system for collision escaping in urban areas. However, in their research, experimental evaluation is still in test phase to achieve better performance.

Collision avoidance is an emerging area of in the boarder prospect of Intelligent Transportation System to meet the demand of fourth industrial revolution (IR 4.0). Some remarkable works have been done so far and also going on (Mahayuddin and Saif 2019), but most of the existing works lack some important features that should have been covered which are addressed to this problem. All the previous methods and approaches for vehicle collision avoidance are invaluable in vision-based research field. Despite the commendable work, some of them do not follow a complete solution and have huge dependencies on external factors. Many of the previous work deals with sensor-based experiments focusing either on the front-end or rear-end of the vehicle. Some experiments include external hardware such as sensors, pro-active head warning equipment for their experimentation. This research proposed collision warning model where ratio between vehicle distance and width of the blob were considered for generating probable notion to correctly identify probable collision. Proposed model does not require any other equipment like sensors for measuring the distance between vehicles.

12.3 RESEARCH CONTRIBUTION

Previous works done by various researchers solved various issues of collision avoidance. However, effective model in terms with low cost and low configuration, robustness depending on various environments are still long way to cover which is in great demand for safety in the highway, busy roads to ensure least accidents due to save valuable lives. This research aimed to develop and investigate an effective model for cautionary vehicle detection and generating warning if there is any probable collision. Cautionary vehicles are detected using the proposed collision avoidance model by measuring the distance between vehicles for probable collision. This research demonstrates following contribution:

A. Proposed model differs from other methods in a way that it does not require any other equipment like sensors for measuring the distance between vehicles.
B. Proposed collision avoidance model used ratio between vehicle distance and width of the blob to generate an approximate notion about the distance between the vehicles in order to correctly identify probable collision.

12.4 PROPOSED MODEL

The proposed model takes image data in the form of video sequence as frames mentioned in Figure 12.2. A thousand vehicles recognizing data were put in a Extensible Markup Language (XML) file, along with many common non-vehicle roadside objects such as a lamppost, traffic signal, human, etc. This research used

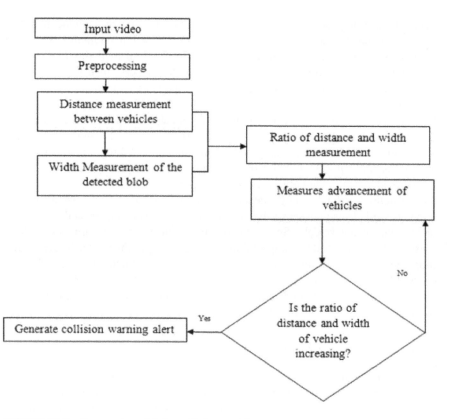

FIGURE 12.2 Proposed model for collision avoidance.

Haar Cascade Classifier for the classification of vehicles correctly. Then, Haar Cascade Classifier was used to detect the shape of vehicles given in any circumstances based on scenarios. In this context, at first, vehicles were detected using shape analysis which was previously followed by some preprocessing steps like taking input video sequences from IP cameras as frames; denoise steps as morphological preprocessing with normalization. After that blob extraction process was demonstrated using rectangle drawing in order to show the region of interest (ROI). Proposed methodology estimates two parameters i.e. distance and width as the basis to state for core evaluation to justify weather a vehicle is cautionary or not. Distance is estimated among source vehicles and others vehicles from various sides, that is rear end, front end, etc. Besides, proposed research measures the width of the detected blob. After that, a ratio is measured based on distance and width which later used to compare with adaptive threshold optimization [25] mentioned equation (12.1).

$$\theta = \psi - \frac{\psi \times (\log_2(N) + 1)}{100} \tag{12.1}$$

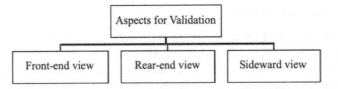

FIGURE 12.3   Three aspects for validation of the proposed model.

Here, N denotes a total number of pixels in a video frame. The threshold value is denoted as θ. The mean value of pictorial intensities is denoted as ψ. If the ratio crosses the threshold, source vehicles will receive and generate a warning alert for the blob of the corresponding vehicle as a cautionary vehicle.

12.5   EXPERIMENTAL RESULTS

Proposed research performed validation into three perspectives, that is, front-end view, rear-end view, sideward view shown in Figure 12.3.

The proposed collision avoidance model considered measuring the distances between two vehicles, where experimental results demonstrate a relationship between the actual width of the blob and the distance of vehicles from source vehicles. Data validation refers to the correct identification of the vehicles, various directions, emitting other obstacles appear in the roads. The classifier used by this research was trained as such it divided the captured video into a stream of frameworks. These frameworks were then processed so that they could produce the image of a vehicle. When it could correctly identify a vehicle, the frameworks were then again merged into a video.

12.5.1   EXPERIMENTAL SET UP

For detecting probable vehicle collision, live video were captured with the help of cameras from inside of the subject vehicle. These videos should be coming from different angles and ends so that collision can be avoided at any side of the subject car. The live video footage was then analyzed to detect vehicles around the subject vehicles. The approximate distance between the subject vehicles and other vehicles were then measured using proposed model and if there was any probable collision, warnings were generated.

12.5.2   HARDWARE SET UP

Proposed model used six IP cameras, two laptops and two smart phones for experimentation. The purpose for using smartphone was to create mobile hotspot, i.e. Wi-Fi network. Six IP cameras were used from six different angles to detect vehicles simultaneously. Besides, warning system was installed in the laptop to generate warning about probable collisions.

12.5.3 Software Set Up

Proposed research used C# programming language for experimental analysis. In this context, IMAGE PROCESSING LAB (IPLAB) available at "http://www.aforge.net/" was embedded with Visual Studio 2012 using C sharp programming language to analyze real-time scene and detect vehicles (Saif and Mahayuddin 2018; Saif et al. 2013a; Saif et al. 2014).

12.6 DATASETS

This research used live video data for validation which represents a diverse pool of vehicles from various viewpoints. An IP camera captured images of passing vehicles from all directions from the host vehicle. Various scenarios were taken into consideration, i.e. frontal collision avoidance, rear-end collision avoidance, side-by-side collision etc. Besides, various condition like velocity, acceleration rate, deceleration rate, maximum deceleration time, maximum braking time, maximum response time, distance between cars etc were also taken into consideration. Frame size in the experiment was 320 × 190.

12.6.1 Results

This research performs measurements based on true positive, false positive, false negative, precision rate, detection rate or recall rate, false alarm rate (Saif et al. 2013b; Saif et al. 2014). True Positive or TP means detected regions that correspond to a moving object. False Positive or FP means detected regions that do not correspond to a moving object. If the moving objects cannot be detected then the performance metric is named as False Negative or FN. Measures of detection rate and false alarm rate involve measures of parameters like True Positive, False Positive and False Negative (Saif et al. 2015; Saif et al. 2013b). In addition, this research measures Computation Time (CT) for executing the proposed model. This research achieved detection rate of 98.89% to generate a warning for collision avoidance in real time. In addition, the proposed research received a false alarm rate of 1.01% with an average computation time of 180.79 ms mentioned in Table 12.1.

12.6.2 Comparison with Previous Research Results

Accuracy or success rate by Meyer et al. (2020) addressed dual-objective problem of controlling underactuated autonomous surface vehicle to follow priori known

TABLE 12.1
Experimental Results for the Proposed Model

Detection Rate (%)	False Alarm Rate (%)	Average Computation Time
98.89	1.01	180.79

path and received accuracy rate of 97% initially depending on reward trade-off parameter. However, although they could increase accuracy rate by decreasing the reward trade-off parameter which was not realistic due to the lack of real-time validation under various detection perspectives as mentioned in Figure 12.3. Besides, Meyer et al. (2020) performed the analog experiments in 2D. In this context, Havenstrøm et al. (2020) received an initial average accuracy rate of 62% by applying proximal optimization was used to train the neural networks which depends on reward trade-off parameter. However, they did not consider sensor noise during experimentation. Peng et al. (2020) received an accuracy rate of 95.9% for near crash scenario by analyzing the effective driver intention, vehicle motion and traffic environment on current driving safety. However, in their database, influence of multi factors on the driving risk was not fully addressed. Only longitudinal driving safety situation assessment was processed and evaluated. The proposed model by this research achieved accuracy rate of 98.89% which higher than previous research mentioned in Figure 12.4. In addition, consideration of three perspectives mentioned in Figure 12.4 indicates higher robustness comparing with previous research.

Results received by the proposed model from the experimentation were satisfyingly met the expected goals as the main goal was to pursue higher accuracy in order to avoid collision for vehicles of all shapes and sizes, emerging from any direction. Classifier designed by the proposed research impacts to receiving higher accuracy for the vehicles of any dimension and moreover, could detect collision from all three ways, i.e. front, rear-end and sideways mentioned in Figure 12.3. So, aspects of the validation for the proposed model were environmental variations, detecting multiple objects for the same scene or various scenes, various sizes of the vehicles which indicate better robustness comparing with previous research mentioned in Figure 12.4.

The experimentation performed by this research with a number of critical and useful aspects is expected to be used for industrial usage collision avoidance applications in the future. Critical evaluation of the data confirms the effectiveness of the proposed model. Both the data obtained from experimentation, proposed model is expected to contribute highly in the area of research of deep learning architectures

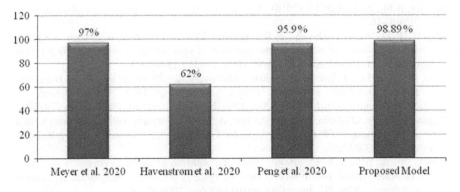

FIGURE 12.4   Detection rate between previous research and proposed model.

and in the broader aspects of designing intelligent transportation system to meet the demand of fourth industrial revolution (IR 4.0).

12.7 CONCLUSION

This research proposed an efficient collision warning model to avoid collision in real-time for the intelligent transportation systems in the context of meeting the demand of fourth industrial revolution (IR 4.0). This research proposed a collision warning model where ratio between vehicle distance and width of the blob was used to generate an approximate notion about the distance between vehicles in order to correctly identify vehicles. Various scenarios were taken into consideration during experimentation, i.e. frontal collision avoidance, rear-end collision avoidance, side-by-side collision. In addition, various conditions like velocity, acceleration rate, deceleration rate, maximum deceleration time, maximum braking time, maximum response time, the distance between cars, etc were also taken into consideration during experimentation. This research performed efficient measurements by obtaining data from video in real time. However, main challenges were faced due to vehicles' sizes, shapes, weather, road condition, speed of the vehicles and various directions. These issues were handled by the proposed model even though there were some misidentifications of the vehicles. In future, more experimentation will be demonstrated to justify the optimum performance in more rural and urban scenarios by the proposed model which is expected to contribute illusively to fulfill the demand of Fourth Industrial Revolution (IR 4.0) for designing an intelligent transportation system.

ACKNOWLEDGMENTS

The authors would like to thank Universiti Kebangsaan Malaysia for providing financial support under the "Geran Universiti Penyelidikan" research grant, GUP-2020-064.

REFERENCES

Abdalla, A.M., & Abaker, M. (2016). A survey on car collision avoidance system. *System*, 2(6), 1–10.

Ahn, H., Rizzi, A., Colombo, A., & Del Vecchio, D. (2016). Robust supervisors for intersection collision avoidance in the presence of uncontrolled vehicles. *arXiv preprint arXiv:1603.03916* https://doi.org/10.1007/s12555-018-0768-4

Chen, M., Shih, J.C., & Tomlin, C.J. (2016). Multi-vehicle collision avoidance via Hamilton-Jacobi reachability and mixed integer programming. *IEEE 55th Conference on Decision and Control (CDC)*, 1695–1700. https://doi.org/10.1109/cdc.2016.7798509

Dagan, E., Mano, O., Stein, G.P., & Shashua, A. (2004). Forward collision warning with a single camera. *IEEE Intelligent Vehicles Symposium*, 37–42. https://doi.org/10.1109/ivs.2004.1336352

Gandhi, T., & Trivedi, M.M. (2006). Pedestrian collision avoidance systems: a survey of computer vision based recent studies. *IEEE Intelligent Transportation Systems Conference*, 976–981. https://doi.org/10.1109/itsc.2006.1706871

Havenstrøm, S.T., Rasheed, A., & San, O. (2020). Deep reinforcement learning controller for 3d path-following and collision avoidance by autonomous underwater vehicles. *arXiv preprint arXiv:2006.09792*

Kedareswar, P.S., & Krishnamoorthy, V. (2015). A CAN protocol based embedded system to avoid rear-end collision of vehicles. *IEEE International Conference on Signal Processing, Informatics, Communication and Energy Systems (SPICES)*, 1–5. https://doi.org/10.1109/spices.2015.7091439

Lee, D., & Yeo, H. (2015). A study on the rear-end collision warning system by considering different perception-reaction time using multi-layer perceptron neural network. *IEEE Intelligent Vehicles Symposium (IV)*, 24–30. https://doi.org/10.1109/ivs.2015.7225657

Lee, P.S., & Wang, L.L. (1994). Collision avoidance by fuzzy logic control for automated guided vehicle navigation. *Journal of Robotic Systems, 11*(8), 743–760. https://doi.org/10.1002/rob.4620110807

Mahayuddin, Z.R., & Saif, A.F.M.S. (2020). Augmented reality based AR alphabets towards improved learning process in primary education system. *Journal of Critical Reviews, 7*(19), 1–15.

Mahayuddin, Z.R., & Saif, A.F.M.S. (2020). A comprehensive review towards segmentation and detection of cancer cell and tumor for dynamic 3D reconstruction. *Asia-Pacific Journal of Information Technology and Multimedia, 9*(1), 28–39. https://doi.org/10.1 7576/apjitm-2020-0901-03

Mahayuddin, Z.R., & Saif, A.F.M.S. (2020). Efficient hand gesture recognition using modified extrusion method based on augmented reality. *TEST Engineering and Management, 83*, 4020–4027.

Mahayuddin, Z.R., & Saif, A.S. (2019). A comparative study of three corner feature based moving object detection using aerial images. *Malaysian Journal of Computer Science, 2019*, 25–33. https://ejournal.um.edu.my/index.php/MJCS/article/view/21461

Mahayuddin, Z.R., & Saif, A.S. (2014). A comparative study of three corner feature based moving object detection using aerial images. *Malaysian Journal of Computer Science*, 25–33.

Mahayuddin, Z.R., & Saif, A.S. (2019). A comprehensive review towards appropriate feature selection for moving object detection using aerial images. *International Visual Informatics Conference*, 227–236. https://doi.org/10.1007/978-3-030-34032-2_21

Mahayuddin, Z.R., Saif, A.S., & Prabuwono, A.S. (2015). Efficiency measurement of various denoise techniques for moving object detection using aerial images. *International Conference on Electrical Engineering and Informatics (ICEEI)*, 161–165. https://doi.org/10.1109/iceei.2015.7352488

Meyer, E., Robinson, H., Rasheed, A., & San, O. (2020). Taming an autonomous surface vehicle for path following and collision avoidance using deep reinforcement learning. *IEEE Access, 8*(41466-41481). https://doi.org/10.1109/access.2020.2976586

Mukhtar, A., Xia, L., & Tang, T.B. (2015). Vehicle detection techniques for collision avoidance systems: a review. *IEEE Transactions on Intelligent Transportation Systems, 16*(5), 2318–2338. https://doi.org/10.1109/tits.2015.2409109

Nakamura, T., Nakayama, T., Uno, N., & Yamamura, K. (2016). A vehicle behavioral analysis of the signal pre-warning information provided to the driver. *Journal of Traffic and Transportation Engineering, 4*(1), 11–17. https://doi.org/10.17265/2328-2142/201 6.01.002

Peng, L., Sotelo, M.A., He, Y., Ai, Y., & Li, Z. (2020). A method for vehicle collision risk assessment through inferring driver's braking actions in near-crash situations. *arXiv preprint arXiv:2004.13761*

Saif, A., & Mahayuddin, Z.R. (2018). Moving object segmentation using various features from aerial images: a review. *Advanced Science Letters, 24*(2), 961–965. https://doi.org/10.1166/asl.2018.10667

Saif, A., Prabuwono, A., & Mahayuddin, Z. (2013). Adaptive long term motion pattern analysis for moving object detection using UAV aerial images. *International Journal of Information System and Engineering*, *1*(1), 50–59. https://doi.org/10.24924/ijise/2 013.04/v1.iss1/42.51

Saif, A., Prabuwono, A.S., & Mahayuddin, Z.R. (2014). Moving object detection using dynamic motion modelling from UAV aerial images. *The Scientific World Journal.* https://doi.org/10.1155/2014/890619

Saif, A.F.M.S., & Mahayuddin, Z.R. (2020a). Moment features based violence action detection using optical flow. *International Journal of Advanced Computer Science and Applications(IJACSA)*, *11*(11), https://doi.org/10.14569/ijacsa.2020.0111163

Saif, A.F.M.S., & Mahayuddin, Z.R. (2020b). Robust drowsiness detection for vehicle driver using deep convolutional neural network. *International Journal of Advanced Computer Science and Applications(IJACSA)*, *11*(10), https://doi.org/10.14569/ijacsa.2020.0111043

Saif, A.S., & Mahayuddin, Z.R. (2020). Vehicle detection for collision avoidance using vision based approach: a constructive review. *Solid State Technology*, *63*, 2861–2869.

Saif, A.S., Prabuwono, A.S., & Mahayuddin, Z.R. (2013a). Adaptive motion pattern analysis for machine vision based moving detection from UAV aerial images. *International Visual Informatics Conference*, 104–114. https://doi.org/10.1007/978-3-319-02958-0_10

Saif, A.S., Prabuwono, A.S., & Mahayuddin, Z.R. (2013b). Real time vision based object detection from UAV aerial images: a conceptual framework. *FIRA RoboWorld Congress*, 265–274. https://doi.org/10.1007/978-3-642-40409-2_23

Saif, A.S., Prabuwono, A.S., & Mahayuddin, Z.R. (2014). Motion analysis for moving object detection from UAV aerial images: a review. *International Conference on Informatics, Electronics & Vision (ICIEV)*, 1–6. https://doi.org/10.1109/iciev.2014.6850753

Saif, A.S., Prabuwono, A.S., & Mahayuddin, Z.R. (2015). Moment feature based fast feature extraction algorithm for moving object detection using aerial images. *PloS One*, *10*(6), e0126212. https://doi.org/10.1371/journal.pone.0126212

Saif, A.S., Prabuwono, A.S., Mahayuddin, Z.R., & Himawan, H.T. (2013). A review of machine vision based on moving objects: object detection from UAV aerial images. *International Journal of Advancements in Computing Technology*, *5*(15), 57.

Saif, A.S., Prabuwono, A.S., Mahayuddin, Z.R., & Mantoro, T. (2013). Vision-based human face recognition using extended principal component analysis. *International Journal of Mobile Computing and Multimedia Communications (IJMCMC)*, *5*(4), 82–94. https://doi.org/10.4018/ijmcmc.2013100105

Samiee, S., Azadi, S., Kazemi, R., Eichberger, A., Rogic, B., & Semmer, M. (2016). Performance evaluation of a novel vehicle collision avoidance lane change algorithm (pnyt.). *Advanced Microsystems for Automotive Applications*, 103–116. https://doi.org/10.1007/978-3-319-20855-8_9

Trivedi, M.M., Gandhi, T., & McCall, J. (2007). Looking-in and looking-out of a vehicle: computer-vision-based enhanced vehicle safety. *IEEE Transactions on Intelligent Transportation Systems*, *8*(1), 108–120. https://doi.org/10.1109/icves.2005.1563609

Ujjainiya, L., & Chakravarthi, M.K. (2015). Raspberry—Pi based cost effective vehicle collision avoidance system using image processing. *ARPN Journal of Engineering and Applied Sciences*, *10*(7), 3001–3005.

Winkler, S., Kazazi, J., & Vollrath, M. 2016. Driving with a multi-stage warning system in the head-up display–how do drivers react upon it. *Proceedings of the Human Factors and Ergonomics Society Europe Chapter 2015 Annual Conference* http://hfes- europe.org (141–153).

Yin, X., & Wang, M. (2015). Research on safety distance mathematical model of pro-active head restraint in rear-end collision avoidance system. *International Journal of Security and Its Applications*, *9*(1), 347–356. https://doi.org/10.14257/ijsia.2015.9.1.33

Index